Praise for the Book

'For me, as a proud Bangalorean, this book beautifully highlights what makes the city so special. The columns are filled with captivating historical insights, vibrant contemporary culture, and engaging trivia that reflect the city's unique charm. Roopa masterfully captures the spirit of Bangalore, offering a heartfelt reminder of why this city holds such significance for so many of us.'

– ROHAN BOPANNA, Grand Slam Champion and Padma Shri honoree

'Roopa Pai is a rare breed of perspicacious and exuberant storyteller who unearths rare nuggets of information time and time again in her now famous and eagerly awaited fortnightly column. *Becoming Bangalore*, Roopa Pai's anthology on the city, is a masterful exploration of the city's metamorphosis. With her characteristic élan and insight, Roopa navigates the complex interplay of history, culture and modernity that define Bangalore, and renders this volume a veritable treasure trove. This collection is an indispensable *vade mecum* for anyone seeking to grasp Bangalore's *sui generis* charm.'

– RAJA CHANDRA URS, son-in-law of Maharaja Jayachamaraja Wadiyar, and archivist of his life, work and legacy

'What an absolutely delightful read this was! With each tale, my love for all things Bangalore got a fresh lease of life. Roopa weaves her own memories and snippets from her life with chronicles from a time gone by, providing, with both her research and her prose, a new dimension to this warm, beautiful, cosmopolitan city that I have lived in all my life. Every story was a walk down a familiar alley with little surprises lurking around corners. This work is an expert narrative, uniquely told, that throws light on how the world at large and the people who called it home across centuries shaped this vibrant city.'

– HEMAMALINI MAIYA, Managing Partner, MTR

'Roopa's *Becoming Bangalore* mirrors the eclectic spirit of Bengaluru in both style and content. Her words draw you into the city's heart, blending vivid historical snapshots with her memories and musings. It's like strolling through Bengaluru with a friend who knows its hidden stories – an intimate journey through the beloved place we call home.'

– AMOGHAVARSHA J.S., award-winning filmmaker

'Roopa's book is a mosaic of stories – each story forming another piece of the soul of the city. A captivating collection, captured in her brilliant prose, with the insight and charm that only an old Bangalorean could bring.'

– RAMJEE CHANDRAN, author and host of *The History Of Bangalore* podcast

Becoming Bangalore

STORIES THAT SHAPED A HOMETOWN

ROOPA PAI

hachette
INDIA

First published in 2025 by Hachette India
(Registered name: Hachette Book Publishing India Pvt. Ltd)
An Hachette UK company
www.hachetteindia.com

1

The essays in this book first appeared in the *Hindustan Times* Bengaluru edition in the fortnightly column 'Beloved Bangalore' between 2021 and 2024, and are included with the kind permission of the newspaper.

Inside illustrations by Priya Kuriyan
Images on pages 73, 77, 193, 229 and 299 from *Koravanji*, and the *Aparanji* logo on page 72 published with the kind permission of M. Shivakumar.

ISBN 978-93-5731-621-7

Hachette Book Publishing India Pvt. Ltd
4th & 5th Floors, Corporate Centre
Plot No. 94, Sector 44, Gurugram – 122003, India

Typeset by Manmohan Kumar, Delhi

Printed and bound in India
by Manipal Technologies Limited

MIX
Paper | Supporting responsible forestry
FSC™ C043100
FSC www.fsc.org

To the city that raised me, and to everyone who believes in the singular power of curiosity, collaboration, and a capaciousness of mind and heart in building inspiring communities, cities and countries

Contents

Season 3: September~October~November * *African Tulip*

Season 4: December~January~February * *Pink Trumpet*

1

Love and the City

When R. Sukumar, editor of the *Hindustan Times*, whom I had briefly worked with at *Business Today* close to three decades ago, got in touch with me in early 2021, asking if I would write a fortnightly column for the newly launched Bengaluru edition of the *Hindustan Times*, I agreed without a second thought – when Bangalore is the subject, that is invariably my response. I did not realize, when I was writing this opening piece, how much discipline a column would demand of me, and I certainly did not anticipate that I would still be writing 'Beloved Bangalore' close to four years later.

Yet here I am, still loving the delicious excitement every second Monday brings as I sit at my laptop in the city that Kempegowda birthed, and wonder what I will write about this time.

It's a rum thing, but for all the surreal never-beforeness that has transpired in the weird year between Valentine's Day 2020 and the same day in 2021, a visitor to Bangalore from another dimension who had only walked the city's streets on those two days might never have guessed at it, so resolutely has 'normalcy' begun to return to these parts. (There are the masks, of course, but that the visitor may dismiss as yet another unfathomable fashion trend.) And since, for reasons divine, (un)hygienic or plain mysterious, this is our happy situation today, we're kicking off this column on the city by celebrating nammooru's trysts with that exhilarating, enervating emotion – love – and the colour it is most associated with – red.

Cut to antediluvian time – always good to begin at the beginning – when gods and goddesses freely roamed the earth. Up in the frozen wastes of the Himalayas, the ascetic Shiva's unrelenting tapas was upsetting the balance of the world, which thrived on union and procreation. Alongside, he himself was having a similar effect on the daughter of the mountain, Parvati. Concerned, the gods sent Kama, the god of love, to create a diversion. Choosing an opportune moment, Kama let fly his flower-laden arrows. The ruse worked, but not in quite the way the gods had hoped. Furious at having his tapas disrupted, Shiva reduced Kama to ashes and ignored Parvati altogether.

Realizing that her only chance of getting Shiva interested was to go toe-to-toe with him in his own department, and that putting a little distance between them might help that process along, Parvati moved south, to the spectacular rocky landscape beside the River Tungabhadra. There, on the Hemakuta hill, she began her own austerities. In due course, intrigued despite himself, Shiva came seeking the great tapasvin known in those parts as Pampe, and they were married. Ever since, that land has been known, after Pampe, as Hampe.

(Right, that's the love part, but what does it have to do with Bengaluru? Wait for it.)

In the fourteenth century, under the brothers Harihara and Bukka, the great empire of Vijayanagara was established, with Hampe at its centre. In 1537 CE, an ambitious chieftain of Yelahanka, with the permission of his emperor Achyuta Deva Raya at Hampe, broke ground for the raising of a brave new city called Bengaluru. The ceremony took place in what would go on to become Bengaluru Pete (or market; say *pay-tay*), an area of roughly a square mile, enclosed by a mud fort, at the heart of today's 286-square-mile urban sprawl. (To give you a sense, the Pete was located between what we know as the Krantivira Sangolli Rayanna Railway Station – the shorter 'City Railway Station' serves just as well – and Mysore Bank Circle in the north and the City Market in the south, between Halasuru Gate police station and the Corporation building in the east and the TCM Royan Road in the west.)

And this chieftain, he met his one true love in the Pete? Perhaps, but history is silent on that. What we do know is that his name, like the airport's, was Kempegowda, which translates from the Kannada to 'Red Chief'. You see? The city's founding father was named for the colour of love itself!

Which is perhaps one of the reasons why this city, across the five centuries of her existence, has been loved so fiercely, by kings and commoners, scientists and students, pensioners and paramours, those who dream up grand ideas and those who back them. And her capacious, liberal heart has given love back, in equal measure.

It's never too early, nor too late, to walk her streets and hear her stories. Let us go then, you and I.

March~April~May

Gulmohar

Delonix regia, flagrant crimson,
Summer's queen, flamboyant, winsome,
Comes in with springtime, goes out with the rain,
Sets Bangalore skies and pavements aflame.

2

SUMMER IN BANGALORE

How the City Was Greened

Bangalore is built on a series of granite hills, which do not provide the most ideal substratum for trees to thrive. But the city's pleasant climate has always proved most suitable for growing flowers, fruits and vegetables, and not just native species either. Encouraged, rulers and administrators through the ages brought in expert gardeners, botanists and horticulturists, and imported exotic species from around the world, to bring their green dreams to life in the red earth. To this day, despite untrammelled growth and urbanization, the city remains defiantly verdant.

Summer comes early to Bengaluru. It announces its impending arrival in the steadily dwindling heaps of dry leaves piled up at the kerb each morning by conscientious BBMP pourakarmikas – signalling the winding down of our brief and very dry tropical 'fall', in the brazen gold of the *Tabebuia* blooms that burst forth, on cue, across the city, and in the more frequent hum of the neighbour's generator as BESCOM begins to flex muscles long idle.

By far the most ubiquitous herald of the hot season, however, is the collective moan that goes up from Bangaloreans as the mercury hits 32°C. The refrain never changes – 'What's happened to this city, man? It's SO hot!' and 'It's all the construction, bro – this city is being overrun!' And, inevitably, the traitorous capitulation – 'This year, I'm buying an AC.'

Yet summer in the city has its compensations. Not only is it mercifully short – the rain comes in early May – but it is also a riot of colour. It's the impossibly fresh green of the massive rain trees (originally from South America) coming back into leaf, the wispy blue–violet of the jacaranda (native to Latin America and the Caribbean), best viewed against a bleached summer sky, the masses of pale pink blossoms draping the canopies of tall *Tabebuia rosea* trees, and, come mid-April, the heart-lifting sight of the *flamboyant*, aka the gulmohar (from Madagascar), bursting into crimson flame.

How did a landscape of granite hills and valleys bang in the centre of the southern Indian peninsula become home to exotics from across the world? Who were the bestowers of this largesse? Well, kings, for one, beginning with that formidable eighteenth-century father–son duo – Hyder Ali and Tipu Sultan – who, in the midst of their relentless military campaigns, found the mind space to be aesthetes.

It was Hyder who, in 1760, set up the royal pleasure garden of roses and cypresses that grew into our Lalbagh, identifying and employing a Tamil-speaking community of expert green thumbs called the Tigalas to maintain it. This was not the first Lalbagh, though – the original, a Mughal garden–inspired charbagh, was in Hyder's capital of Srirangapatna, and included apple and pear trees.

Tipu had wider-ranging interests, and having the French as allies enabled him to cast his eye globally. From Mauritius, in 1798, his ambassadors brought chests of nutmeg and cloves that were then carried across the Western Ghats from the ports. Earlier, from the Cape of Good Hope, where his officers had docked on their way back from a successful mission to Versailles, they had returned with spices, camphor, oak and pine. From the sultan of Turkey, Tipu procured fig trees that thrived in the temperate climate of Bangalore. From Australia, soon after it was formed in 1788, he brought in eucalyptus, his curiosity ignited by everything he'd heard about them.

Avocados from Mexico and pomelo (chakkota in Kannada) from China and Thailand also found a place in his gardens. The chakkota he planted outside the Devanahalli fort where he was born, and the conditions turned out to be so suitable for this vitamin C–loaded, pink-fleshed fruit that the 'Devanahalliya chakkota' (the chakkota of Devanahalli) came to be immortalized in a popular Kannada poem for children, 'Hannu Maaruvavana Haadu' (The Song of the Fruit Seller), written by teacher, freedom fighter and farmer Kayyara Kinhanna Rai over 150 years later. Now the fruit even has its own GI tag!

Look out for the laden carts the next time you are headed to the Nandi Hills in chakkota season!

If 'The Song of the Fruit Seller' declared that Devanahalli produced Karnataka's best pomelos, which fruits do you reckon other towns and regions in Karnataka, like Nanjangud, Kodagu (Coorg), Bidar, Madhugiri, Belagavi, Ganjam, Tumkur, Dharwad, the Malnad region, and of course, Bangalore, were famous for? In order, the small, fleshy, sweet banana called rasabaale, orange, guava, pomegranate, sapota (chikoo), fig, jackfruit, aapoos (Alphonso) mango, pineapple, and. . .apples! You would be hard put to find a single apple tree in Bangalore today, but a hundred years ago, apple orchards were not an uncommon sight. (*For more information about Bangalore apples, see page 14.*)

3

TIPU SULTAN DIED ON 4 MAY 1799

How the Chow Chow Came to Bengaluru

The death of Tipu Sultan ended a glorious era of resistance in south India to the rise of the British Empire. With Tipu out of the way, a vast tract of the peninsula became available for exploration to British geographers, geologists, surveyors, mapmakers, botanists and others. Several pioneering scientific projects, including the Great Trigonometrical Survey (GTS) of India, began as early as 1800, when a pilot for the GTS was carried out in Bangalore by Lt Col William Lambton. Another project that was immediately undertaken was the study of the flora in Tipu's beloved Lalbagh, where, 80 years later, the chow chow was first acclimatized.

Bangalore's darshinis are justifiably famous for their chow-chow bhath, a dish that features a little mound of khara bhath alongside a little mound of kesari bhath, each held together by tuppa (ghee) and love. But the chow chow in the title of this column has nothing to do with bhath; it refers to the 'Bangalore Brinjal' or the *seemebadanekaayi,* whose mild taste lends it a versatility happily exploited in the Karnataka kitchen.

How did the Jamaican chocho or chayote, introduced to the Old World via the so-called Columbian Exchange (a mega-swap of grains, vegetables, culture, ideas, and human beings between West Africa, the Americas and the rest of the world, following Christopher Columbus's path-breaking voyage of discovery and domination in 1492 CE), morph into the Bangalore Brinjal? Thereby hangs a tale of some remarkable nineteenth- and twentieth-century botanists and horticulturists.

It was Scottish physician and naturalist Francis Buchanan who opened the floodgates. Retained by the governor general of India, Lord Wellesley, to survey south India, following the tragic fall of Tipu Sultan in 1799, Buchanan set to his task with alacrity, recording in his report on the sultan's beloved Lalbagh, already bursting with species from across the world – 'I think there can be little doubt, but that in this country (of Mysore) all the valuable plants of the Levant would succeed.'

Following Buchanan's report, Lord Wellesley ordered that Lalbagh be appropriated for a botanical garden, a place to cultivate 'useful plants' (over pretty ones, thus confirming that the British were a nation of shopkeepers) from different parts of the country, under the stewardship of Benjamin Heyne, a Scottish botanist. Heyne introduced such species into the gardens as coffee, durian, rambutan, mangosteen, potatoes, and even grapes (for winemaking, what else?).

Over the next three decades, Lalbagh passed back and forth between the East India Company, private British owners and the maharajas of Mysore. In 1831, the Company wrested control of Mysore back from the king, and Lalbagh passed into the care of the chief commissioner of Mysore, the much-admired Sir Mark Cubbon (yup, he who the other park is named after).

An 'Agricultural and Horticultural Society of Bangalore', set up by a few keen Europeans, managed the space for a few years, enthusiastically growing wheat, barley, oats and even sugarcane. Finally, in 1856, on the recommendation of Hugh Cleghorn, conservator of forests in the Madras Presidency, Lalbagh officially became the Government Botanical Gardens, and began its long and fruitful association with its more celebrated counterpart, the Royal Kew Gardens in London.

Beginning with botanist William New, who took over as superintendent of Lalbagh in 1858, every superintendent – John Cameron, Gustav Krumbiegel, H.C. Javaraya, and M.H. Mari Gowda – either came from Kew or was trained at Kew. Between them, they planted, studied, fussed over and 'acclimatized' hundreds of non-native plant and tree species to Indian conditions, before despatching them to the far corners of the country to be cultivated for commercial purposes.

On Herr Krumbiegel's watch, some of those trees – the prettiest ones – left the Lalbagh experimental nursery to line Bangalore's avenues. His masterstroke – the idea of 'serial blossoming' – has ensured that there are always trees in bloom on the streets of Bangalore, whatever the season.

And what of the chow chow? That was John Cameron. Having received samples of the light green pear-shaped vegetable from Sri Lanka, he proceeded to plant them in Lalbagh, and was so taken with the vegetable's possibilities that he brought in all his powers of persuasion to ensure that Bangalore's reluctant farmers cultivated it.

Et voilà! The Bangalore Brinjal was born!

John Cameron also introduced apple cultivation to Bangalore in 1887, importing 17 varieties to see which ones would take. Only one did – the Rome Beauty. Seeds were distributed free to farmers, and cultivation began in right earnest. In 1910, there were close to 1,000 acres of land under apple cultivation in Bangalore alone! By 1920, however, the dream had died – air pollution from the rising number of motor vehicles on the city's streets had put paid to the apple crop. Yup, even a century ago, Bangalore traffic had a bad rap.

4

IN MAY 1799, COL ARTHUR WELLESLEY, 1ST DUKE OF WELLINGTON, TOOK OVER AS GOVERNOR OF SERINGAPATAM AND MYSORE

A City Birthed by Mosquitoes

I was first introduced to Wellington boots, or wellies, by Enid Blyton, my most favourite author as a child. Like with everything else Blyton wrote about, I immediately wanted a pair for myself – what a treat not to have to squelch home through muddy puddles of 4 p.m. Bangalore rain in my 'bubbling' Bata keds! Many years later, I learnt that wellies were named after Arthur Wellesley, 1st Duke of Wellington, who got his shoemaker to change the design of his Hessian boots so that they would be more fashionable. Even later, I was gobsmacked to discover that at the fag end of the eighteenth century, the Iron Duke, then a young man, had walked around MY city in his unfashionable Hessians!

Which is all fine and dandy, but how do mosquitoes come into this story? Seriously? Can there be a Bangalore story without them?

April is the cruellest month, breeding not lilacs but mosquitoes out of the open drains that the summer heat cooks to a ripe stench in pockets across the city. Of course, official mosquito season is after the rains, but Bengaluru's tenacious little devils clearly never got the memo. Like disoriented Magi, they come bearing gifts in every season – dengue, chikungunya, malaria, or, at the very least, a nightly dose of aggravation.

What is not widely known, however, is that we owe this very city – or at least a large and central portion of it – to mosquitoes. No, seriously. This is how that went down.

After the Fourth Anglo-Mysore War had ended with the fall of Tipu Sultan in 1799, the young and formidable Col Arthur Wellesley, who had brought up the rear in the final battle, was appointed governor of Seringapatam (Srirangapatna) and Mysore. Chuffed at adding the annihilation of the Tiger of Mysore to his résumé, the 30-year-old insisted on moving into Tipu's airy summer palace, Dariya Daulat, in Srirangapatna. From there, he charted the rise of the empire, routing the mighty Marathas in the Second Anglo-Maratha War, and effectively securing the Deccan for the East India Company.

Even though the Indian peninsula had proved a happy hunting ground for Wellesley, drilling him in battle strategies that would serve him well in the military campaigns he would lead in the future, he grew weary of life in the tropics (several prolonged and debilitating bouts of diarrhoea may have sealed the deal). In 1805, along with his older brother, Lord (Richard) Wellesley, who had just retired from his position as governor-general of India, he sailed for home. In 1815, now extensively decorated and raised to the peerage, he defeated Napoleon in the Battle of Waterloo.

Uh-hunh, the celebrated Duke of Wellington was none other than our Wellesley, who earned his early stripes fighting Tipu in these parts!

Soon after Wellesley quit Srirangapatna, a petition went out to the maharaja of Mysore from the hapless British regiments left behind, requesting a piece of land more salubrious than the one they had been condemned to. The mosquito pestilence on the island was not to be borne, they pleaded, and they were tired of losing brother soldiers to the scourge called malaria. In 1807, the maharaja granted them a parcel of land 6 km east of the Bengaluru Pete, near the Ulsoor Lake, and – ta-da! – the Bengaluru Cantonment (which grew to contain today's MG Road, Brigade Road, Infantry Road, Cavalry Road, Artillery Road, Shivajinagar, Commercial Street, Richmond Road, Residency Road, Fraser Town and much, much more) was born!

Up for another bit of Wellesley–Bengaluru trivia? So, Assaye Road, which leads to the HQ of the Madras Engineering Group (originally the Madras Sappers, founded 1780) by the Ulsoor Lake, is named after a legendary 1803 battle in the Second Anglo-Maratha War, in which a small band of British and Indian regiments, including the Sappers, defeated the much larger Maratha army. The win came at great cost to Wellesley – he lost hundreds of men – but it remained one of his 'great victories'. Years after his triumph at Waterloo, when asked which he considered his best battle, the Iron Duke would reply, unhesitatingly – 'Assaye'.

By the way, the harried Seringapatam petitioners had no idea that mosquitoes and malaria were related. In fact, no one in the world had figured it out yet. It would take close to 90 years, and another British army officer stationed in Bengaluru, to crack that one.

The Iron Duke is remembered in Bangalore by Wellington Street in Richmond Town, and by the Beef Wellington (a dish created in his honour after his victory at Waterloo), which can be ordered at several restaurants in the city.

5

GANDHIJI VISITED BANGALORE IN APRIL 1927

For the New Year, an Old Bapu Memory

Gandhiji visited Bangalore five times between 1915 and 1936. His longest stay was in 1927, which this column briefly chronicles. But the funniest story about him comes from his 1936 visit. The renowned violinist Vidwan T. Chowdiah (the grand, violin-shaped 1,100-seater concert hall in Malleswaram is named after him), had just finished a command performance for Bapu, who was enthralled. That's when our local wit, the playwright T.P. Kailasam, observed, tongue firmly in cheek, 'Bapu, he is a violinist. But you are a non-violinist.' Bapu burst out laughing, while everyone else, including Chowdiah, looked on, bewildered.

'Yuga yugaadi kaledaroo Ugadi marali baruthide (Countless yugas may come and go, but the Ugadi festival always returns),' wrote the beloved Jnanpith Award–winning Kannada lyrical poet Dattatreya Ramachandra Bendre, in the '60s, assuring us of the exuberant, periodic and inevitable return of springtime, not just in Nature but also in human fortunes. In the 1963 film, *Kulavadhu*, prolific playback singer S. Janaki sang the words straight into Kannadiga hearts, where they have remained as the signature song of the season. Each year around the beginning of April, on the morning that follows the new moon night of Phalguna, when the moon of Chaitra enters its waxing phase against the backdrop of honge and neem blossoms and mangoes heavy on the bough, Ugadi returns, just as the poet promised, bringing joy and hope, infusing the bitterness of our overburdened lives with a hint of sweetness.

But April also marks another, much less acknowledged, anniversary on the Bengaluru history timeline – it was in April 1927, almost a century ago now, that Mahatma Gandhi came to the city, on his doctor's express orders, for some much-needed R&R. Earlier that year, he had collapsed from a mild apoplexy, a minor stroke, brought on, as the struggle for Swaraj gained momentum, by overwork, exposure, incessant travel and severe hypertension. Contravening medical advice, 57-year-old Gandhi was back on the road no sooner than he was back on his feet, addressing rallies across the country about, variously, khadi, non-cooperation, self-rule and self-reliance.

In April, however, when temperatures across the country began to soar, Dr Jivaraj Mehta put his foot down. Reluctantly, Gandhiji agreed to move – to 'Bangalore or some such place' – for a couple of months. He ended up staying until early August, making that stint his longest one ever outside the Sabarmati Ashram.

Why Bangalore? Then as now, the city's pleasant weather was legendary. Plus, Bangalore wasn't entirely unfamiliar to Gandhiji – he had already visited on two occasions – in 1915, very soon after he had returned to India from South Africa, to inaugurate the Mysore Social Service League, an organization set up by Kannada writer, thinker and reformer D.V. Gundappa, and again in 1920. Even more importantly, Gandhiji and the then Maharaja of Mysore Krishnaraja Wadiyar IV, shared a great mutual respect. Alighting on 19 April at the Yeshwantpur Railway Station as the maharaja's honoured guest, a frail Gandhiji conducted a prayer meeting on the railway platform for the crowds gathered to welcome him, before he was whisked away to the seclusion of Nandi Hills.

At Nandi Hills, Gandhiji chose Oaklands, the smaller, more isolated bungalow of Francis Cunningham (yes, the same Cunningham after whom the road is named – he had been private secretary to Sir Mark Cubbon in the nineteenth century) for his recuperation, over other grander ones. Forty-five days later, on 5 June, much improved in health but still awaiting a clean chit from his doctor, he moved to Bangalore, into the Kumara Krupa Guest House, itching to get back into the whirl of things.

Gandhiji made many visits to many institutions in the city in the two months that followed, but the one he visited most often, thanks to a serendipitous meeting with William Smith, was the Imperial Institute of Animal Husbandry and Dairying (today, the National Dairy Research Institute [NDRI]), of which Smith was director. Signing into its visitors' book as 'a farmer from Sabarmati', he spent several happy hours there, learning about the latest innovations in dairy technology. He even posed with the institute's rock star, an Ayrshire–Haryana cross-breed cow called Jill, who had birthed 16 calves and was reputed to yield over 5,000 litres of milk a year. That picture that still hangs at the institute, to commemorate both Jill and her famous visitor.

'You mention Kailasam meeting Gandhi in your well-written column. Did you know that Kailasam wrote a poem on Gandhi? Here it is.'

— M. SHIVAKUMAR, FOUNDER–EDITOR OF KANNADA WEEKLY HUMOUR MAGAZINE *APARANJI*

•

The Recipe

Into a bare handful of bone and skin
Pour just an ounce of flesh and blood;
Put in a heart as love-full as sea in flood,
Likewise, a mind profound and free from sin;

Fix on two jumbo ears, two goo-goo eyes,
Paint on a smile of babe at mother's breast;
Enclose a soul that caps Himavat's crest
And speaks with tongue that honey's sweet defies;

The 'stuffing'? Goat's milk, soya beans and dates!
Now, fill to brim with suffering humans' tears
And bake this dish in gaol for umpteen years;
Remove and garnish with pariah mates;

Wrap up in rags, prop up with lithe bamboo
And serve: The World Redeemer, OUR BAPOO!

— T.P. KAILASAM

6

THE ALMOST CENTURY-OLD RUSSELL MARKET
WAS BEAUTIFULLY RESTORED IN MARCH 2023

A Vibrant Market at the Heart of the Cantonment

Everyone has their favourite market – mine was the open-air, stone-flagged Malleswaram Market, now sadly missed in its original form, at 15th Cross, Sampige Road. I was first introduced to the market as a toddler, riding on my uncle's shoulders or carried in my grandfather's arms. Its sights and scents and sounds – the sugandharaja and roses in the lush garlands; the piles of thickly strung Mysuru mallige (GI-tagged local jasmine) and kanakambara in the baskets outside; the walk down the steps into the sunken market area; the glistening, freshly watered mounds of fruits, vegetables and soppu (leafy vegetables); the voices raised in cheerful bargaining; and so much more – are part of my fondest memories of childhood.

Ugadi is here, and Bengaluru's traditional markets are bursting with flowers, the promise of sweet summer mangoes, and tender neem leaves waiting to become part of the philosophical deliciousness of bevu-bella. A new year should herald new (re)beginnings; appropriately, the famous Russell Market, one of the city's oldest, is welcoming Bengalureans to experience its delights post a long-overdue makeover.

With its Indo-Saracenic onion-bulb domes, Islamic arches and very British clock tower, the palatial market building looks incongruous among present company. When it first came up in 1927, however, it made a perfectly gracious and necessary addition to the Cantonment. It was T.B. Russell, the municipal commissioner of the time, who conceived of a covered structure with separate dry and wet markets; a one-stop shop for flowers, exotic 'English' fruits and vegetables, meat and fish to serve British homes and kitchens.

But Commissioner Russell was not creating something new – he was only aggregating and organizing a marketplace that had operated in the same area for at least a century. When Major General Arthur Wellesley, part-architect of the decisive English victory against Tipu Sultan in the Fourth Anglo-Mysore War, departed for England in March 1805, the regiments he left behind in Srirangapatna urged the maharaja of Mysore to grant them a more salubrious piece of land somewhere else in the kingdom for a new Cantonment. Chitradurga and Channapatna were considered, but in the end, the British familiarity with Bengaluru Pete (the old city) won out.

There was still the question of where exactly the Cantonment would be built. Astoundingly, it was a 23-year-old military engineer who was charged with the responsibility of not only finding a suitable location, but also of designing the entire Cantonment. In his memoir *Twelve Years' Military Adventure in Three Quarters of the Globe*, published in 1829, John Blakiston himself admits that his services in quelling the Vellore Mutiny of 1806 being accorded a 'higher value than strictly merited' by the powers-that-be, he was 'ordered up to Bangalore'.

The lad proved equal to the task, however. Contending that the Cantonment needed to be close enough to the Pete (for provisions and services) while remaining splendidly isolated from it, and that height was an advantage given the region's topography, he picked a mile-long ridge running east to west – where the British army under Lord Cornwallis had camped during the 1791 siege of the Bengaluru Fort – to build it on. (MG Road and Cubbon Road, the heart of the erstwhile Cantonment, lie on that ridge). In under a year, he had constructed barracks for two European and five native regiments, and even built a hospital! Blakiston enjoyed his three-year stay in Bangalore, declaring that its climate, situation, production and society 'rendered it by far the pleasantest and most agreeable residence in the peninsula.'

In a couple of decades, the Cantonment had grown and spread, bringing in its wake migrant labour, service staff, and tradesmen from Madras and other surrounding areas, who were accommodated in the valleys that the ridge sloped into on its north and south sides. One of the first areas occupied was a small existing settlement called Bilekalli, adjacent to which an informal marketplace, the precursor to Russell Market, began to thrive in the late 1820s. By and by, that area came to be known as Blackpally (whether that was the mandatory British mangling of a local name, a racist reference to the local people who lived there, or a tribute to the capable John Blakiston is anyone's guess). At some point after Independence, Blackpally was bestowed the name of a Maratha hero who had briefly called Bengaluru home, and became Shivajinagar.

'Lovely snippets of history! I had no idea there used to be a Bilekahalli adjoining Russell Market, before the area came to be called Shivajinagar. My Bilekahalli is near IIM Bangalore, close to where I live and work.'

— VIDYA MANI, CO-FOUNDER OF AN INDEPENDENT CHILDREN'S BOOKSTORE IN SOUTH BANGALORE

•

'Very nice reading about my favourite Russell Market. I went there regularly on my Suvega after finishing half-day school on Queen's Road to get my provisions of vegetables and fruits. It all seems so long ago now.'

— SHAKUNTALA PAI, HEADMISTRESS OF THE HAMSADHWANI SCHOOL FOR HEARING AND SPEECH IMPAIRED IN THE '80S AND '90S

7

HAJEE ISMAIL SAIT WAS BORN ON 7 MARCH 1859

The Munificent Memon of Mosque Road

I grew up City-side, in the neighbourhoods of Kumara Park and Malleswaram, in the '70s and '80s. To me, the Cantonment, apart from Cubbon Park, MG Road and Commercial Street, might well have been a different planet. I made my acquaintance with Mosque Road only years into adulthood, when meat-eating friends took me along to show me where they disappeared each evening during Ramzan, and why. There wasn't very much for vegetarian me to eat, but the lights, the crowds, the appetizing smells and the thoroughly festive mood were delightful revelations to someone who had hitherto believed she knew her city.

With Ugadi almost upon us, the sublime beauty of those Bengaluru March days when, as Dickens put it in *Great Expectations*, 'it is summer in the light and winter in the shade', are no longer ours. It is still a good time, though, to remember a son of the soil, born in another, long-ago March. This merchant–philanthropist has a hospital, a street and one of the city's best-known mosques named after him, all located in the neighbourhood of Pulikeshi Nagara (Eh? Oh, all right, let's call it by its original name, Fraser Town). We are speaking, of course, of Fakhr-ut-Tujjar Hajee Sir Ismail Sait.

In 1870, 11-year-old Ismail Sait and his family moved from Mysore to the Bangalore Cantonment. Only four years later, tragedy struck – Ismail's father passed, leaving the family bereft. Drawing on his mercantile Cutchi Memon genes, the boy stepped up to the plate, and soon had a very successful store – The English Warehouse – up and running on St Mark's Road, selling all manner of goods imported from England, from milk powder to machinery.

(The Memons were historically part of Sindh's Lohana business community. Facing hostility from their neighbours, the 700 families who accepted Islam in the fifteenth century were forced to leave their native land. The Memons who settled in Bhuj, in Gujarat's Kachchh region, came to be known as the Cutchi Memons. Under British rule, the Cutchi Memons moved to the empire's commercial centres across India and the world to ply their trade.)

In the decades that followed, young Ismail went from strength to strength. Branches of the Warehouse opened in Chennai and Secunderabad. Cornering the market on horse-gram, among other food supplies to the British military, he diversified into timber and kerosene (imported from America through Spencer & Co) as well. Smart investments in the Kolar gold mines reaped rich returns, leading him to establish a distillery and a complementary carbonic acid manufacturing unit in Calcutta. At 22, noticed by the establishment on both sides of the City–Cantonment divide, he had a seat on the board of directors of the Carnatic Mills (which later became the Binny Mills). He would also go on to serve as director of the Mysore Sandalwood Oil Company, the Bhadravati Iron Works and Mysore Sugar.

When the plague hit Bengaluru in the late 1890s, the C&M station was slow on the uptake when it came to establishing new extensions to house the residents of congested Blackpally (today's Shivajinagar). While Malleswaram and Basavanagudi, on the City side, were up and running by 1899, it was only in 1906 that plans for Fraser Town – one of the first 'plague extensions' on the Cantonment side – were approved. But Blackpally residents weren't convinced – not until Ismail Sait (and others) invested in the extension's growth and development, and created enough excitement for people to move in.

Neither the honorific 'Hajee', nor the title Fakhr-ut-Tujjar ('The pride of merchants'), bestowed on him by the maharaja in 1919, nor the knighthood conferred by King George V in 1923, were consequences of Ismail Sait's business success, however. It was his philanthropy that did it – apart from setting up the Gosha hospital for women in purdah and the beautiful mosque in Fraser Town that gives Mosque Road its name, he made generous endowments to the Aligarh Muslim University, the Mysore University, the Victoria Hospital and the St Martha's Hospital, apart from several orphanages, schools and reading rooms across the country.

When you are scarfing down iftar delicacies on Mosque Road with the rest of Bengaluru the next time Ramzan rolls around, make sure you spare a thought for the good Hajee.

'At a time when the community is being battered by a systematic campaign of hatred and prejudice to discredit and weaken it, your paean to Hajee Sir Ismail Sait was refreshing and so timely. I can only hope that the essence of Bangalore's composite culture that we all love and bask in will not be destroyed forever by these inimical forces. As a fellow author and Bangalorean, and a Cutchi Memon to boot, I felt I just had to reach out to you.'

— SAEED IBRAHIM, AUTHOR OF *TWIN TALES FROM KUTCCH: A FAMILY SAGA SET IN COLONIAL INDIA*

8

SATI SULOCHANA, THE FIRST KANNADA TALKIE, WAS RELEASED ON 3 MARCH 1934

The Filmy Ways of Gandhinagar

In the memories of my extended family on my dad's side, Gandhinagar is inextricably linked with celebrations at Sukh Sagar, the OG Gujarati-run eatery that, in our opinion, served the best chaat and pav bhaji this side of the Vindhyas. But I also went to Gandhinagar for other reasons – my aunt, a lecturer in library science, took me with her to Sapna Book House (the only one in town at the time), where she went to choose books for her college library, and I tagged along with mum when she occasionally drove to the Janatha Bazaar for her monthly groceries, gawping at the 60-ft high movie-star cutouts outside the dozens of theatres on KG Road. But I never watched a film at any of them.

On 13 April 2022, the most expensive Kannada film ever made – *KGF: Chapter 2* – opened to rave reviews across India. To date, it has raked in an incredible 1.2k crores, a dozen times over its production budget, making it the highest-grossing Kannada film, and the third highest-grossing Indian film, of all time. The wholehearted pan-Indian acceptance of a homegrown Kannada film series has been a shot in the arm for the Kannada film industry, whose glory days hitherto lay in the '70s and '80s, when Bengaluru's Gandhinagar was where the lights, cameras and action were at.

Lying as it does at the junction of Kempegowda I's sixteenth-century fort town and the erstwhile British Cantonment, and the home of both the 'Majestic' Bus Stand (officially, Kempegowda Bus Terminal) and the City Railway Station (officially, Krantivira Sangolli Rayanna Railway Station), Gandhinagar has welcomed visitors to our fair city for several decades now. Since 2016, it has also housed the Kempegowda Interchange, the point of intersection of the two lines of the Bengaluru metro, making it a unique multi-modal transport hub at the city's heart.

But the heart of Gandhinagar itself wasn't always a bus terminus; it was a tank. City founder Kempegowda I raised the original Bengaluru in 1537 to the south of this tank, so that it would be well supplied with water. Remarkably, the Dharmambudhi tank would continue to fulfil this function until the end of the nineteenth century. In 1889, when Prince Albert Victor, grandson of Queen Victoria, visited Bangalore to lay the foundation stone of the Lalbagh Glass House, he emerged from the City railway station to a royal welcome that included a Bharatanatyam performance – on a raft of boats anchored in the middle of the Dharmambudhi tank!

In the decade after, as the city's water demands grew, the tank began to deplete. In 1894, the Hesaraghatta Reservoir, created to be the primary water source for Bengaluru, was completed, killing any incentive to replenish Dharmambudhi. Part of the tank bed was soon turned into a space for cultural activities and political gatherings – in 1931, none other than Jawaharlal Nehru made a fiery speech there. In 1969, the now-dry lake bed was repurposed into the Majestic Bus Station.

Meanwhile, in 1934, the first Kannada talkie, *Sati Sulochana*, was released. None of the post-production was done in Bengaluru, however; it was Madras, with an already well-established cinema scene, that would serve for the latter until the '70s. In 1954, the beloved superstar and Kannada cultural icon, Dr Rajkumar, made his explosive debut as the eponymous hero of *Bedara Kannappa*, ushering in the golden age. By the time the Majestic Bus Station (why Majestic? Because that was the name of a well-known theatre that stood close by) began operations, the city had no less than 149 cinema halls, 14 of them on Gandhinagar's KG Road! To cater to every moviegoer in a city that had always welcomed immigrants, Bengaluru's theatres screened movies in at least six languages, and continue to do so today.

The thriving domestic market soon convinced filmmakers that the city needed its own production infrastructure. With its proximity to theatres and transportation – film reels had to be physically delivered to theatres – Gandhinagar was the natural choice of location. For the next 40 years, the neighbourhood would reign as the nerve centre of 'Sandalwood'. Until, inevitably,

change arrived in the shape of digital filmmaking and multiplexes. Today, only five theatres still function on KG Road, and most studios have moved to the city's south-western reaches, around Nagarabhavi and Rajarajeshwari Nagar. For now, Gandhinagar has slouched off into the sunset.

'Interesting way to connect the old and the new. By the way, so happy for Sandalwood to have those superhits – *KGF: Chapter 1* and *2*, *Kantara*, and even the smaller but much-loved *Charlie 777*. Kannada films have allowed Telugu and Tamil films to overshadow them for too long.'

— VENKY DATLA, FOUNDER, CREYA LEARNING, HYDERABAD

9

SHIVAJI DIED ON 3 APRIL 1680

A Chhatrapati in the City

Growing up, a wedding in the family invariably meant a saree-shopping expedition to Chikpete, in the wake of mum, grandmum and assorted aunts. I did not really enjoy those outings, but bore them stoically because there was usually some delicious compensation to look forward to – a chilled glass of sugarcane juice, hot-hot bajjis from a street-side vendor, or a 'plate' of darkly glistening jamuns (we never called them gulab jamuns). It was only when I went to college, down the road from Chikpete, that I became a regular visitor, trawling Avenue Road for '10 years' solved question papers' guides, Sultanpete for an amazing variety of handmade paper, and Raja Market for shiny feminine baubles.

I was only following an old Bangalore tradition – three centuries before me, a teenaged Maratha boy with far bigger dreams had enjoyed the delights of the same streets with his own friends.

Ever wondered why an imposing statue of an equestrian Chhatrapati Shivaji Maharaj, apparently storming the ramparts of yet another fortress freshly fallen to his sword, stands at the Bhashyam Circle by the Sankey Tank? Or why a well-known neighbourhood in the heart of the Cantonment is named after this same personage? After all, wasn't Shivaji a seventeenth-century Punekar who, with a ragtag army scrabbled together from peasants and artisans and petty tradesmen, successfully challenged the mighty Mughals and, with his audacious guerrilla tactics, changed the rules of war in the subcontinent? What did he have to do with Bangalore?

As it turns out, a fair bit. And as is often the case with trails gone cold, a good place to begin is. . . *cherchez la femme*! In Shivaji's case, the *femme* in question was a Saibai Nimbalkar, whom our hero travelled to Bengaluru to wed, when he was only 12. Now, the girl herself wasn't from this city, but Shivaji's mum, Jijabai, thought it good form that the boy's father, Shahaji Bhonsale, who was living here at the time, be involved in the proceedings, so that he may bless the couple (and hopefully host the whole shindig as well).

Why was Shahaji in Bengaluru, though? Thereby hangs a tale of a shrewd buccaneer who survived – nay, thrived – in the fluid politics and constantly shifting borders of the Deccan by switching his loyalties, at a dizzying pace, between the various kingdoms that were jockeying for control of the region. Among them were the five Deccan sultanates – Ahmadnagar, Berar, Bidar, Bijapur and Golconda – that had come together in one grand show of unity to decimate Vijayanagara at the Battle of Talikota in 1565. By the time 12-year-old Shahaji appeared on the scene in 1606, already commanding a unit in the Ahmadnagar army in which his father had also served, the sultanates had once again fallen out. By 1625, when Shahaji was appointed to a senior position in the same army and awarded the jagir (fiefdom) of Pune for his services, beady Mughal eyes had also come to settle on the region.

Over the next decade, Shahaji moved between serving Ahmadnagar, the Mughals and Bijapur – an asset to the side he was on and a nuisance to everyone else. In 1636, a peace treaty was signed between Bijapur and the Mughals. One of the conditions, laid down by Emperor Shah Jahan himself, was that the bothersome Shahaji be banished from the northern Deccan and Pune. Reluctantly, Shahaji handed Pune to his young heir, Shivaji, and hung out in the Konkan, biding his time. His luck turned in 1638, when he helped the fierce Bijapur commander, Ranadullah Khan, capture Bengaluru and its surrounds from the third Kempegowda, and received the jagir of Bengaluru for his pains.

So, naturally, when Jijabai asked about a Bengaluru wedding for their son in 1642, Shahaji accepted with alacrity. The boss' son's nuptials were quite a show, if legend is to be believed, and likely happened somewhere in Chikpete, within the mud fort that Kempegowda I had built over a hundred years before to house his new capital. After which, the newly-weds, much taken with this fine city, stayed on for a couple of years, with Shivaji shadowing his dad, learning from him not only the intricacies of administration but also the importance of gardens, which Shahaji loved commissioning, in the civilizing of a city.

By rights, Bengaluru should have raised memorials to the senior Bhonsale, but much like Shahaji himself, cities and communities like to ally themselves with winning horses. *C'est la vie.*

'Wah! The Chhatrapati and namma ooru! Learnt of this for the first time.'

— RAMYA SRINIVASAN, BANGALOREAN SETTLED IN AHMEDABAD

Circa 1674, Shivaji's half-brother, Venkoji, who had grown up in Bengaluru, shifted base to Thanjavur and founded the Thanjavur Maratha dynasty, which would last well into the nineteenth century before it fell to the British. Two famous people from the Thanjavur Marathi community were V.P. Madhava Rao and T. Ananda Rao (T stands for Thanjavarkar) both of whom served as diwans of Mysore in the twentieth century. The former also served as diwan of Travancore and Baroda; the latter, who invited Sir M. Visvesvaraya to take over as diwan after him in 1912, has a famous circle along the Race Course Road named after him.

10

WHITEFIELD METRO LINE WAS INAUGURATED IN MARCH 2023

It's Whitefield Ho! Via Namma Metro

In the '70s and '80s, the word Whitefield only brought up one visual in Bangalorean minds – the curly haired, miracle-performing godman Sathya Sai Baba. His ashram, Brindavan, inaugurated in 1960, was located next to the Whitefield Railway Station, at an unimaginable distance – 24 km – from the city. (My dad worked at MICO Bosch, 7 km from home, and people were always commiserating with him about his commute.)

Everything changed in 1996, when the still sleepy village exploded into the Whitefield we know, with the opening of the International Tech Park, the petri dish in which Bengaluru's – and India's – transformation into a global tech hub was brewed.

It's March, and right on cue, Bengaluru's avenues and parks have turned to gold as the *Tabebuia aurea* has exploded into bloom across the city. Shortly, Bengalureans will lapse into their annual summer pastime of moaning about the heat, but for now, as the gentle, perfumed breezes of Phalguna waft through the verdure, setting a-quiver the new, shiny, deliciously fresh green leaves of peepal and honge and rain tree against perfect blue skies, everything is just dreamy.

In some city circles, however, an imminent event is raising excitement levels to fever pitch – the Bengaluru Metro Rail Corporation Limited (BMRCL) has confirmed that a new 13-km extension of the east–west Purple Line will soon become operational. That extension will connect the centuries-old settlement of Krishnarajapuram, named after the nineteenth-century king of Mysore, Krishnaraja Wadiyar III, with the more recent, and more curiously named, suburb of Whitefield.

It was Krishnaraja III's successor, Chamarajendra Wadiyar X, who generously allocated 3,900 acres of land 12 miles east of the Bangalore Cantonment and two miles south of the Kadugodi (now Whitefield) railway station for the poorer Eurasian and Anglo-Indian people of the city, in response to a petition filed in 1882 by David Emmanuel Starkenburgh White, a retired Anglo-Indian civil servant and founder of the Eurasian and Anglo-Indian Association of Southern India. It was in his honour that the settlement was called Whitefield, and not, as is popularly believed, because it was a community of white, or at the very least, half-white, people.

Mr White had hoped, even in the face of huge scepticism that anyone could make farmers out of Eurasians (the nineteenth-century term for the community we today know as Anglo-Indians, who were the offspring of marriages between Indian women and British men), that promoting industrial and agricultural pursuits among his community would make them self-sufficient, but things did not turn out in quite the way he had envisioned.

The *Mysore Gazette* of 1897 mentions that even in 1889, there were only 25 families in Whitefield, six of them non-resident. The village proper had a spread of 30 acres, divided into 24 plots, arranged in two concentric circles around the village green, but only 12 cottages had been built there. There was a school with 31 students, and a Protestant Church, where regular Church of England services were conducted. Some residents had indeed taken up dairy farming and some others poultry farming, but the land lay fallow around them – many houses were only weekend getaways, to indulge their owners' passion for hunting in the Whitefield wilds!

Whitefield's fortunes changed when Asia's largest hydroelectric project at the time began operations in Shivanasamudram in 1902 to supply power to the rich gold mines at Kolar, further east of Whitefield by about 50 miles. The railway line allowed people to live in Whitefield and commute to the mines for work, and the village began to fill up. But it would remain a sleepy settlement well outside the Bengalurean mind space until the mid-'90s, when it became home to the city's first tech park, ITPL. Since then, Whitefield has mainly been known for the torturous difficulty of getting to it.

All that is set to change in a few weeks with Namma Metro access. Once that happens, put that metro card to good use – go attend a service at the old Protestant church (now the Memorial Church Anglican), founded in 1886. It stands right next to the Whitefield Club (founded in 1905) on the rim of the old village green, between the Inner Circle and the Outer Circle, 1.5 km south of the Hope Farm Bus Stop.

'Thanks for your fortnightly "research papers" on what a true resident of Bangalore needs to know. The FAPS (Frank Anthony Public School) brass band and the string chamber orchestra of the Bangalore School of Music have performed quite a few times in Whitefield, both at the club and the Memorial Church.'

— MAESTRO V. NARAYANASWAMY, RESIDENT CONDUCTOR OF THE BSM CHAMBER ORCHESTRA FOR OVER 30 YEARS

•

'Thank you for this! We have newly been allowed into Bangalore thanks to the metro, and we are bursting with excitement on this side of town. After 15 years of moving back, my husband and I are talking about visiting Bangalore spaces!'

— NITYA RAMAKRISHNAN, 'WHITEFIELD RISING' AND 'THRIVE'

KARAGA IS CELEBRATED ON THE FULL MOON NIGHT OF THE MONTH OF CHAITRA, IN MARCH OR APRIL

Bengaluru Karaga: When Draupadi Comes to Town

'There are several reasons why the festival (Karaga) has become so popular. First, the community that performs the main roles in the festival is part of an alliance of backward caste communities in Bengaluru. Secondly (...) 60–70 per cent of the city's population works in the informal sector, so it represents their aspirations, their rights towards the city and their vision of what urban is (...) we cannot always talk urbanism from above. And the fact that we have different religions, castes and communities celebrating this festival together proves something to us today – India has had a composite culture at the urban level for vast swathes of time and we should celebrate that.'

– *Dr Smriti Srinivas, author of* Landscapes of Urban Memory: The Sacred and the Civic in India's High-Tech City (2001), *in an interview to sahapedia.org*

Some 800 years ago, around the time that the Bhakti Movement was reaching its zenith in south India, an unusual temple was raised on a rocky ridge in the centre of the southern Indian peninsula. Unusual, because its chief deity was neither Shiva nor Vishnu, between whom the loyalties of the south were divided, but the Pandava queen Draupadi. The temple was built by the Tigalas, a Tamil-speaking, water-worshipping, flower-growing people who believe themselves to be her descendants.

Three hundred years or so later, circa 1537 CE, a chieftain of Yelahanka called Kempegowda I was looking for a suitable site to build himself a new capital city. How much of a role the temple played in his choice of location is moot, but Kempegowda not only built his city, which he named Bengaluru, around the temple, but also invited the small community of Tigalas to come and live in its vicinity, in an enclave that came to be known as Tigalarapete.

The new city, keen to take advantage of its strategic location – equidistant as it was from the eastern and western coasts – concerned itself at first with trade and commerce rather than with flowers and gardens. Perhaps the few Tigalas who were already in the city found work in Kempegowda's 'Kempu Thota', located in the general region of today's Lalbagh, where flowers were cultivated for worship, but not many more came to live here.

That happened around 1760, when the garden-loving Hyder Ali became the de facto ruler of the kingdom of Mysore and turned Kempu Thota into Lalbagh, a sultan's pleasure garden, laid out in the Mughal tradition, with terraces and water features, and walking paths lined by cypress trees and flower beds. His son Tipu Sultan filled Lalbagh with trees both local and exotic, many of them fruit-bearing ones. Both Hyder and Tipu leaned heavily on the Tigalas' green fingers to make the magic happen.

The rise in the numbers and status of the Tigala community brought the centuries-old temple to Draupadi into the centre of the city's public life. The annual 11-day festival of Karaga, during which the Tigalas worship Draupadi as Adi Shakti, the feminine, dynamic aspect of the primordial cosmic energy, rose in prominence to become a vibrant community festival that involved all its citizens. In a city that was not built along a river and was at a great distance from the sea, a festival that worshipped the Goddess in the form of water quickly found resonance.

This April, on the full moon night of Chaitra, the Tigalas will gather once again, as they have done for centuries, in the centre of the old city, at the temple to Draupadi (ironically called the Dharmaraya Swamy Temple, after her oldest husband), to welcome the Goddess on her annual visit to the earth. The priest designated to be the bearer of the Karaga (unbaked mud pot) will wait patiently, in his saffron saree and bangles (for he is channelling the Goddess herself), for her to manifest in the water in the pot.

And when she does, somewhere in the wee hours, the rejoicing will begin, and the 'dik-di, dik-di' chants of the sword-wielding Veerakumaras, the soldiers designated to protect her, will fill the air. Followed by the Veerakumaras, the priest, carrying the three-foot high, flower-bedecked Karaga on his head, will proceed to circumnavigate the old city through the milling crowds, paying his respects not only at various temples along the route, but also, in a time-honoured symbol of communal harmony that has defined this city, at the dargah of the eighteenth-century Sufi saint Hazrat Tawakkal Mastan.

'And what of the food frenzy in every bylane after the shops down shutters and before Draupadi Amman ventures out, each street competing with the other in trying to please the devout! The free idli, dosa and rice bhath provide the much-needed energy to jostle and elbow the others while running along with the Karaga. On my last visit, I had eaten well, and passed out in front of a shop until the screaming crowds woke me up, haha!'

— DEEPAK K.G., OLD BANGALOREAN WITH THREE CATS

12

INDIA'S FIRST SATELLITE, ARYABHATA, WAS LAUNCHED ON 19 APRIL 1975

The Man Who Built a Satellite in a Shed

National Public School, Indiranagar, where my children studied, is located very much in the vicinity of the organizations, agencies and laboratories – ISRO, NAL, HAL, Liquid Propulsion Systems Centre and the UR Rao Satellite Centre – that are the heart and head of India's aviation and space programme. Naturally, the school community included many children whose parents were, to put it simply (and perhaps inaccurately), space scientists. But a large majority of the children were unaware that the man who had cobbled together India's very first satellite lived in the unpretentious house opposite the back gate of their school, or that his name was Udupi Ramachandra Rao.

Last week, as the Vikram lander descended into a graceful, precise, soft landing on the dark side of the moon, Indian hearts exploded in pride. This week, let us shift our attention away from the lander to Chandrayaan-3, the satellite that carried it there, and to the story of India's satellite dream, which began in 1972 in six rough industrial sheds outside Bengaluru.

The problem with space technology is that countries guard their knowhow fiercely – there's very little, and very sketchy, information available in the public domain. In 1966, therefore, Vikram Sarabhai, then director of the Indian National Committee for Space Research (INCOSPAR), invited one of his former PhD students at the Physical Research Laboratories (PRL) Ahmedabad, who had been researching solar cosmic-ray phenomena while working with Pioneer space probes and Explorer satellites at MIT, to return and head the satellite engineering team Sarabhai was putting together. The brilliant young man who bought into the dream and would later be hailed as India's Satellite Man was 34-year-old Udupi Ramachandra Rao.

When U.R. Rao took over the satellite programme, he was the only one on the team to have ever seen a satellite. At that time, the satellite engineering team was divided between the Thumba Equatorial Rocket Launching Station (TERLS) near Trivandrum, and PRL in Ahmedabad. The untimely death of Sarabhai in 1971 brought Satish Dhawan to the helm of ISRO (INCOSPAR became ISRO in 1969). Unwilling to give up his job as director of the Indian Institute of Science (IISc), Dhawan negotiated for ISRO to move to Bangalore, providing the perfect opportunity for Rao, who had spent his boyhood in Ballari and the little village of Adamaru in Udupi, to decide to move the satellite centre here as well.

It wasn't easy. The unionized labour force at TERLS went on the warpath, refusing to allow any equipment to be moved out. In Bangalore itself, premises had to be found. At first, the IISc gymkhana was co-opted; later, the Karnataka government offered Rao a few sheds at the brand-new (read: entirely lacking facilities) Peenya Industrial Area outside town. In a dazzling feat of jugaad, involving thermocol, vinyl and, presumably, duct tape, one of those dusty, asbestos-roofed sheds was converted into the 'clean room' required for satellite activity.

In those sheds, between 1972 and 1975, a young and inexperienced but passionate team of scientists and engineers – average age: 26 – put together, under Rao's dynamic, inspiring, impatient leadership, India's very first satellite, Aryabhata. It was a magnificent feat – no other country had built a satellite in under three years. The famous picture of Aryabhata being transported on a bullock cart was scoffed at in the American press, which questioned a poor country's need for a space programme. Rao explained it years later as another brilliant example of jugaad. The spacecraft had to be tested for electromagnetic capability and interference in an open area, but metal trucks threw off reflections that interfered with the satellite's antenna. Someone came up with the brilliant idea of using a wooden bullock cart to transport it instead – *et voilà*!

In 2017, at the age of 85, after overseeing the design of 18 more satellites, accelerating the development of satellite launch vehicles like the ASLVs and PSLVs during his decade-long tenure as chairman of ISRO, and becoming the first Indian to be inducted into the International Astronautical Federation's 'Hall of Fame', the much-decorated U.R. Rao died with his boots on. Since then, the ISRO Satellite Centre in Bengaluru, which he so capably raised on the wings of a dream and a prayer, and where all the Chandrayaan satellites were built, has carried his name, and now goes by UR Rao Satellite Centre.

'Very nice article. I had gone to meet Dr Rao, in 1975, soon after joining NAL (National Aerospace Laboratories). I accompanied Dr Beckers, the UNDP expert working with us, to see the legendary sheds in Peenya. Did look a joke at that time!'

– DR B.R. PAI, FORMER DIRECTOR OF NAL

•

'I had the opportunity to work with Dr U.R. Rao many years ago, when I worked for Prism Publications, on a book called *Space and Agenda 21: Caring for Planet Earth*. It was a wonderful experience – he was a most unassuming man.'

– MAHESH NANJUNDAIAH, SENIOR SALES MANAGER, SIMON & SCHUSTER INDIA

13

ROYAL CHALLENGERS BANGALORE (RCB) WOMEN WON THEIR MAIDEN WPL IN MARCH 2024

A Stadium Located at (and in) the City's Heart

Cricket is not a sport I follow closely, but I have found myself in the stands at Chinnaswamy Stadium several times over the years, simply because it is a Bangalorean thing to do. Most recently, I watched Ellyse Perry demolish the Mumbai Indians and usher RCB Women to the playoffs of WPL 2024, a tournament they eventually won with great aplomb – Ee sala Cup nammadu! – beating their male RCB counterparts to it. What I did not know, and discovered to my utter surprise while researching this piece, was that the Mr Chinnaswamy after whom the stadium is named was one of the founders of the MES College of Arts, Commerce and Science in Malleswaram, my alma mater for two wonderful years of pre-university.

Last week, the M. Chinnaswamy Stadium exploded with joy as our girls in red and blue, the floodlights glinting off their sequinned jersey numbers, took the game away from the UP Warriorz in their campaign for the WPL 2024 trophy. It was a bittersweet moment for RCB fans, for the match also marked the girls' last WPL 2024 game in their home stadium. For over two weeks, the long lines outside and the roars inside had demonstrated convincingly that women's cricket was no longer the poorer cousin of the men's game, at least as far as the Bengaluru fans were concerned. The win was also a nice tribute to the beloved stadium that celebrates its 50th anniversary this year.

Technically, the foundation stone of the Chinnaswamy Stadium, originally called the Karnataka State Cricket Association (KSCA) Stadium, was laid in 1969. But if you believe that a cricket stadium truly comes to life when it hosts its first Test match, that honour was granted to our stadium only in 1974. Excitement reached fever pitch as the match dates approached, but the stadium was far from complete, its eastern stands no more than wooden planks held up by casuarina poles. In response to a High Court directive to ensure public safety, the KSCA bolstered the poles with thousands of cement bags, a precious, rationed commodity in those times, and the show went off without a hitch.

In that first match of their India tour, Clive Lloyd's West Indians, including Alvin Kallicharran, debutants Gordon Greenidge and Vivian Richards, and Andy Roberts, thrashed M.A.K. Pataudi's boys, among them Sunil Gavaskar, Farokh Engineer, and Karnataka greats E.A.S. Prasanna, B.S. Chandrasekhar, Brijesh Patel and G.R. Viswanath, by a whopping 267 runs. That was probably when the curse was laid – since then, Chinnaswamy Stadium has had the reputation of being a happy hunting ground for visiting teams.

Luckily for us, Pakistan has bucked that trend – of the three times they have faced off against India here, India has only lost once – at Sunny Gavaskar's swansong Test in 1987, and that by a whisker. In a spruced-up, floodlit stadium, at the quarter-finals of the 1996 ODI World Cup, India registered a resounding win. The third encounter in 2007, a Test match remembered mainly for Sourav Ganguly's career-best innings of 239, ended in a draw.

The relatively small size of the ground has proved a headache for bowlers, a joy for hitters and an absolute delight for the capacity crowd of 32,000. And yet, this was where local lad Anil Kumble, cheered on by his home crowd, bagged his 400th Test wicket, sneaking past Australian Simon Katich's defences in 2004. An admiring city commemorated the achievement by renaming the Oriental Circle, located just outside the stadium, Anil Kumble Circle.

Speaking of renaming, when did the KSCA Stadium become the M. Chinnaswamy Stadium? And who was Chinnaswamy, anyway? A Mandya-born lawyer and passionate cricket fan, Mangalam Chinnaswamy, born 124 years ago this March, served the KSCA for close to four decades, first as secretary and then president, until his retirement in 1990. Alongside, from 1960 to 1980, he also held office at the BCCI, serving as its president from 1977 to 1980. It was he who convinced the Mysore government to allot a parcel of land by the historic Cubbon Park for the stadium, and lease it to the KSCA for one hundred years. This busy, busy man was also one of the founders of the city's MES group of educational institutions.

In 1987, four years before he passed and much against his wishes, the KSCA Stadium was renamed the M. Chinnaswamy Stadium in honour of his services to the beautiful game. Now you know.

'Excellent! I was there reporting in 1987 and some of us had dinner with Gavaskar after – it was his way of saying goodbye, although he didn't announce his retirement until much later.'

— SURESH MENON, CRICKET COLUMNIST, SPORTSWRITER, AND FORMER EDITOR OF *THE INDIAN EXPRESS*

•

'The flat where I live now is part of a building on 16th Cross, Malleswaram, that was constructed by Mr Chinnaswamy's son after demolishing their old house. Guess what the building is called? Cricket House!'

— SUCHITRA DEEP, ARCHITECT AND URBAN ACTIVIST

14

BASAVA JAYANTI IS TRADITIONALLY CELEBRATED IN APRIL—MAY

Dehave Degula: The Game-Changing Ideas of Basavanna

I was brought up Lingayat, by liberal, gender-blind parents. My mother ensured that her children learnt to sing several vachanas composed by Basava, the twelfth-century poet, philosopher, administrator and social reformer whose followers the Lingayats are. One vachana that has endured as one of my favourites, both for the simplicity of its expression and the profundity of its sentiments, is 'Ullavaru Shivalayava Maaduvaru' (The rich build temples), from which the line 'Dehave Degula', the body itself is the temple, is taken. 800 years after it was first written, that ringing declaration still feels like an uplifting, empowering benediction.

To Indians who grew up in the 1980s, Republic Day brings a specific whiff of nostalgia – watching, on Doordarshan, the RD parade, livestreamed from foggy Rajpath. That tradition is now past, but a more local RD tradition endures – the excitement around the Flower Show at Lalbagh. The show's theme in 2024, so the Horticultural Department tells us, was: 'Philosopher–poet–saint Basavanna, and vachana literature.'

That's ambitious, but there is no denying the ever-present need to showcase Basavanna's liberal, inclusive ideas in every kind of forum. Especially because, despite his likenesses gracing two prominent locations in the city – the eponymous Basaveshwara Circle in High Grounds, and more recently, the forecourt of the Vidhana Soudha – so few Bengalureans know much about the life and work of this towering public figure who drove radical social reform in twelfth-century Karnataka.

Born circa 1106 to a Shaiva Brahmin couple of Basavana Bagewadi (in Bijapur district), then part of the powerful Western Chalukya Empire, Basava, so the story goes, rejected the trappings of his caste and left home as a boy to seek guidance at the feet of Ishanya Guru at Kudalasangama (in Bagalkote district). Here, at the confluence of the Krishna and Malaprabha rivers, he spent many happy years, exploring metaphysics alongside more temporal subjects, equipping himself for a life in the world.

So deeply would Kudalasangama impact Basava that he would not only dedicate all his vachanas – moral and philosophical ideas, poetically expressed in colloquial Kannada – to Kudalasangama Deva, his name for the formless Absolute, but would also return here for solace in times of doubt and distress. Of such times there were many, for Basava challenged social inequities, ritualistic worship, animal sacrifice, and caste and gender discrimination at every turn, which did not endear him to the self-appointed guardians of social order.

Fortunately, he had the support of the Kalachuri king Bijjala II, a Chalukya feudatory who toppled his masters and occupied their capital of Kalyana (today, Basavakalyana, in Bidar) in 1156 CE. Basava served Bijjala as his prime minister, using his position to enable social change. One of his firmest convictions, 'Kaayakave Kailasa' (Work Is Worship), dignified the meanest work – and its practitioners – garnering him a large and loyal following among the working classes. The other, that worship did not need temples, saw him encourage his followers, the Sharanas, or Lingayats, to wear an ishtalinga, the symbol of a personal god, on their person, so that they could worship anywhere.

Basava's Anubhava Mantapa (Pavilion of Experience), both a democratic concept and a physical space, offered people of all castes and genders a platform to express themselves in speech and poetry – this last fostered a genre of Kannada devotional and philosophical literature, rooted in social reality, called vachana sahitya. This 'spiritual parliament' was presided over by the low-caste mystic–saint Allamaprabhu, and included the convention-defying female poet–saint Akka Mahadevi. Thus empowered, the Sharanas began to rise against injustice: a revolution was ripe in Kalyana.

The tipping point was Basavanna officiating at the wedding of a Brahmin girl to a low-caste boy, circa 1167. Unable to hold off the orthodox factions any longer, and furious with Basava for overstepping, Bijjala allowed the brutal large-scale massacre of Sharanas to happen on his watch, and was assassinated. Horrified, Basava fled to Kudalasangama, where he died soon after.

Today, the Lingayats make up about 17 per cent of Karnataka's population, and the state has elected 10 chief ministers from the community. What really deserves celebrating, however, is that, some 900 years after they were so violently opposed, Basava's humanistic ideas endure and continue to inspire. And not just as flower show themes, either.

'I was astounded when I read your piece on Basavanna and followed it up with some additional reading. What a man! And outside Karnataka, probably not known too well. Do follow this up with a book about him.'

— ANANDO BANERJEE, VORACIOUS, CATHOLIC READER FROM DELHI

•

'I loved the choice of the title "Dehave Degula" at a time when massive temples are being built. Basavanna stands tall in every age.'

— RAGINI UMESH, READER FROM BANGALORE

•

'A Christian friend of mine strongly believes that Basavanna/Veerashaiva ideology is the only fitting answer to divisive politics. And that only Karnataka has the potential for such a response.

Oh, also, this response from a Bangalore friend: *Dehave is probably better spelt Daehavae. My Indiranagar crowd is pronouncing Dehave to rhyme with behave*!'

— RENU MUKUNDA, SOCIAL DEVELOPMENT SPECIALIST BASED IN TUMKUR

15

THE VESTING ORDER FOR THE TATA INSTITUTE WAS SIGNED ON 27 MAY 1909

Mr Tata and His World-Class Scientific Research Institute

23 November 1898

Esplanade House, Bombay

Dear Swami Vivekananda,

I trust you remember me as a fellow traveller on your voyage from Japan to Chicago. I very much recall at this moment your views on the growth of the ascetic spirit in India, and the duty, not of destroying, but of diverting it into useful channels.

I recall these ideas in connection with my scheme of a Research Institute of Science for India (...). It seems to me that no better use can be made of the ascetic spirit than the establishment of monasteries or residential halls for men dominated by this spirit, where they should (...) devote their lives to the cultivation of sciences – natural and humanistic.

Do you think you would care to apply yourself to the mission of galvanizing into life our ancient traditions in this respect? (...)

Yours faithfully

Jamsetji N. Tata

(In response, the good Swami pleaded his inability to take Jamsetji up on his kind offer.)

In October 2021, jubilant reports in the Indian media recorded that the Indian Institute of Science (IISc) in Bangalore had broken through to the list of the world's top 100 universities in the prestigious Times Higher Education rankings. That made the IISc (often referred to as the Tata Institute) the top-ranked Indian university, a position it has maintained through most of the 115 years of its existence.

How did India's first institute of advanced science research and education, endowed by a Bombay industrialist, come to be located in Bangalore? The answers are contained in a series of events that led to three eminences – industrialist Jamsetji Tata, the Diwan of Mysore Seshadri Iyer, and Swami Vivekananda – crossing paths over a decade.

In the early 1890s, given that Mysore had been a vibrant centre for sericulture ever since the time of Tipu Sultan, Jamsetji approached the diwan of Mysore with the idea of setting up a silk farm in the state. Seshadri Iyer not only helped Jamsetji procure land in Bangalore (today, the area, close to Jayanagar's South End Circle, is still referred to as the Tata Silk Farm) but also arranged for governmental subsidies, and a great mutual respect developed between the two men.

In 1893, Swami Vivekananda sailed to America to speak on Indian philosophy at the World's First Parliament of Religions in Chicago. On the deck of the steamship *Empress of India,* sailing from Yokohama to Vancouver, he ran into his co-passenger Jamsetji. In the course of many long conversations, Jamsetji told the Swami that he was thinking of importing matches from Japan, and that he was travelling to America in search of technology that would make India a strong, industrialized nation. To Jamsetji's surprise, the Swami entirely endorsed his views on industrialization and the need for Indians to develop a scientific temper. He urged Mr Tata, however, to manufacture matches in India itself and offer a livelihood to the poor, exclaiming, 'How wonderful it would be if we could combine the scientific and technological achievements of the West with India's asceticism and humanism!'

The Swami's words exploded into Jamsetji's consciousness. Casting about for a project that would bring the Swami's vision to life, he zeroed in on education, specifically the vacuum that existed where institutes of higher education in science were concerned. In 1898, in a move that stunned his fellow industrialists, he set aside 14 buildings and four landed properties in Bombay for an endowment to establish a science university, and presented his proposal to the new viceroy, Lord Curzon. The viceroy was sceptical – were there enough Indians qualified for such advanced scientific training? Plus, what opportunities for employment would they have in a country that had no industries of its own?

Still, Curzon referred the proposal to the Royal Society in England, which, in 1900, sent out William Ramsay (who would win the Nobel Prize in Chemistry in 1904) to do a viability report. Ramsay not only approved the project but also recommended Bangalore, with its great weather, access to mineral reserves (including gold and iron ore), imminent electrification, and perfect location between Madras and Bombay, as the best place to locate the institute. Meanwhile, Jamsetji had been in touch with his friend Iyer, looking for support for his grand dream. The diwan recommended the project to Maharani Vani Vilasa Sannidhana, who unhesitatingly promised any support the institute might need, on the condition that it be situated in Bangalore.

The fates had conspired – it was to be Bangalore! In 1909, the Institute of Research opened its doors in our city. Sadly, neither Jamsetji, nor Iyer, nor Swami Vivekananda, was around to see the day.

'We are not aware if any project at once so opportune and so far-reaching in its beneficent effects was ever mooted in India, as that of the postgraduate research university of Mr Tata.'

— SWAMI VIVEKANANDA IN *PRABUDDHA BHARATA*, A MONTHLY HE HAD FOUNDED, IN APRIL 1899

16

THE WORLD PREMIERE OF RICHARD STRAUSS'S *FOUR LAST SONGS*, SPONSORED BY J.C. WADIYAR, WAS PERFORMED AT THE ROYAL ALBERT HALL ON 22 MAY 1950

Strauss, Medtner and the Maharaja: A Musical Love Story

My first memory of Jayachamaraja (J.C.) Wadiyar comes from a large black-and-white photograph that used to hang over the doorway to the inner rooms of my maternal grandparents' house. It was a picture from the late '50s, after J.C. had taken over as the first governor of the unified Mysore State. In his signature dark glasses and rich Mysore peta, J.C. was prominent in the picture, but my attention was always on the two sombre young girls, 12 and 10, standing in front of a microphone to his left, a mass of Mysuru mallige flowers in their pigtails, dressed in matching silk 'langa-blouse' sets.

My grandparents never tired of telling us what a very special occasion it was – my mum and aunt, singing one of the maharaja's own compositions for him.

Of all the adjectives one could use to describe the last maharaja of Mysore, Jayachamaraja Wadiyar (J.C.), the clunky 'multidimensional' is probably the most appropriate. 'Maverick' is another.

Passionate about hunting, J.C. was a crack shot. His people were wont to come calling when there was a man-eating tiger about, and he usually arrived in person for the job, his teenage daughters in tow (for what sort of princess did not shoot and ride?).

Academically bright and high-achieving – his principal at Mysore's Maharaja College described him as 'a prince among students' – he inexplicably found Kannada a struggle and needed extra tuitions in the subject! Sanskrit came more easily, perhaps because of his deep interest in Advaita philosophy; he composed 108 kritis to Chamundeshwari, patron goddess of Mysore and family deity of the Wadiyars, in that language, some of which have become an integral part of the repertoire of Carnatic musicians everywhere.

Which brings us to the one overarching love of J.C.'s life – music. Coming from a family where music had played a central role in lives both private and public ever since Vijayanagara fell in the sixteenth century – the Wadiyar kings saw themselves as the natural inheritors and guardians of Vijayanagara's cultural legacy, particularly Carnatic music. This in itself was no surprise, but he took it a step further – if his predecessor, Nalvadi, could play eight instruments, including the veena, sitar, mridangam, the saxophone and the piano, all while nurturing a variety of talented musicians, across genres, in his court, J.C. went international.

Growing up, J.C. was a gifted pianist and a huge fan of European classical music (in fact, his exposure to Carnatic music began only well after he became king). In college, he dreamt of training under Russian virtuoso Sergei Rachmaninoff, but was forced to abandon that thought when his uncle's sudden passing made him king at 21. No matter, there were other ways to indulge his passion.

Like becoming the first president of the Philharmonia Concert Society, which funded a series of philharmonic concerts – the Mysore Concerts – at London's Royal Albert Hall in 1950–51. Like putting together in the Mysore Palace – in the words of the legendary British classical music record producer, Walter Legge – 'a record library containing every imaginable recording of serious music'. Like sponsoring never-before recordings of works by brilliant European composers, thus 'making it possible for music lovers throughout the world to learn, enjoy and study works which, but for this young Indian prince's knowledge and love for music, would never have been recorded...'

There's more. In 1949, the great German composer, Richard Strauss, passed away, leaving behind a last grand work – *Four Last Songs.* Before he died, he wrote to his favourite soprano, Kirsten Flagstad, requesting that she lend her voice to it, and perform it with a 'first-class conductor and orchestra'. When J.C. heard of Strauss's last wish, he was galvanized into action. In 1950, thanks to the generosity of a king he had never met, halfway across the world from him, Strauss's piece was performed –

NIKOLAI MEDTNER

by Flagstad, with a first class conductor and orchestra accompanying her, at the Royal Albert Hall.

And then some. When J.C. had visited Rachmaninoff in his youth, the maestro had introduced him to the compositions of his friend and compatriot Nikolai Medtner. J.C. had found them electrifying. Unfortunately, Medtner's work hadn't found much of a following in Europe, where he lived in abject poverty. Until, in 1946, J.C. founded the Medtner Society to enable the recordings of all of the composer's works as a gift to the world. Despite his failing health, Medtner managed to record all three of his piano concertos, and in gratitude, dedicated the third to the maharaja.

Heart-warming, what?

J.C. was not the son, but the nephew of the maharaja before him, the great Krishnaraja Wadiyar IV; his father was the king's younger brother, Kanteerava Narasimharaja. J.C.'s sister, Rani Vijaya Devi, a very accomplished concert pianist herself, went on to found the International Music and Arts Society in 1974 to 'augment Bangalore's cultural scene' by providing a forum for both Indian and international musicians and artistes. The society is still active.

17

WATER CRISIS IN BANGALORE, MARCH 2024

Desperately Seeking Water: An Old Bengaluru Story

When a water crisis broke in the city in March 2024, new Bangaloreans fretted, wrung their hands and blamed, in no particular order, the administration, builders, climate change and the traffic (this last from sheer habit). Meanwhile, old Bangaloreans, responding to an atavistic instinct, shrugged, pulled their largest water storage containers out of the mothballs and battened down the hatches. When you live on a hill, this kind of thing is par for the course.

In keeping with the long-standing Bengalurean inability to begin any March conversation without referring to the 'unbearable' heat, let us talk about a related topic – thirst, the raging summer thirst of 14 million people in an elevated city through which no river runs. The current water crisis has brought that thirst back into sharp focus, but it has always been this way in Bengaluru, or at least, ever since it became a city to reckon with, circa the mid-nineteenth century.

In 1806, with a generous grant of land from the maharaja of Mysore, Krishnaraja Wadiyar III, the British began the building of a Cantonment to the east of the sixteenth-century Bengaluru Pete. Beginning 1831, when the maharaja was dismissed and the kingdom came under direct British rule, temperature-controlled Bangalore became the seat of administration, proceeding over the decades to outpace every other town in the kingdom, on every front. People poured into the city from every direction, hungry for employment and, inevitably, thirsty for water.

In 1881, after 50 years of petitioning, Mysore got what it wanted – another Wadiyar on the throne. But Chamarajendra X walked into a fraught situation – his diwan, C.V. Rangacharlu, confirmed that Mysore had lost 20 per cent of its population and livestock in the devastating famines that had racked the state from 1876 to 1878, brought on both by unseasonal rains that destroyed the ragi crop in Kolar and Bengaluru, and drought from a series of failed monsoons. Water security, not just for agriculture but also for drinking, became a serious priority for the Mysore government.

K. Seshadri Iyer, who succeeded Rangacharlu as diwan in 1893, was less concerned about Mysore's water needs – with the Kaveri flowing alongside, the city had a well-established source of drinking water – than about burgeoning Bengaluru's. In 1891, with the Ulsoor Tank, which supplied water to the Cantonment, entirely contaminated, and Chief Engineer Richard Sankey's experiment to create a new source of water supply within the city (today's Sankey Tank) having failed, Iyer, along with British engineers, identified a spot on the closest river, the Arkavathi (which rises in the Nandi Hills before flowing west and south to join the Kaveri at Mekedatu), for a new reservoir. The Hesaraghatta Reservoir, 18 km outside the city, was inaugurated in 1894; the era of piped water had begun.

By 1921, Bengaluru's population had grown from around 3.6 lakhs (estimate) to close to 5 lakhs (1921 census), already stretching the capacity of Hesaraghatta. In 1933, just a year after the inauguration of the state-of-the-art Krishna Raja Sagar (KRS) Dam across the Kaveri in Mysore, a new reservoir was inaugurated across the same Arkavathi, at Thippagondanahalli (TG Halli), 35 km away to the west of the city at Magadi. This project, like the KRS Dam, was initiated by another Mysore diwan, Sir M. Visvesvaraya. In a repeat performance, the T.G. Halli reservoir reached capacity by 1956, when the city's population stood at one million.

In 1974, right after Mysore became Karnataka and the city's population hit 2 million, the government took a bold decision – they would pump water into Bengaluru from the Kaveri, a whopping 100 km away, and 500 m below the city's average elevation to boot. It worked! Today, the inner core of the metropolis still drinks deeply and contentedly of Kaveri water, having all but forgotten its longtime lifeline, the Arkavathi. But the 110 once-villages around the core, which became part of the City Corporation in 2008 and include such eminences as Electronic City, Whitefield, Bellandur and Kengeri, are in crisis now.

Not for long, hopefully – Phase V of the Cauvery Project, which will bring these 'villages' into Kaveriamma's sweet embrace, was inaugurated on 16 October 2024.

The Sound of Music

Have you ever stopped to think what the most beautiful sound in the world is? Let Hardy keep his opinion that it is the song of a thrush on a bleak winter's night. Let Wordsworth swear by the melancholy strain of his solitary reaper. The people on my street beg to differ.

To us, as indeed to any Bangalorean, the sound which puts a spring in our step and a sparkle in our eye is the sound of water gushing (a little exaggeration never hurt anyone) out of a tap.

No sound when the tap is opened implies this is going to be one of those no-bath, paper-plate days. An asthmatic wheezing gives rise to the hope of steel plates at dinner. And a gurgle like the clearing of a throat – maybe if I bunk the first hour of college, I can have a bath!

— EXCERPT FROM A 'MIDDLE' CARRIED IN THE *DECCAN HERALD* ON 30 APRIL 1991, WRITTEN BY ROOPA RAJANNA (MY ALLITERATIVE MAIDEN NAME)

18

KORAVANJI WAS LAUNCHED IN MARCH 1942

A Kannada Humour Magazine That Is Pure Gold

I first met Shivakumar Uncle when I was seven or eight. Like many other middle-class couples in Bangalore, my parents belonged to a Lions Club, of which he was also a member. The club was as much about social service as it was about getting together over drinks and dinner in a family setting. While all the adults were sweet enough, Shivakumar Uncle was special – he always treated me like an adult, and was interested in what I had to say and in what I had been writing.

He still is. When my book *The Gita for Children* was published in 2015, he was among the first to buy a copy. He loved it so much that he translated it into Kannada, of his own accord, in less than a fortnight. Sapna Book House published that translation in 2016.

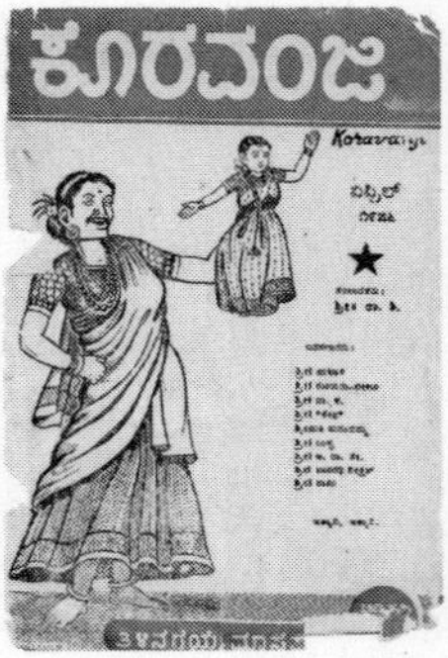

THE FIRST EDITION OF *KORAVANJI*

On 7 October, the Kannada humour magazine *Aparanji* celebrated its 40th birthday, an extraordinary feat for any print publication in the digital age, let alone one dedicated to humour. Through the years, this little independent monthly has held its own against media giants, discovering, nurturing and platforming a gamut of unknown voices, turning them into familiar, beloved names among the Kannada reading public. Its dedicated editor, who not only contributes extensively to the magazine but has overseen every single issue since its inception save for the first eight months, is engineer-entrepreneur M. Shivakumar, affectionately called 'Aparanji Shivu'.

Shivu was about the age *Aparanji* is now when he took over the editorship of a magazine that had, in some sense, been bequeathed to him. For *Aparanji* is only the newer version of an even older, much-celebrated, pioneering humour magazine called *Koravanji*, founded by Shivu's father, Dr M. Shivaram, who wrote under the pseudonym Raashi. Perhaps aptly, *Koravanji* was born in March 1942, during World War II, when there wasn't a lot to joke about.

APARANJI LOGO

Raashi's own funny bone was whetted by his friend and mentor, the great T.P. Kailasam, whom Kannadigas know for his unconventional plays and literary criticism. Kailasam's work was revolutionary in its rejection of extravagant mythologicals as the only kind of Kannada theatre possible – his plays were tongue-in-cheek contemporary social commentaries that first shocked and then delighted audiences. Like many other Kannada writers, Kailasam wrote with as much felicity in English as in Kannada.

ನಮಗೆ ಈಗ ಬೇಕಾದ್ದು - ಶಾಂತಿ - ಶಾಂತಿ - ಶಾಂತಿ.

'WHAT WE NEED NOW IS PEACE, PEACE, PEACE!' – R.K. LAXMAN'S CARTOON IN *KORAVANJI*

Cycling down the streets of Cantonment after work at his very busy clinic in Majestic – in his other life, Raashi was a popular and much-loved doctor – on his way home to Malleswaram, Raashi often caught up with Kailasam for long chats about this and that. One of their favourite topics of discussion was the British humour magazine, *Punch*. In fact, it was *Punch* that inspired Raashi to start a similar magazine in Kannada. In this endeavour, the young doctor found a wonderful collaborator in journalist, writer and academic Prof. Na(rayana) Kasturi, who was then teaching in Mysore.

During *Koravanji*'s early days, Na Kasturi contributed as many laugh-a-minute pieces – jokes, skits, social satire, limericks and his unique 'Anarthakosha' (anti-dictionary), which involved hilarious definitions of common words – as Raashi himself. He also brought in a young, artistically inclined student of his at Maharaja's College, who had taken up a BA there after he had been rejected by Bombay's J.J. School of Art, to provide the occasional cartoons and illustrations. The student's name was R.K. Laxman.

Over the next 25 years, *Koravanji* (Kannada for a female fortune teller of Karnataka's nomadic Korava tribe) went on to build a loyal community of readers and humour writers, including such luminaries as T. Sunandamma, Sriranga (Adya Rangacharya), Kefa (A.V. Keshava Murthy), A Ra Se (A.R. Sethurama Rao), G.P. Rajaratnam, Dasharathi Dikshit, A.K. Ramanujan, and occasionally, Dr Shivaram Karanth himself. The language of the magazine was colloquial and informal, an organic mix of Kannada and English, and the satire sharp, but the humour was always 'clean', which gave *Koravanji* a very special place in the Kannada literary firmament.

In 1967, citing a lack of funds, Raashi sent *Koravanji* 'back to the forest'. In 1981, as he lay ailing in bed, A Ra Se came to visit Raashi, and urged him to allow him to bring *Koravanji* back. Raashi assented but requested that the magazine be renamed *Aparanji* instead. Eight months later, soon after Raashi had passed, his son Shivakumar took on the editorial mantle. To this day, the iconic magazine, now also available online at aparanjimag.in, is put together in the very same house in Malleswaram that Raashi built.

'Lovely. Na Kasturi, who was Raashi's collaborator on *Koravanji*, was a Palghat Iyer who learnt Kannada in his mid-'20s and went on to become one of the twentieth century's most famous Kannada humorists! Another example of how much "anya-matrubhasha" people (people whose mother tongue isn't Kannada) have given to Kannada literature and culture. It would not have been possible if Kannadigas hadn't accommodated everyone from the get-go.'

— MADHAV AJJAMPUR, AUTHOR OF *THE POLLEN WAITS ON TIPTOE*, A COLLECTION OF KANNADA POET-LAUREATE DA RA BENDRE'S POEMS IN TRANSLATION

19

DR RAJKUMAR DIED ON 12 APRIL 2006

Bangarada Manushya: The Legacy of Dr Rajkumar

I was fortunate to grow up in the golden age of Kannada cinema. Dr Rajkumar was my grandmother's favourite, so I got to watch all his films. At home, she had his songs playing constantly off her two-in-one; they became the background music to my childhood. But it wasn't just his acting, screen presence, or voice that endeared Rajkumar to me or my fellow Kannadigas; it was the fact that we all believed, we *knew*, that he was a good man.

To cricket fans, 15 November, smack-dab in the middle of Karnataka's birthday month, is the date on which Sachin Tendulkar debuted in international cricket in 1989. Last week, it also became the date on which Virat Kohli broke his hero's record, when he completed an incredible 50 ODI centuries. To Kannadigas, the day marks a bittersweet anniversary – it was the day on which, in the year 2000, their beloved Annavaru, Natasarvabhouma Dr Rajkumar, who had been abducted and held hostage for 108 days by the dreaded bandit Veerappan, was finally released.

Veerappan knew what he was doing when he picked his hostage. For almost 50 years, the matinee idol, born Singanalluru Puttaswamaiah Muthuraj, had dominated the Kannadiga imagination as a towering symbol of Kannada identity. Whether it was the parts he essayed in his 200-odd films – including historical Kannada heroes like Wadiyar king Ranadheera Kanteerava, Chalukyan hero Pulikeshi II, Krishnadevaraya of Vijayanagara, and Kadamba ruler Mayurasharma – or his iconic songs, some of which, like 'Huttidare Kannada Naadinalli Huttabeku' and 'Naanaaduva Nudiye Kannada Nudi', became quasi state anthems, everything Rajkumar did reiterated his commitment to the language and the region. The fact that it was all done gently, with great pride but an admirable lack of jingoism, endeared him even to non-Kannadigas; although he never acted in a non-Kannada film as a matter of principle, his films were remade 58 times, in no fewer than nine languages!

Rajkumar's rise in Kannada cinema in the '50s had a Saleem Sinai-esque quality to it – it mirrored the rise of the common identity that the just-cobbled-together Mysore State was striving for. He played a significant part in cementing that identity – his ability to play characters across socio-economic divisions and geographies of Karnataka made him a unifying figure, one that people from all over the state could get behind. From his debut film as leading man, *Bedara Kannappa* (1954), which spoke up against caste discrimination, to his last film *Shabdavedi* (2000), which cautioned youth about the dangers of drug abuse, he was also an on-screen crusader against social evils, which gave him an unimpeachable, saint-like status in the eyes of his fans, whom he always respectfully referred to as Abhimani Devarugalu (gods in the shape of fans).

His disciplined and publicity-shy off-screen life only served to bolster that image. Known to wake at 4 each morning, he spent an hour or two practising yoga, a lifelong passion, before spending a similar amount of time practising his music. (His early training in classical music, as a child artiste with the famous Gubbi Veeranna theatre troupe, saw him recording over 300 songs for films and 200 other devotional songs in adulthood; in 1992, he became the only Indian actor to win the National Film Award for Best Male Playback Singer). Unlike other matinee idols of the south, he never contested the elections, contending that the love of fans should not be used to garner power for oneself.

Dr. Raj Kumar Poster

Rajkumar's quiet, philosophical side was beautifully balanced by his fun, swashbuckling side, so exuberantly on display in so many films. Who can forget him as Bhadra in *Sampattige Sawaal*, riding a buffalo and singing 'Yaare

Koogaadali' with such joie de vivre? Or as the dashing CID 999 in the 1978 superhit *Operation Diamond Racket*, playing a desi James Bond? Even those who are entirely unfamiliar with his work will know the opening lines of a nightclub song from the movie that went viral after his death in 2006 – 'If you come today, it's too early, if you come tomorrow, it's too late…'

That is not meant to be taken seriously – it's never too late to come to the magic of Dr Raj.

'Perhaps the first Rajkumar film I watched was *Bangarada Manushya*, which I watched in 1973 in Chamundeshwari Theatre, Mysuru, when I was in grade 3 (I remember having a Gold Spot during the interval). Rajkumar was also my uncle's patient (like us, he belonged to the Ediga Gowda community). Once, when he was visiting my uncle in Mysuru, people got wind of it and a huge crowd assembled outside. Rajkumar had to go to the balcony and sing a few lines of the song "Naaniruvude Nimagaagi" before they dispersed.'

— T.N. HARI, EXECUTIVE CHAIRMAN – STEER WORLD, AUTHOR AND GROWTH ADVISER

•

'You have captured the essence of Dr Raj in such few words – congratulations. My list of favourite Rajkumar songs includes "Baanigondu Yelle Yellide" and "Cheluveya Nota Chenna", among many others. A thousand namaskaras to him.'

— DR KIRAN RAO, FORMER PROFESSOR AND HEAD, DEPARTMENT OF CLINICAL PSYCHOLOGY, NIMHANS

June~July~August

Champaka

Magnolia champaca, ephemeral blessing,
For monsoon hair, a fragrant dressing;
Butter-yellow, red-gold, by the basketload,
Luring Gowri-habba shoppers on Sampige Road.

20

THE FIRST ELECTRIC BULB WAS SWITCHED ON IN BANGALORE IN AUGUST 1905

How Bangalore Entered the Electric Age

It was the City, the part of Bangalore administered by the maharaja, that got electrified before the British Cantonment – officially the Bangalore Civil and Military Station – did. How come? Actually, the original plan did include the electrification of the C&M Station – in fact, there were two substations set up there versus just one in the City. But bureaucracy intervened, with the military authorities expressing concern about the route of the transmission lines, and the telegraph department raising objections about the possible interference that the electric lines may cause with their own telephone lines. There was also much hand-wringing all round about the number of trees marked for chopping down. Clearly, even 120 years ago, Bangalore was Bangalore-ing.

Perhaps the worst collective nightmare of 'civilized' humanity in the twenty-first century, far worse than a pandemic even, is the notion of someone, some*thing*, pulling the plug on electricity, so consummately are our lives designed around that precious, priceless resource. What makes this absolute dependence so remarkable is that incandescent bulbs – and everything that came after – are such a recent invention; Thomas Edison only patented them in 1880. By 1882, determined that his bulbs would 'light up the world', he had torn up the streets of Manhattan's Lower East Side to set up the world's first power station and set alight a small chunk of the city.

Edison's power station was steam-powered, but just a few days after it began functioning, the world's first hydroelectric power plant became operational in Appleton, Wisconsin. That project was initiated by a huge Edison fan, a local paper manufacturer called H.J. Rogers.

Only 20 years later, in 1902, owing to the efforts of a visionary diwan and a supportive queen, Asia's largest hydroelectric power plant began operations thousands of kilometres across the seas. The spectacularly beautiful setting for this station, where the River Kaveri thunders down a 100 m cliff in a wide arc of waterfalls, was called Shivanasamudra. It was Mysore's maharani, Vani Vilasa Sannidhana, who had floated the global tender to build the plant, and, hold your breath, it was Edison's company, General Electric, that won the contract, marking the entry of the first American MNC into India!

Diwan Seshadri Iyer's decision to put Mysore's money behind a brand-new technology was driven both by commerce and a willingness to experiment with what was cutting-edge (a culture that has endured in the entrepreneurial climate of today's Bangalore). In 1897, India's first hydel power station – Sidrapong – had been commissioned near Darjeeling, and

Mr Iyer did not see why Mysore should lag behind. Plus, Messrs John Taylor and Sons Limited, the mining company that had struck gold at Kolar, had been at his ear, enumerating the ways in which electricity could galvanize gold extraction from Asia's deepest mines. The diwan did not hesitate – work on the power station began in 1898.

An engineering challenge soon threw a spanner into the works – power would be generated in Shivanasamudra, to the south-west of Bangalore, but was needed in Kolar, to the north-east of the city, a full 147 kms away! Nowhere else in the world had power been transmitted across such vast distances, but GE proved itself equal to the task. By 1902, the mineshafts in the Kolar Gold Fields were buzzing with electricity.

And what of the city that found itself lying so fortuitously in the path of these lines? It was a no-brainer – in 1904, Nalvadi Krishnaraja Wadiyar, who had now taken over from his mum, green-lighted a scheme for the electrification of Bangalore.

On 3 August 1905, at precisely 6.30 p.m., a great gasp went up from the crowds gathered in the streets leading to the historic Bangalore Fort beside the Victoria Hospital as 104 lamps went on as one, making Bangalore, in one fell swoop, one of the very first cities in India and Asia to receive the glorious gift of electric light.

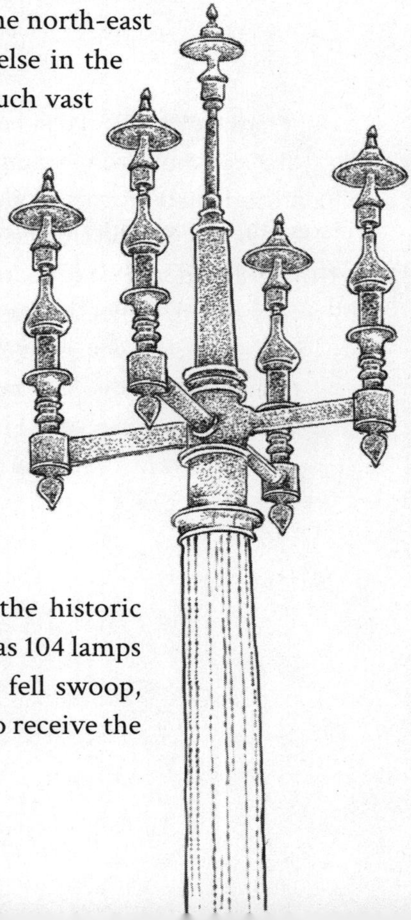

Unfortunately, no trace remains today of 'M station', the transformer house by the City Market where the first switch was thrown, but the next time you are driving down MG Road towards Trinity Church, don't miss eyeballing the old stone building that comes up on your left at the Dickenson Road junction – that there is the B Station, which, after it came up in 1907, lit up the night for Bangalore Cantonment.

From the time of the Rendition (the return of political authority to the maharaja from the British) in 1881, the kingdom of Mysore saw unprecedented progress under the stewardship of very capable diwans. Fortunately for Mysore, the one who served the longest, from 1883 to 1901 – Kumarapuram Seshadri Iyer – was also one of her best. A visionary who was also famously short-tempered, Iyer drove the modernization of the kingdom with a passion. Although he passed away just a few months before the Shivanasamudram hydroelectric project began operations, he is honoured in the name of the station – Sir Seshadri Iyer Hydel Station – to this day.

21

RONALD ROSS PUBLISHED HIS PIONEERING FINDINGS IN AUGUST 1897

The Surgeon Major Who Cracked Malaria

In the last quarter of the nineteenth century, the kingdom of Mysore was racked by famine and disease. Barely limping back to recovery after the Great Famine of 1876–78, which took millions of lives in Madras, Bombay and the princely states between them, Bangalore was struck by a cholera epidemic in 1895, and three years later, by a severe outbreak of the plague. Fortunately, although Bangalore was infested with mosquitoes, the weather ensured that it wasn't as malarious a city as others in India. And yet, this was where a mosquito-obsessed British surgeon, who eventually won the Nobel Prize for Medicine, conducted his first investigations into the transmission of malaria.

It's 2021, and everyone – in the ooru and elsewhere – is an epidemiologist, holding forth on spike proteins, triple mutations, reproductive numbers and aerosol transmission. It's hard to believe that it was only in the 1880s that the link between germs and disease was first proved, by the great Louis Pasteur.

Only a few years after that, in 1894, an article in the august *British Medical Journal* by a Dr Patrick Manson, proposing the so-called Mosquito–Malaria theory, went, um, viral. Dr Manson, who had worked in the tropics for several years, was celebrated for his work in identifying the female Culex mosquito as a 'vector' (carrier and transmitter) of filaria (elephantiasis). In an age when most others held that malaria was caused by inhaling miasma, a foul-smelling fog that rose from rotting things (the name 'malaria' itself comes from the Latin 'mal aria' – literally, 'bad air'), he believed that the malarial parasite, plasmodium, was also transmitted by mosquitoes. Unfortunately, he was now retired and far away from regions where malaria was endemic, and could not prove his theory.

However, there were many bright young doctors in the colonies willing to pick up the gauntlet. One of them was Ronald Ross, a surgeon major in the Indian Medical Service. Born in Almora to Scottish parents just three days after the First War of Indian Independence broke out in 1857, Ross, who was educated in England, returned in 1882 for a posting in the Madras Presidency. The very next year, he took over as the acting garrison surgeon of the Bangalore Civil and Military Station, and had his first brush with namma mosquitoes.

It happened this way. Frustrated by the mosquitoes that made life hell in his bungalow (off South Parade, today's MG Road), Ross set out to find their source, and found it in a barrel of water by his bedroom window, teeming with mosquito larvae. By simply tipping the barrel over, he won himself a temporary peace (and, with his mentor Manson, toyed for a while with the theory that people contracted malaria by drinking water contaminated with mosquito larvae).

The fascinating story of how Ross nailed the transmission route of the malarial parasite from human to human via the digestive system of the female Anopheles mosquito (part of it involved paying the the local people to get bitten by mosquitoes!), a breakthrough that won him the Nobel Prize in 1902, is unfortunately beyond the scope of this column. Instead, here are a few Ronald-Ross-in-Bangalore highlights:

- In 1890, Ross returned to Bangalore as staff surgeon, occupying a bungalow opposite the Bangalore Golf Club. In 1894, frustrated with how his malaria research was going, he returned to England for a sabbatical, getting there just after Manson's article appeared in the *BMJ*. Intrigued, he went off to meet Manson, and, thoroughly inspired, returned to India and malaria research in 1895. The rest is history.
- Apart from his malaria passion, Ross also had his responsibilities as surgeon major. From 1895 to 1897, he served here as an officer on special sanitary duty, living, during a cholera outbreak, in a tent on the grounds of the West End Hotel. In those two years, he overhauled garbage clearing systems, had wells disinfected, improved drainage systems and posted marshals for early flagging of cases in congested areas of the Cantonment, like Ulsoor and Shivajinagar.
- Ross published his findings on the mosquito–malaria connection first in the *Indian Medical Gazette* in August 1897. They were published in the *British Medical Journal* only in December the same year.

- The 173 letters that Ross and Manson exchanged between 1895 and 1899 – Ross's 'Eureka!' moment came in 1897 – are today considered one of the world's great scientific correspondences. Many of those letters were written from Bangalore Station. Pretty cool, huh?

> As the plateau is about 2,700 ft above sea level, the climate is almost Italian in character – fairly hot and dry in March, April and May, much cooler with the early rains in May, not over-hot nor very wet during the big rains, and with a delightful, clear and cool winter. The ground is green most of the year. There are the Cubbon Park, the beautiful Lai Bagh Garden, the Club, endless games, and a pleasant military social life. A picture of pleasure remains in my mind: the sun, the gardens and pillared villas, the cleanly dressed natives, and the open-air, aristocratic life of the British – as goodly a place, probably, as there is in the world.
>
> – A DESCRIPTION OF BANGALORE FROM *MEMOIRS, WITH A FULL ACCOUNT OF THE GREAT MALARIA PROBLEM AND ITS SOLUTION*, BY RONALD ROSS, PUBLISHED IN 1923

AGHA ALY ASKER'S DESCENDANT, FOUAAD MIRZA, BECAME THE FIRST INDIAN FINALIST IN THE OLYMPICS EQUESTRIAN INDIVIDUAL EVENTING ON 2 AUGUST 2021

A Persian Horse Trader in Bangalore

Although it is bang in the centre of town, in the heart of Richmond Town, I have never visited Johnson Market. But since I was in college, I have heard meat-eating friends, mostly male, rave about the delights of the beef seekh kabab rolls at a legendary eatery called Fanoos, which began life as an Iranian street-side kiosk in the small, crowded lanes of the market in 1975. The market itself, 'Russell Market's poor cousin', came up in 1929, on land that had once been used to stable the fine thoroughbreds of Agha Aly Asker, the scion of a Persian family of horse traders, who had first arrived in Bangalore as a young man, over a century before the market was built.

What thread of whimsical destiny could possibly connect a barely overheard conversation in a smoke-filled chaikhana in Shiraz, Iran, in 1824, and Bangalore's iconic Town Hall, built over a century later, in 1935? Let's find out, shall we?

Sipping on his chai at that crowded hostelry on that fateful day back in 1824 was a young man of 16, eyes bright with adventure. His family were landed gentry that had made their fortune breeding and trading in thoroughbreds, and he and his brothers had just returned from an exhilarating ride. They were lucky to find themselves a table, even if it happened to be right next to one occupied by a noisy group of horse traders like themselves, from the port city of Bushehr.

The young man didn't mean to eavesdrop, but the conversation at the next table was electrifying. It seemed the men had just returned from Hind, where they had made an incredibly profitable sale to the British East India Company. Word was that the Company, now in control of most of Hind, needed all the horses they could get. His imagination fired, the young man persuaded his brothers and his formidable father to fall in with his plans. Soon after, with 200 horses in tow, the brothers sailed for Hind, making tracks for the kingdom of Mysore.

In time, with the business established, the older brothers returned to Iran. The youngest, Agha Aly Asker, however, fell so in love with Hind that he not only made it his home but left behind a grand legacy, including one particularly famous descendant, in the city of Bangalore.

When Asker arrived in Mysore in 1824, a young Mummadi Krishnaraja Wadiyar was in charge, with a British Resident overseeing things. Things were about to change, however. In 1831, following a series of upheavals, the Company wrested control of Mysore for itself. By this time, however, the largely unlettered Aly Asker had formed a strong bond with the sophisticated, literary maharaja.

In 1834, Mysore came under a new commissioner called Mark Cubbon, who was passionate about horses, keeping 60 in his own stables. Quite naturally, Asker and Cubbon got on like a house on fire. The unique position he held in both these men's lives would eventually lead Asker to help Mysore avert a terrible disaster.

In 1848, Lord Dalhousie took over as governor general of India. Resurrecting a highly unpopular policy called the Doctrine of Lapse, which stated that the kingdom of any ruler who did not have a direct male heir would lapse to the Company, he began to use it aggressively, annexing princely states like Satara, Sambalpur, Udaipur, Nagpur and Jhansi by 1854. With Mummadi having failed to produce a son, Mysore was in the direct line of fire. It was Aly Asker, so the story goes, who parleyed unofficially with Cubbon on behalf of the maharaja, suggesting that it would do the Company more harm than good to annex a stable, prosperous princely state like Mysore using the unpopular doctrine. Convinced, Cubbon used the same argument with his higher-ups, and Mysore remained independent.

What of Aly Asker's legacy to Bangalore, where he lived? Well, Mark Cubbon was so taken with Asker's home (it stood opposite the Fatima Bakery on Richmond Road) that he requested him to build one hundred similar bungalows! Acquiescing, Asker bought up large tracts of land in the present Richmond Town, Cantonment and High Grounds areas, and built those bungalows, gentrifying the city. Unfortunately, none of them still stands, but there is a street off Miller's Road that continues to bear the name of the redoubtable horse trader from Shiraz.

And the Bangalore Town Hall? That story, and the story of Asker's famous descendant, is revealed in on page 171.

At the 2020 Tokyo Olympics, 29-year-old Bangalorean Fouaad Mirza became the first Indian to make it to the final of the equestrian event called Individual Eventing. Fouaad was already an Arjuna Awardee, having won two silver medals at the Jakarta Asian Games in 2018, besides many other international championships. Considering that he is the grandson of Syeda Mirza and Major Mohammed Mirza, who was not only the great-grandson of Agha Aly Asker but also himself part of the Indian Army's 61st Cavalry, it is perhaps not that surprising that Fouaad has a way with horses. Oh, also, his dad, Dr Hasneyn Mirza, is one of India's top equine veterinarians. More horse sense!

THE BANGALORE TORPEDO PLAYED A SIGNIFICANT ROLE IN THE WORLD WAR II NORMANDY LANDINGS OF 6 JUNE 1944

The Thambis Who Built the Bangalore Torpedo

In a city packed with great microbreweries, pubs and bars, one establishment has remained relentlessly popular for over 30 years. Locals love its 'old Bangalore vibe', and visitors its delicious bar menu, but everyone agrees that its unbeatable USP is the view from – and the microclimate of – its terraces on the 13th floor of the Barton Centre on MG Road. You can certainly order a 'Bangalore Torpedo' – a cocktail built of 'Bangalore's best beer, gin, anise and lemonade' – when you visit, but know that a later, but more 'authentic', version of the said cocktail has been served at the MEG (Madras Engineers Group) mess, located in the regiment's HQ beside the Ulsoor Lake, since 2015. That one, created to commemorate the centenary of the invention of the actual Bangalore Torpedo by a Scottish colonel of the regiment, contains single malt Scotch whisky, cardamom jaggery, star anise spiced apple juice, tea, and a slice of a Bangalore orange.

Bet you've never thought, *really* thought, about barbed wire. But it is barbed wire that is at the heart of today's fascinating Bangalore story. Before we plunge into it, therefore, some context.

Barbed wire was patented in the 1870s, when settlers in the American Midwest were looking for a cheap and effective way to fence their crops and their livestock. But people soon began to see how barbed wire could also be a quick and effective deterrent to troop movement in war – neither men nor horses could get through coils and coils of barbed wire ('entanglements') simply placed in a wide swathe in the path of a marching army, without injuring themselves grievously. Plus, machine guns had very little impact on this kind of fortification, given how much empty space it incorporated. Entanglements were used very effectively in the Second Boer War (1899–1902) in South Africa and the Russo-Japanese War (1904–05).

Rewind to peninsular India in 1780. The British, taking stock after a humiliating loss to Nawab Hyder Ali in the First Anglo-Mysore War (1767–69), decided to incorporate into the Madras Presidency army a dedicated force of 'combat pioneers' – a corps that went ahead of the rest to reconnoitre and execute engineering tasks – build bridges, dig trenches or 'saps' for cannon to be brought within range of enemy forts, and dig and pack 'mines' with explosives to create breaches in fort walls. Accordingly, in 1780, two companies of 'Madras Pioneers' (aka Madras Sappers, today the Madras Engineer Group or MEG) were raised at Fort St George. They rendered yeoman service to the British Army, helping them win the final war against Tipu Sultan in 1799, and contributing significantly to Arthur Wellesley's famous victory against the Marathas at Assaye in 1803.

In 1834, after a series of campaigns in India, Egypt, Java and Myanmar, the Madras Sappers moved to Bangalore to help the British build the new

Civil and Military Station here. But their international campaigns continued unabated – Afghanistan, Persia, the Opium Wars in China. . . By the turn of the century, they, like sappers everywhere, were coming up more and more against an unrelenting new enemy – barbed wire. It was Colonel R.L. McClintock of the Royal Engineers, while he was attached to the Sappers at Bangalore, who finally made the breakthrough against the menace in 1912, creating the – drumroll please! – Bangalore Torpedo.

The advantage of the Bangalore Torpedo – or simply, 'Bangalore' – which is basically a 5 ft–long tube packed with an explosive charge, is that it can be screwed onto more (empty) pipes of similar length to create a, say, 25 ft pole. This pole can be pushed along the ground from a trench towards the entanglement, and then detonated. The explosion creates a 3- to 4-metre breach, while the sapper stays far away and safe.

It seems like a simple enough device, but the Bangalore was so effective that it is still being produced, in more sophisticated versions, well over 100

THE ROUSING SLOGAN OF THE MADRAS REGIMENT, THE OLDEST INFANTRY REGIMENT IN THE INDIAN ARMY

years after it was invented. It played a starring role in World War I, in the D-Day landings of American troops on Omaha Beach (watch Tom Hanks yell, in *Saving Private Ryan*, 'Bangalores! Bring out them Bangalores!'), in World War II, and in the 1973 Yom Kippur War, where the Israeli Army used it to clear paths through Syrian minefields.

As for the Thambis, as the Sappers are affectionately known, they are still here, in the MEG HQ abutting Assaye Road (ever wondered why the road was called that? Now you know!) by the Ulsoor Lake. At 244 years of age, they are the oldest corps of engineers in the Indian Army.

Being the first of the 'Indian' British regiments that travelled overseas to fight wars (at a time when Hindus believed that 'crossing the seas' was tantamount to becoming an outcaste), the Thambis of the MEG were also among the earliest to lose all consciousness of caste. On long campaigns abroad, the Sappers also became accustomed to eating and drinking together with other Sappers, whatever their caste or religion, another practice that was strictly forbidden in Hindu society. The Madras Sappers archives record that when an inspecting officer once asked a Thambi what his caste was, he answered proudly, 'Sapper caste, Sir!'

PS: The War Memorial at the junction of Brigade Road and Residency Road, which the British installed in 1919, commemorates soldiers and officers of the Madras Sappers who lost their lives in various foreign fields during World War I.

24

J.C. WADIYAR WAS BORN ON 18 JULY 1919, AND WAS PROCLAIMED KING ON 3 AUGUST 1940

An Appreciation Post for Jayachamarajendra Wadiyar

My paternal grandmother came from Mysore, raised by a family who regarded Maharaja Nalvadi Krishnaraja Wadiyar (1902–40), Jayachamarajendra's uncle and predecessor, as a godlike figure. She married a Gandhian from Tumkur who denounced monarchy, fought for freedom and went to jail often, leaving her (very capably) holding the babies, before he was elected to the Lok Sabha in 1952. Despite their opposing ideologies, my grandparents had a happy marriage.

On his part, my maternal grandfather was a superintendent of police who had served the maharaja and the colonial government. And yet, my two grandfathers shared a very cordial relationship. I was fortunate to hear different perspectives on the freedom struggle and the maharajas when I was quite young – it helped me imbibe, unconsciously, that there were always several sides to a story.

This being our Independence Day month and all, here is an appreciation post for Jayachamarajendra (J.C.) Wadiyar, the last maharaja of Mysore and the first ruler (among the nearly 600 that flourished at the time) to sign, on the 6 August 1947, the Instrument of Accession, which allowed Mysore to become part of the Dominion of India. Years later, when the then chief minister hailed his decision as a 'sacrifice', J.C. would say, simply, 'I do not look upon it as such. If destiny had decreed that over the past few centuries the progress and prosperity of the people of this beloved state should be in the hands of the Wadiyars of Mysore, then that same destiny now ordains that the time is ripe for the people, now grown to full political stature in a free democratic republic, to rule themselves... the rule of the maharajas has indeed fulfilled its purpose, the purpose of making the people fit to rule themselves.'

Such a gracious response was not only unsurprising but expected from this particular ruler. After all, he came from an illustrious line of 'rajarshis', saintly kings who truly saw *vox populi* as *vox Dei.* As far back as August 1881, when the British restored the monarchy to the Wadiyars after 50 long years, his grandfather, Chamarajendra Wadiyar X, had made a startling proclamation – rejecting the opportunity to be an absolute monarch, he would install instead a Representative Assembly for Mysore, a first among Indian princely states. In 1907, J.C.'s uncle, the great Nalvadi Krishnaraja Wadiyar, enlarged the assembly and brought in a Legislative Council, a 'house of elders', to create a bicameral legislature. To J.C., therefore, giving up his rights as king was only an inevitable progression of something his own predecessors had set in motion.

J.C.'s father, Kanteerava Narasimharaja Wadiyar, was an excellent public speaker and polo player, who, playing alongside his older brother Nalvadi as part of the Mysore team, brought the state many sporting laurels. He – Narasimharaja – was also passionate about books and music, particularly jazz, and passed those passions on to his children, particularly to J.C. and his sister Vijaya Devi, who would reminisce many years later that their father always introduced the two of them as 'my two highbrow children'.

Not having any children of his own, Nalvadi adopted his brother's only son, J.C., as his heir. And that was how Jayachamaraja Wadiyar, who by rights was only third in line to the Mysore throne, got to be its 25th occupant.

(As an aside, this – having to resort to adoption because of the absence of a natural male heir – has happened bizarrely often in the history of the Wadiyars. The current head of the royal family, Yaduveer Wadiyar, is himself adopted – the previous head, J.C.'s son Srikantadatta, died without leaving an heir. Legend has it that it was a wronged seventeenth-century queen's curse that brought this about, but that story will keep for another time.)

J.C. was king for only 10 years, from the age of 21 to 31 (he remained king until India became a republic, on 26 January 1950), taking over after both his natural and adoptive fathers passed in 1940; dying young is another hallmark of the Wadiyar men. But his imposing presence,

JAYACHAMARAJENDRA WADIYAR, THE LAST MAHARAJA OF MYSORE

both literally (he was over 6 ft tall) and metaphorically, and his cosmopolitan, liberal outlook made a significant impact not just on his own state but on the world of Western classical music as well.

What? Yes! J.C. not only fulfilled the dying wish of Richard Strauss but also introduced to the world a brilliant Russian composer he discovered and rescued from obscurity. But more about that on page 63!

Music of all kinds – Western classical, jazz, Carnatic classical – was a passion with J.C. But so was sport – he was a crack shot, played a great game of tennis and was a competent horseman to boot. In 1960, when he was serving as governor of the new unified Mysore State, Ramanathan Krishnan, India's top tennis player, made it to Wimbledon, seeded 7th. It was J.C. who provided the talented 23-year-old the financial assistance he needed through the tournament. Krishnan stormed into the men's semi-finals a couple of weeks later, where he lost to the top seed, Australian Neale Fraser.

25

PATIENT ZERO OF THE GREAT PLAGUE OF BANGALORE ARRIVED ON A TRAIN FROM BOMBAY VIA HUBLI ON 11 AUGUST 1898

The City-Side Origins of Bengaluru's Café Society

My father was a bon vivant. At 17, moving to Bangalore from the family estate in Tumkur to study mechanical engineering, he succumbed happily to the forbidden delights of the Cantonment – primarily beef fry and beer at Parade Café (now Koshy's) – while frequenting Udupi Sri Krishna Bhavan in the City for 'SKC' (sweet-khara-coffee) with more conservative friends. Once he had graduated, he moved to Germany, and later to France, where he learnt to love schnitzel, frankfurters and warm baguette. By the time he returned two years later to get married and settle down, he was part-European. My dad brought us flowers on our birthdays, took us to Plaza and Rex to watch 'good English movies', and treated us to 'a nice dinner out' on special occasions. And he always chuckled when fellow Kannadigas, as is our wont, referred to a restaurant ('it's resth-o-ron, not rest-o-rent!') as a hotel.

When the first outlet of (the admittedly oddly named) Café Coffee Day (CCD) opened on Bangalore's Brigade Road in 1996, no one could have imagined how iconic a brand CCD would grow to become. But to the new, shiny, dial-up-internet generation that came of age in the '90s, that outlet, which was the country's first so-called 'cybercafé', was the coolest hangout in town. Years later, CCD would be hailed as the pioneer of Bangalore's booming café society.

Try that claim out on an old-timer, however, and you will be sent away with a flea in your ear. They will have you know that it was in fact Koshy's, or Parade Café, founded way back in 1952, that was the city's original Indian-owned café.

Dig into the city's history a wee bit, however, and you will find that the genesis of the beloved slurping-coffee-while-shooting-the-breeze Bengaluru tradition predates Koshy's by half a century, and lies not in the erstwhile Cantonment but in the bylanes of the City, in the shape of K.T. Appanna's Hindu Coffee Club (HCC). Here is the short version of the story.

The plague that swept through the City in 1898 emptied homes of women, children and the elderly, all of whom were sent away to more salubrious locales, leaving the men who were still standing with little access to fresh and hygienically prepared food. The city municipality established free kitchens, but the upper castes did not warm to the idea of breaking bread with the hoi polloi. Among the first to see the opportunity was probably Avani Narsing Rao, who, before the year was out, set up a little establishment selling Brahmin-made food. A few years later, teenage entrepreneur K.T. Appanna, who had lost his father to the plague, set up his hotel, featuring meals cooked by his widowed mother (2 annas per meal, with 7 rupees covering all meals for a month).

Appanna's hotel soon became very popular, not least because of the aroma of balekai bajjis that emanated thence around 4 p.m. every evening, an 'after-office snack' innovation the young man had introduced. Circa 1906, Appanna moved his hotel to Chikpete, added benches and tables (most other 'hotels' were 'standing only') and rebranded it the Hindu Coffee Club. Their palates now habituated to 'hotel food', the men came in droves.

By 1908, the HCC had blossomed into a cultural centre, where a motley group of vidvaans, professors, bureaucrats, journalists and writers would gather between 6 and 7:30 each evening, analysing Carnatic classical music, arguing loud and long about the recent split in the Indian National Congress, hauling the Mysore administration over the coals, discussing the scriptures and making dozens of rarely realized plans to 'improve' the common people.

In 1916, K.T. Appanna founded the Modern Hindu Hotel (the HCC had been closed for a while, reeling under the weight of vast unpaid debts from its exclusive clientèle) near Ananda Rao Circle, with the full encouragement of the diwan of Mysore, Sir M. Visvesvaraya, who, believing that Bangalore needed more hotels to serve the needs of the hordes of outside talent that streamed daily into the growing city (sounds familiar?), had convinced the maharaja to offer all manner of sops to the hospitality industry.

The Modern Hindu Hotel was the first hotel to cater to people of all communities and religions. So respected was Appanna that his mentee, Seetharama Rao, founder of the legendary Dasaprakash chain, set up a Modern Hindu Hotel in 1928 in Mysore with the former's blessings, but chose not to go into business in Bengaluru, so that the two would never be in competition with each other.

'In those days, if anyone went out to eat at a restaurant, people used to say, "Ivanu haalaada, jaati ketta (he is ruined now, he has lost his caste)." In such an environment, it must have taken a lot of courage for people like Appanna to set up an eatery. Thank you for reminding us of Bangalore's early F&B entrepreneurs.'

— MALLIKARJUNA D.G., PHOTOGRAPHER, JOURNALIST, AND WINNER OF THE SAHITYA AKADEMI AWARD FOR TRAVEL WRITING IN KANNADA

•

'I had often wondered why so many of the old cafés and restaurants had Hindu or Brahmin in their names. Now I know.'

— MANOHAR D. RAO, ENTREPRENEUR, TECH AND MANAGEMENT CONSULTANT, AND PROFESSIONAL BRIDGE PLAYER

26

B.L. RICE WAS BORN ON 17 JULY 1837

Benjamin Lewis Rice: Grandsire of Kannada Epigraphy

I returned to my hometown in 2004, after 12 years away in other cities in India and abroad, to find that all had changed, changed utterly. My laid-back city had exploded, embraced capitalism with a vengeance and made space for the tens of thousands of dreamers newly arrived at her gates. I was happy for her, but occasionally went looking for my old Bangalore. One of the spaces where I found it beautifully preserved was in a heritage home, close to where I had grown up, that was now enjoying a new lease of life as a multi-brand boutique called RainTree. In this column, meet that home's most famous resident.

Two roads diverge in Bangalore's High Grounds, once you're past the Bangalore Golf Club grounds and at the point where the Make-In-India lion stands, frozen in mid-roar. You could, like most people, zoom down the one that plunges towards the Palace Grounds, or you could take the road less travelled to two stately buildings – the ITC Windsor Hotel on the far side, and a smaller beauty set in a large garden, bearing the legend 'Pen Rhiw' ('top of the hill' in Welsh). The second is hallowed ground, for it was once the home of Benjamin Lewis Rice, Mysore's pioneer of archaeological research, epigraphist par excellence and much-loved educationist.

Lewis was born in Bangalore in July 1837, the same year that his father, Rev. B.H. Rice, arrived here from England to take up duties as pastor of the Pettah Chapel (now the Rice Memorial Church) on Avenue Road. With both his parents deeply involved in the management of a residential school for Indian girls, Lewis grew up in an academic environment, mingling with the locals and speaking fluent Kannada. At 11, he was sent off to school in England, where he eventually graduated with a BA, and gained employment. Homesick for Bangalore, however, he was preparing for the Indian Civil Service exams when the serendipitous offer of the post of principal at the new Bangalore High School (which later became the iconic Central College) brought him back at age 23.

Over the next six years, under Rice's stewardship, the school, and his own reputation as an educationist, grew and flourished. In 1866, as inspector of schools, he proceeded with alacrity to travel extensively across Mysore state on his trusty steed, getting up close and personal with its culture and people. As acting director of public instruction (a lucky break – the actual director went on long leave in 1868), he drew up a much-admired blueprint for a 'hobli system' of indigenous schools, where each hobli (cluster of villages) had its own school, funded, managed and staffed by people of that hobli.

Lewis's great bond with, and understanding of, the land, language and people of Mysore, and his talent for meticulous documentation, did not go unnoticed. In 1873, he was tasked with the herculean effort of compiling the *Mysore Gazetteer*, an exhaustive survey of the history, ethnography, geography, flora, fauna, religion, language and literature of the state, and each individual district. The set of two volumes, each a doorstopper at 1,000 pages, continues to be the pre-eminent authority on the subject. He also went on to author the equally hailed *Coorg Gazetteer.*

A few years earlier, the commissioner of Mysore, Lord Bowring, asked for Lewis's assistance with translating some 150 stone inscriptions that he had had photographed. Lewis was not familiar with the old Kannada script, but his interest piqued, he put together a team of local scholars and got to work. When *Mysore Inscriptions*, a comprehensive translation and interpretation of the inscriptions, was published in 1879, it created a sensation, introducing Mysoreans, for the first time, to the significance of the epigraphical wealth that lay mostly neglected around them.

In 1884, B.L. Rice was appointed the first director of Mysore's brand-new Department of Archaeology. Until his retirement in 1906, he worked tirelessly on unearthing the rich history of the state, and published, among many other important works, his 12-volume magnum opus *Epigraphia Carnatica*, containing commentaries on 9,000 inscriptions in Kannada, Tamil, Sanskrit and even Prakrit (from three Ashokan rock edicts, circa 300 BCE, that he had personally discovered near Chitradurga).

For his magnificent contributions, B.L. Rice is hailed by grateful Kannadigas to this day as *Shasana Pitamaha* – grandsire of epigraphy.

In 1891, while trawling the area around Chitaldrug (Chitradurga), B.L. Rice made a stunning discovery – an edict, the first of its kind in Karnataka, bearing the name of an ancient Indian emperor called Devanampriya. Rice considered this the most glamorous find of his career, because it extended the boundaries of Devanampriya's empire farther south than anyone had supposed.

In 1915, archaeologist C. Beadon discovered a similar edict in the town of Maski in Raichur, Karnataka, which opened with the line – *'Devanampriya Ashoka (proclaims thus).'* It was a thrilling, Rosetta-Stone moment for Indian history – finally, there was incontrovertible evidence that Devanampriya and the emperor Ashoka of Buddhist lore were the same person.

27

MASTI VENKATESHA IYENGAR, A BASAVANAGUDI LOCAL, WAS BORN ON 6 JUNE 1891, AND DIED ON THE SAME DAY 95 YEARS LATER

The Literary Leanings of Basavanagudi

I grew up a Malleswaram girl, which means that I will always insist, in public, that Gandhi Bazaar has nothing on 8th Cross. But the two months I spent at the BMS College of Engineering as a 17-year-old, before I moved to a different college, made me fall in love with Basavanagudi's wide, tree-lined avenues, its gracious old bungalows, the fruit bats in Bugle Rock Park, and the to-die-for idli and chutney at Brahmin's Coffee Bar. Over the last few years, ever since I undertook a project to translate into English 100 poems of the late, great K.S. Nisar Ahmed, whose first poetry collection was titled *Manasu Gandhi Bazaar-u* – The mind is (as chaotic and as wondrous as) Gandhi Bazaar – I have grown even fonder of Basavanagudi, even though I visit it less.

CTR or Vidyarthi Bhavan (VB)? The quintessentially Bengalurean debate about where the city's best benne masaal *dose* is to be found is as old as the two neighbourhoods where these venerable establishments are located. While Malleswaram residents stoutly defend the almost century-old Central Tiffin Room, Basavanagudi diehards swear by VB, founded in 1943.

The battlelines are more porous than most imagine, however. A few weeks ago, VB put out a provocative ad that seemed to suggest that a branch was soon opening at Malleswaram. The jubilation on social media, much of it from Malleswaram residents, clearly revealed that there are quislings on every team. So did the howls of indignation that went up when VB announced that their ad had only been a bit of mischievous punning; they had no intention of opening a branch anywhere.

If there is no clear winner – and may there never be one – in the best *dose* challenge, the same isn't true of the number-of-Kannada-litterateurs-per-square-km challenge, which Basavanagudi wins hands down. Such greats as poet D.V. Gundappa, Jnanpith awardee Masti Venkatesh Iyengar, journalist P. Lankesh and contemporary poet K.S. Nisar Ahmed have graced its streets and markets, and are celebrated with sculptures and portraits at local hangouts like the Bugle Rock Park and Brahmin's Coffee Bar. (Mercifully, Brahmin's does not offer *dose*. It is renowned for its idli and chutney, which pits it fiercely against Malleswaram's Veena Stores. It never ends.)

Even the Kannada Sahitya Parishat (now located next door, in Chamarajpet) was conceived at a conference held at Basavanagudi's Government High School grounds, way back in 1915! The Parishat was the brainchild of (who else but) Sir M. Visveswaraya, who worried that the Kannada language was losing its integrity, what with Kannada speakers in the then provinces of Madras,

Bombay, Hyderabad and Coorg taking on the inflections and vocabulary of the local languages into their conversation and writing.

The first president of the Parishat was H.V. Nanjundayya, highly respected ethnographer, former chief justice of the Chief Court of Mysore and almost-diwan of the kingdom. In 1916, after he retired from government service, this brilliant man would also serve as the first vice chancellor of Mysore University. The only twist in this story is that Nanjundayya himself was a Malleswaram man; it is his erstwhile residence, at the junction of 13th Cross and 4th Main, that now houses the Government Girls' School.

One of the other founding members of the Parishat, Bellave Venkatanaranappa, was a hardcore Basavanagudi groupie. As far back as 1901, this professor of physics, contending that the residents of the new extension needed a place to spend time 'in a jolly manner', set up the Basavanagudi Union and Service Club (BUSC), the city's very first 'native' version of the British 'gentlemen's club'. Unsurprisingly, only men were admitted, and the hefty membership fee (one rupee) ensured that the 'riff-raff' was kept out. In 1907, with a generous donation from the maharaja, the club found its forever home opposite the Tagore (literature again!) Circle.

The BUSC is often referred to as the Masti Club, after its most famous member ('Kannadada aasti, namma Masti' – Kannada's treasure, our Masti), for it was in these halls that the savant was to be found of an evening, shooting the breeze with his cronies over a game of cards. So adored was Masti and such a fixture at the BUSC that K.S. Nisar Ahmed composed an entire poem describing Masti's slow walk down the D.V. Gundappa Road to and from the club each evening, an ode as much to the man as the (very literary) neighbourhood.

Apart from its literary brigade, the most famous resident of Basavanagudi was perhaps Dr Hosur Narasimhaiah (better known by his initials, H.N.), a freedom fighter, physicist and fierce rationalist, who founded the Bangalore Science Forum in 1962, and served as principal of the famous National College, Basavanagudi, and vice chancellor of Bangalore University. In 1936, as a student at National High School, he was hand-picked for a most important job – Gandhiji was visiting the school, and H.N. was to translate Gandhiji's speech, in real time, into Kannada. That interaction had such a huge impact on the boy that he dropped out of college in 1942 to join the Quit India Movement, went to jail for nine months and wore khadi for the rest of his life. Apart from all his other achievements, H.N. is remembered for his very public battles with and denunciation of popular godmen such as Sathya Sai Baba and Shivabalayogi.

28

THE FOUNDING PLAQUE OF FRASER TOWN WAS UNVEILED IN AUGUST 1910

The English Bureaucrat Who Tutored Maharajas

Force of habit is one thing, but old Bangaloreans have a real penchant for retaining the use of old names for streets and neighbourhoods, never mind that they hark back to a colonial past. It has been almost a century since the 200-acre public park in the centre of the city was christened Chamarajendra Park, but precious few of us refer to it as anything other than Cubbon Park. Auto-drivers will look quizzically at you if you mention Field Marshal KM Cariappa Road, Maj Thimmayya Road, or Nam Srikantaiah Circle; they know them as Residency Road, Richmond Road, and South End Circle. The same fate is visited upon neighbourhoods – Sarvagnanagar and Pulikeshinagara still have an unfamiliar ring compared to Cox Town and Fraser Town. This last – not the neighbourhood but the man after whom it is named – is the subject of this column.

On 16 April, the all-night Shakti Utsava, the main event of the 300-year-old Bengaluru Karaga festival, made a glorious return after a Covid-induced hiatus. Once again, thousands of people belonging to the city's green-fingered, water-worshipping Tigala community thronged the narrow, nearly-500-year-old streets of the old city around the Dharmaraya Temple, to honour the feisty queen of the Kurus, Draupadi.

The Tigalas, who the father–son duo of Hyder Ali and Tipu Sultan had employed to create their thotas (flower- and produce-filled gardens) in the eighteenth century, had always celebrated Karaga. But it was not until F.J. Richards, keen ethnographer and Collector of the Bangalore Cantonment between 1908 and 1912, documented the festival in the journal of The Mythic Society (which he had helped found in 1909) that Karaga was introduced to the larger world.

Now, F.J. Richards had a missus, and it is her name that is on an unassuming granite plaque installed 112 years ago at the corner of Coles Road and Mosque Road in Bengaluru's Pulikeshinagara. The plaque states that it was Mrs Richards who christened the locality – except, she named it after a well-loved British Resident of Mysore, not the valiant seventh-century Chalukya king of Karnataka. That name change was effected in 1988, but most Bengalureans still refer to the locality by its original name, Fraser Town.

Who was this Fraser, then? Stuart Mitford Fraser arrived in India, only 20, in 1884, to serve in the Bombay Presidency as part of the Indian Civil Services. As per usual, he was banished to the 'districts' to cut his administrative teeth, but only five years later, was picked to serve as guardian and tutor to young Yeshwantrao Ghatge, adopted heir of the queen of Kolhapur.

In 1894, Yeshwantrao mounted the throne as Maharaja Shahu. Two years later, Fraser received his new appointment – tutor to 11-year-old Nalvadi Krishnaraja Wadiyar of Mysore, pitched willy-nilly into kingship following the tragic death of his father, Chamarajendra. Until he came of age in 1902, Fraser would stay by the boy–king's side, coaching him in jurisprudence, revenue administration, and more – which he taught through extensive tours of the Mysore country. Interestingly, both Fraser's wards would be hailed as rajarshis – saint-kings – by their people. 'It seems almost incredible,' Fraser recalled in his memoirs, 'that any one officer should have been fortunate enough to know intimately two Indian Princes (...) so alike in inspiring a life-long friendship with (...) their tutor and governor.'

In 1903, as His Majesty's commissioner, Fraser was sent off to negotiate with the Chinese the opening of Tibet's borders with British India. But he was soon back in these parts, as the Resident of Mysore and chief commissioner of Coorg. Apart from discharging his duties honourably, he enjoyed tiger hunting with his daughter in 'this delightful country', narrowly escaped death by wild elephant, and suffered an attack by angry bees. When he was appointed Resident of Kashmir in 1911, a deputation of Coorg luminaries voluntarily travelled over 100 miles in the monsoon to Bangalore to deliver his farewell address.

Between 1905 and 1910, Fraser would also help found The Mythic Society; rescue the Bishop Cotton Boys' School from financial ruin; undertake the expansion, redecoration and, for the first time, electrification, of his official residence (today, the Karnataka Raj Bhavan) to accommodate the future King George V, who came visiting in 1906; and push hard for a new extension north of the Cantonment to move survivors of the plague into. It was that new extension that Mrs Richards, in honour of that fine bureaucrat, christened Fraser Town.

No prizes for guessing who the adjacent extension, Richards Town, is named for.

It wasn't just Mrs Richards who was going around the city laying foundation stones. As wife of the Resident of Mysore and Commissioner of Coorg, Mrs Fraser did too. Two that are still around are the foundation stones of the Anglican Church at Basavanagudi, which Mrs Fraser laid on 8 March 1907, and that of the Fraser Town branch of the Rao Bahadur BP Annasawmy Mudaliar (RBANM's) School, which welcomed Indian children of all castes and creeds, less than a week later, on 13 March 1907.

29

KANTEERAVA NARASIMHARAJA WADIYAR, AFTER WHOM THE STADIUM IS NAMED, WAS BORN ON 5 JUNE 1888

Kanteerava: The Sports Stadium in a Lake Bed

I have never been a sportsperson, or a big watcher of sport. While my classmates headed off to Kanteerava in great excitement for interschool sports meets or training camps or simply to bunk classes, I usually stayed behind, nose buried in a book. But I have always been in awe of sportspeople, and have written often about them. That was how I finally found my way to Kanteerava back in October 2016, right after the Rio Paralympics, to interview high-jump gold medallist Mariyappan Thangavelu for a comic I had been commissioned to script. It was such a high, both meeting Mariyappan and standing on the hallowed track, that I decided I would start playing a sport myself. By the time I had demolished a post-interview masala dosa at Konark Kanteerava, the sweet restaurant in the stadium complex, that good intention, like so many others before it, had vanished without a trace.

On 12 October 2022, the curtains will ring down on the 36th National Games of India, currently underway in Gujarat after an unconscionable seven-year gap.

The very first national-level games, held at Delhi in 1924, were called the All-India Olympic Games, since they were held purely to pick a contingent for the Paris Olympics. It was only during their ninth edition, in 1940, that they were rechristened the National Games.

Until 1970, the Games were held, as planned, every couple of years. Things went a bit downhill after that – in the next 14 years, there would be only one edition of the National Games. Once India had hosted the Asian Games in 1982, however, the lustre returned – the 26th edition, hosted in 1985 in the new, state-of-the-art stadiums of the capital city, were a grand success. A dozen years later, in 1997, Bengaluru got her own opportunity to host the Games.

The city's first real sports stadium, the Kanteerava Stadium, was founded as early as 1946, by the last maharaja of Mysore, Jayachamarajendra (J.C.) Wadiyar. The maharaja himself was a keen sportsman, a crack shot who brought down man-eating tigers while being a passionate conservationist. He also enjoyed his game of tennis, and was instrumental not only in sending Ramanathan Krishnan, the first Indian to make it to the semi-finals of Wimbledon in 1960, to the tournament, but also in intervening on behalf of a young E.A.S. Prasanna, whose father did not want him to travel as part of the team to the faraway West Indies. The new stadium was named after J.C.'s father, Kanteerava Narasimharaja, who had himself been an excellent polo player.

In the beginning, most people referred to the Kanteerava Stadium as the Sampangi Stadium, and with good reason. With its six-lane cinder track, which drew even India's Flying Sikh, Milkha Singh, to train here in 1952, the stadium had come up in what used to be the Sampangi Tank, constructed by Kempegowda and his descendants some 400 years before, to serve the agricultural needs of the fort town. One of the largest in the kingdom, the lake was particularly sacred to the water-worshipping Tigalas, the green-fingered Tamil-speaking horticulturists that Hyder Ali brought over in large numbers from the Tamil country in the eighteenth century.

By the 1880s, however, even though Sampangi's waters were still irrigating ragi fields upstream and paddy fields downstream, Bangalore was being reimagined into a modern city. As the lake became gentrified, with people like Michael Lavelle – who had, quite literally, struck gold in Kolar – moving into lakeside bungalows, and the Bangalore Breweries (estd 1885), the city's first, setting up close by, the Tigalas and other communities who depended on the lake for their livelihood were firmly eased out.

In 1894, with the commissioning of the Hesaraghatta Lake, built specifically to supply piped drinking water to the growing city, Sampangi's relevance as a useful water body fell further. Calls to drain it and turn it into a polo field grew ever more strident, even as the Tigalas resisted. In the end, the polo field won. Whatever was left of the lake – except a tiny portion, which was left over for the Tigalas to worship at during their annual festival of Karaga – was drained by 1937, leaving it free to be turned into a sports stadium in 1946.

It was only 50 years later, when Bengaluru got its opportunity to host the National Games, that the indoor stadium was raised. That catapulted Kanteerava into a whole different league. Today, it is the city's biggest and most popular multi-sport stadium, and the home of the much-loved Bengaluru FC.

'Loved this. Kanteerava is akin to a temple for me, albeit for non-religious reasons. So there has always been some poetry to it having an actual temple on the premises. (Incidentally, I am not alone in that kind of thinking. Most athletes who come there genuflect before stepping on the track.)'

— ARVIND KRISHNAN, FOUNDER, *THE FULLER LIFE* AND *RUNNERS FOR LIFE*

30

ISRO WAS FOUNDED ON 15 AUGUST 1969

The Man Who Brought ISRO to Bengaluru

In the past two decades, with the huge successes of India's space programme, whether we are talking the Mars mission or landing a lunar rover on the dark side of the moon, the Indian Space Research Organisation (ISRO) has captured the Indian imagination like few other government agencies. According to former director K. Kasturirangan, ISRO owes a significant part of its success to a watertight clause in its charter disallowing interference in the agency's running from politicians and bureaucrats. That clause was written in by the second director of ISRO, the genteel, gentle MA in English literature who was known to sweat each comma and semicolon in any piece of communication he sent out. Meet Satish Dhawan, beloved Bangalorean.

On 14 July 2023, as the glorious sight of the Chandrayaan-3 successfully blasting off from Sriharikota filled our hearts and screens, India's national space agency, ISRO, was once again in the global limelight, this time for its efforts to make India only the fourth country in the world to land a spacecraft on the moon's surface. In honour of its successful soft landing on 23 August, let us turn our attention to a soft-spoken, much-loved, hugely admired Bengalurean, the postgraduate in English literature after whom the space centre in Sriharikota is named.

To be fair, Satish Dhawan, who was born in Srinagar and grew up in Lahore, had many other degrees besides the MA in English – a BA in mathematics and physics and a BE in mechanical engineering, both from Punjab University, an MS in aerospace engineering from the University of Minnesota, and a PhD in aerospace engineering and mathematics from Caltech. In 1951, he returned to India and came straight to Bangalore, to join the Indian Institute of Science as a senior scientific officer. Thenceforth, his rise was nothing short of mercurial. A decade later, only 42, he took charge as the IISc's youngest-ever director. He would helm the institute for over 17 years, exerting a huge influence on its intellectual character, and deploying his unique vision to turn IISc from an excellent institute of technology into a temple of application-based research and education.

Prof. Dhawan's own interest in a vast and varied number of subjects, apart from his strong social conscience and a deep love for nature, ensured the setting up of several centres of interdisciplinary research at IISc, including ASTRA (Cell for Application of Science and Technology to Rural Areas) and CES (Centre for Ecological Sciences). In the early '70s, he had just launched a global campaign to recruit the brightest minds as faculty for the institute when India's fledgling space programme suffered a huge setback –

on 30 December 1971, its brilliant architect, and the founder–chairman of ISRO, Vikram Sarabhai, only 52, succumbed to a cardiac arrest.

The idea of ISRO, a government agency that devoted itself to space research, had been mooted by Sarabhai as far back as 1962; in 1969, it took shape as ISRO. With Sarabhai gone, the then Prime Minister Indira Gandhi offered Prof. Dhawan the chairmanship. That was when, in a now-legendary counter-offer, Prof. Dhawan requested two assurances: one, that ISRO would be HQ-ed at Bengaluru, which, following the setting up of Hindustan Aircraft (now Aeronautics) Limited in 1940, and IISc's Aeronautical Engineering Department in 1942, had become the perfect ecosystem for such an organization; and two, that he would be allowed to continue as director of his beloved IISc. The prime minister agreed, and ISRO came to Bengaluru.

Satish Dhawan retired from IISc in 1981 and ISRO in 1984, continuing as chairman of the Indian Space Commission until his death in 2002, 50 years after he had first arrived in the city. It was during his tenure at ISRO that India's first two satellites – Aryabhata (1975) and Bhaskara (1979) – were placed in orbit (by Soviet rockets), and the first indigenously built SLVs (satellite launch vehicles) announced India's entry into the global space club. For all his great achievements as scientist, researcher and institution-builder, however, Prof. Dhawan is cherished far more by his colleagues as a great leader – one who shielded them from public ire when the SLV had a disastrous first outing in 1979, and stayed in the background when the same team, with his encouragement, triumphed the next year, successfully placing Rohini into orbit.

SATISH DHAWAN

'Your article on Prof. Satish Dhawan is short, succinct and factually correct – it was indeed Prof. Dhawan who was responsible for establishing ISRO HQ in Bangalore. Similarly, Prof. U.R. Rao was responsible for moving the Satellite Division of Vikram Sarabhai Space Centre from Trivandrum to Bengaluru to establish a full-fledged centre for spacecraft activities here. I encourage you to write this interesting story as well.'*

— L.V. PRASAD, RETD DEPUTY DIRECTOR, ISRO

•

'My dad always remembered the marked change in ISRO after Prof. Dhawan took over. Where Vikram Sarabhai's approach was passion-driven and intuition-led, sometimes at the expense of due scientific process, Prof. Dhawan's approach was more streamlined and structured – he created processes that could easily be built upon.'

— SRIRAM ARAVAMUDAN, WHOSE FATHER, R. ARAVAMUDAN, SERVED AS THE DIRECTOR OF THE SATISH DHAWAN SPACE CENTRE AND THE ISRO SATELLITE CENTRE

•

'When I was doing my master's in civil engineering at IISc, Prof. Dhawan was its director. In my final exams, I had topped in every subject except pure math, which I had failed. It would have been the end of the road for me had Prof. Dhawan not asked to see my other grades, quizzed me on what I wanted to do in life (build dams for hydroelectric projects, I said) and decided unilaterally that I should receive my degree, since engineers did not need pure math. He was as sharp as he was kind – a great man.'

— H.V. ESWARAIAH, TECHNICAL DIRECTOR (RETD), KARNATAKA POWER CORPORATION LTD

•

'So nice to read this. Two stories about Prof. Dhawan you perhaps know. 1. He kept PM Indira Gandhi's call on hold because he was in the middle of teaching a class at Caltech; 2. He stood up for Kalam after a failed satellite launch. A true legend!'

— SUDHEESH VENKATESH, CHIEF COMMUNICATIONS OFFICER AND MANAGING EDITOR, AZIM PREMJI FOUNDATION

I did write that piece on Prof. U.R. Rao, with Mr Prasad's inputs (see page 47).

31

TWICE OLYMPIAN AHMED KHAN, WHO STARTED HIS CAREER WITH BMFC, DIED ON 27 AUGUST 2017

The Winning Ways of the Bangalore Muslims FC

The period between 1951 and 1962 is considered the Golden Age of Indian Football. It is bookended by two gold medal–winning performances by the Indian team, at the 1951 and 1962 Asian Games. In between the two, at the 1956 Melbourne Olympics, India became the first Asian country to reach the semis. How did Indian football come to dream so big (for it is the dream that always precedes reality)? Arguably, it all began in 1937, when an unknown team from Bangalore called the Bangalore Muslims FC became the first Indian team to lift the prestigious Rovers Cup.

When the iconic playback singer S.P. Balasubrahmanyam succumbed in September 2020 to Covid-related complications, one of the most unexpected tributes to him on Twitter came from the fan club of a football team. 'Thank you, SPB,' it read. 'Thank you for the song that united us all.' The song in question was the disco number 'Santoshakke Haadu Santoshakke' from the 1981 Kannada movie *Geetha*, starring the never-forgotten Shankar Nag. The football team was our own Bengaluru FC. And the fan club was, of course, the very vocal West Block Blues, who belt out this song at every opportunity at The Fortress, aka the Kanteerava Stadium.

In a sporting universe dominated by cricket, Bengaluru FC's dazzling popularity is due (in unequal parts) to the team's excellent performances – unlike with RCB, 'ee sala Cup nammade' (this time, the Cup's ours) is not purely wishful thinking where BFC is concerned; its captain Sunil Chhetri's top-tier footballing skills and personal charisma; its fandom's unrelenting enthusiasm; and the city's long and deep-rooted culture of football excellence. Yes, excellence – it was a Bangalore team that became the first ever Indian club to win the British-founded Rovers Cup in 1937. The name of that legendary team? Bangalore Muslims FC (BMFC).

The Rovers Cup (founded in 1890, suspended in 2001) was not India's oldest football tournament – that honour goes to the Durand Cup, initiated in 1888 by the then foreign secretary of British India, Sir Mortimer Durand. Both tournaments were initially restricted to clubs drawn from military regiments, both Indian and British. Among the Indians, who much preferred field hockey, it was only the Gurkhas who signed up, but the tournament was always won by British regiments.

When World War II broke, British soldiers quit the subcontinent in droves, leaving the field open to Indian and civilian clubs. It was Bengal's

Mohammedan Sporting that lifted the Durand Cup in 1940, but by then, the BMFC had lifted the Rovers Cup – twice! In 1937, they beat Mohammedan 1–0 in the final; in 1938, the Argyll and Scottish Highlanders 3–2. They won it again in 1948, and were runners-up, twice to boot.

Who were these barefoot bravehearts – yes, like most other Indian clubs at the time, they played barefoot! – who called themselves the Bangalore Muslims? For starters, while their players were drawn from all sections of society, they weren't all Muslim. The 1937 squad included four non-Muslim players; it was one of them, Lakshminarayan, who scored the winning goal. Among those who began their careers with the Bangalore Muslims were Olympians Mohammad Abdus Sattar, who not only went on to play for Mohammedan Sporting but also coached the team in later years; Ahmed Khan, best remembered as one of the Pancha Pandavas, the five legendary forwards – along with Mysoreans K.P. Dhanraj and P. Venkatesh – of East Bengal FC; and Mariappa Kempaiah, who had a 12-year stint with the national team and was considered one of India's best midfielders.

But the BMFC was far more than just a winning football team. At a time when the country was beginning to be riven by communal conflict, it represented hope for cooperation and reconciliation. For the Indian National Congress, whose Bangalore chapter organized a grand reception in 1937 to welcome the winning team home, the boys were a living, breathing symbol of their vision of an undivided India.

Remarkably, although currently foundering in the C division of the state-level league, the club still exists, under the auspices of the Al-Ameen Trust. But the 'jalebi' style of play that was their signature – keep possession as far as possible, and dribble, dribble, dribble in circles to tire your opponent out – has slowly but surely passed out of public memory.

Star midfielder of the Indian team of the 1950s and 1960s, BMFC boy Mariappa Kempaiah was, like Tulsidas Balaram, a protégé of legendary national football coach Syed Abdul Rahim (played by Ajay Devgn in the 2024 film *Maidaan*, a biopic on Rahim's life), who spotted him in 1954 when he was playing for Mysore in the Santosh Trophy. Kempaiah went on to represent India at two Olympic Games – Melbourne 1956 and Rome 1960 – and played alongside the greats of Indian football, all coached by Rahim, including Chuni Goswami, P.K. Banerjee, Jarnail Singh and Peter Thangaraj. In January 2024, his biography, simply titled *Olympian M. Kempaiah*, and written by his daughter Sumaa Mahesh Gowda, was released by Sunil Chhetri in a glittering ceremony at the Indian Embassy in Doha.

BYRAMMA ACHIEVED HER FEAT, MOST PROBABLY, IN JUNE OR JULY

The Swimming Sensation of Kempambudhi Kere

I learnt to swim – if such panicked, undignified flailing could be called that – one long-ago summer vacation, in the massive (or so it seemed to the eight-year-old me) pool at the IISc Gymkhana, which I had access to only because my uncle was an alumnus. Although I did not go back to the pool, or learn to swim well until several years later, I followed the accomplishments of my city's swimmers on the sports pages like a good Bangalorean. I still do, and they continue to shine.

It's May, the long-awaited showers have finally – sorta, kinda – arrived, and the blazing crimson of the gulmohars against relentlessly blue skies reassure old Bengalureans that not all of the charms of their remembered city have been lost to 'progress'. May is also summer vacation season, which means the city's many swimming pools – and Bengaluru has more Olympic-sized pools than any other city in the country – are packed with shrieking children, a few of whom, although they don't know it yet, are destined for sporting greatness.

The British legacy of gentlemen's clubs and missionary schools, most of which had their own swimming pools, had ensured that swimming had historically been a preoccupation, albeit an elite one, in the city. It was the opening of two Olympic-sized public pools built by the Bangalore City Corporation in the 1970s, the (recently revived) Kensington Swimming Pool by the Ulsoor Lake, and the Sadashivanagar pool by the Sankey Tank, however, that made it part of the city's mainstream leisure and sporting culture. In the '80s, Bengaluru's pleasant all-year-round weather and the growing interest in swimming saw its champions begin to make a splash at the national level, bringing attention to the city as a potential hub for athlete training. Swim clubs, including the famous Basavanagudi Aquatic Centre (BAC, founded in 1986) and the K.C. Reddy Swim Centre (founded in 1994, now Global Swim Centre) at the Sadashivanagar pool, began to proliferate, their crack swim teams competing at city-wide competitions, raising the overall pitch.

With legendary coaches like Nihar Ameen – he returned home in the early '90s after a stint as assistant coach of the US National Team, and now trains national champions at the Padukone–Dravid Academy – and Pradeep Kumar Sreedharan – national swimming coach since 2005, and head coach at BAC – also pledging their troth to Bengaluru, the sport zoomed into a different league. Many of the country's 28 Olympians, including Nisha Millet, Hakimuddin Habibulla, Shikha Tandon, Rehan Poncha, Gagan Ullalmath, para swimmer Sharath Gayakwad, and most recently, at Tokyo 2020, Srihari Nataraj, are natives of Bengaluru. The latest – and youngest – to join the roll of honour is 14-year-old Dhinidhi Desinghu, who won seven gold medals at the National Games 2023 and broke Indian records with her relay team at the Hangzhou Asian Games.

What most people do not know, however, is that Nisha, Shikha and Dhinidhi are the torchbearers of a proud Bengaluru tradition of record-breaking swimmer girls, the first among whom was a little-known eight-year-old called Byramma. In the 1920s, when the city's many lakes and tanks still thrived, the sixteenth-century Kempambudhi Kere in Chamarajpet, built by city founder Kempegowda I, was reputed to be the deepest and the cleanest. Chosen by the Bangalore Scouts Association as the location for their swim club, it attracted many locals, including Byramma.

The little girl's potential was noticed by coach Srinivasa Rao, who took her under his wing. In July 1935, after putting her through a series of endurance trials, he reckoned his protégée was ready to attempt something big. At midnight, by the flickering of dozens of kerosene lamps, Byramma entered the water to begin her epic swim. She emerged from the lake an incredible 18 hours later, at 6 p.m., having smashed the world record for nonstop swimming. Felicitated by Sir Mirza Ismail, the then diwan of Mysore, and attaining global recognition via the editor of an American children's magazine, who had been among the witnesses to her spectacular feat, Byramma inexplicably faded into obscurity. Until, in 2012, a 70-year-old Bengaluru resident called Vemagal

Somashekhar found a thread of her story in an old newspaper report, followed the very cold trail, collected documentation connected with Byramma's achievement, including a photograph with her coach, and submitted it to the State Archives Department, where it is now, one presumes, safely preserved.

'Very inspirational! The column truly resonated with me because swimming has been my passion now for over two decades. After I was gifted my Siamese twin (my stoma bag, post my episode with colon cancer), I thought I would never swim again. But my son Aniket did his research and bought me 'ostomy swimwear'. I make sure my stoma bag fits cosily into it first, then wear my normal swimming costume over it. As a result of this sartorial tweaking, I am able to swim for 30 to 40 minutes at a time, much to the surprise and delight of my onco surgeons!'

— RAMENDRA KUMAR, AWARD-WINNING WRITER, STORYTELLER AND INSPIRATIONAL SPEAKER

•

In his 1807 book, *A Journey from Madras through the Countries of Mysore, Canara and Malabar*, Scottish surgeon, surveyor and botanist Francis Buchanan-Hamilton classified the many man-made water bodies he saw in Bangalore and Mysore thus: a katte, he said, was a small reservoir supplying water for cattle, a kunte was a square cavity dug into the ground, and a kere, like the Kempambudhi Kere mentioned in this piece, was a large reservoir used for watering lands around it.

33

S.V. SETTY'S BIPLANE DESIGN FOR A.V. ROE WAS PUBLISHED IN JULY 1912 IN THE CALCUTTA MAGAZINE, *MODERN REVIEW*

That Magnificent Mysorean and His Flying Machines

Any talk of aircraft always brings back memories of Bangalore's lovely, much-missed old HAL airport (off today's Old Airport Road), where everyone went to receive assorted aunties and uncles visiting from the 'States'. To those of us who lived to the west of Cubbon Park, going to the airport, 10 km away in the east, felt like an expedition – we dressed up, loaded the camera with film, and even packed snacks for the ride (and garlands for our foreign-returned relations)! Then the buying of the entry tickets, the excitement of watching the plane land and the absolute thrill of spotting our relatives, newly descended from the skies, walking from the runway towards us.

This column goes back to where it all began, to a remarkable but little-known young man from nineteenth-century Mysore who can legitimately lay claim to the title of 'India's first aviator'.

As an (admittedly torturous) exercise in self-control, let us desist from speaking today of the two topics uppermost in the Bangalorean mind – the weather and voting day – and speak instead of the deep human yearning to 'slip the surly bonds of Earth, and dance the skies on laughter-silvered wings.' Let us speak, in particular, of a remarkable aviator from Mysuru, who, two decades before the great J.R.D. Tata famously piloted the 'first flight in the history of Indian aviation' from Karachi to Bombay in 1932, had danced the skies in planes he himself had helped design.

Given that he was born in 1879, flying hadn't always been on Srirama Venkatasubba Setty's bucket list. After completing his bachelor's degree in arts at Maharaja's College, Mysore, he enrolled at the engineering college at Guindy, Madras, from where he transferred to the storied Thomason College (later IIT Roorkee), excited by the prospect of getting a degree in a new discipline – electrical engineering. Graduating in 1906, he joined the Mysore PWD (Public Works Department) and was happily occupied for the next few years.

In 1909, Setty won a scholarship to the prestigious Faraday House, a London engineering college funded by the industry well before electrical engineering became de rigueur at universities. The diploma course included industry internships, and Setty had a grand time learning about power generation and distribution.

However, it was impossible to be a mechanical-minded young man in England at the time and not be swept up in dreams of flying. On 17 December 1903, the Wright Brothers had completed the world's first manned and powered flight over the dunes of Kitty Hawk, North Carolina. On 25 July 1909, the year that Setty arrived in England, French aviator Louis Blériot became the first to fly a plane across the Channel, bringing the excitement closer home. In 1911, thanks to a generous Mysore patron, S.V. Setty was able to stay on in England and join A.V. Roe and Company (founded in 1910; later Avro), among the first British aircraft building companies, as an 'apprentice and unpaid draughtsman' (according to the sign accompanying his picture at the Museum of Science and Industry in Manchester).

One of the great (and dangerous) compensations of the job was the opportunity to test and fly planes, which Setty, who had also enrolled at the Avro Flying School at the Brooklands Airfield in Surrey, made gleeful use of. But the planes were unreliable and crashed often. A designer at heart, Setty took it upon himself to fix the problem. The test flight of the biplane with Setty's design, piloted by the man himself, so impressed Aussie aviation pioneer, John Duigan, that he immediately booked one for himself. That biplane became the prototype of the Avro Duigan, which in turn was the inspiration for the Avro 500 and the famous training aircraft, the Avro 504, which was produced more than any other military airplane during World War I.

In June 1912, out of funds and unable to complete the flying hours required for a pilot's licence, Setty returned home. The delighted diwan of Mysore, Sir M. Visvesvaraya, installed him forthwith as superintendent of the kingdom's first technical school in Bangalore. That school, in 1917, became Mysore's first School of Engineering. Today, it continues to flourish as the University Visvesvaraya College of Engineering (UVCE).

S.V. Setty dreamt of building India's first aircraft in Bangalore, but World War I (1914–18) put his plans on hold. In 1918, the Spanish Flu swept through Bangalore, felling a fifth of the city's population, including, tragically, India's first aviator himself. He was only 38. Setty must have manifested that vision hard, though – in 1940, India's first aircraft factory, Hindustan Aircraft Limited, did come up in the city, just as he had hoped.

'Read this while in the clouds on a plane, Roopa Aunty! Lovely piece. Setty made his short life memorable – that's simply DOPE. This article makes me proud to be a Bangalorean once again!'

— MAHI SASTRY, RUNNER, POET AND ASPIRING DATA ANALYST

•

'What a stunning story! And what a premature end to such promise! On a side note, I'm once again delighted to know a little bit more about the deep and wide influence of Sir M.V.'

— JASJEET KAUR, WHO WONDERS HOW SHE CAN GIVE SOMETHING BACK TO THE CITY THAT GIVES SO MUCH OF ITSELF TO ALL WHO COME HERE

34

DECCAN HERALD WAS FOUNDED ON 16 JUNE 1948

Liquor into Printing Ink: A Newspaper Story

To old Bangaloreans, *Deccan Herald* (*DH*) was a morning habit as addictive, and as beloved, as the day's first cup of coffee. But my relationship with *DH* is rather more special than anyone else's – when I was only 17, *DH* carried a piece I had sent them as a 'middle' (a short, humorous, slice-of-life piece on any theme) on their Op-Ed page, granting a young, aspiring writer the singular, unassailable high of her very first byline. I even got paid a goodly sum – 200 rupees – for my contribution. I will never forget how the phone was ringing off the hook that morning, with friends and family calling to congratulate my mum – you see, everyone we knew read *Deccan Herald*!

On 16 June 2023, one of Bengaluru's well-loved, much-respected and most enduring institutions, synonymous with the city itself, turned a robust 75. Like many others of that vintage in the Cantonment, this one also started life on what used to be South Parade (today's MG Road). And like so many other well-known institutions in the city – schools, hospitals, film production houses, sports centres and horse racing – this one too was bankrolled by a local liquor baron.

If you want to split hairs over it, Kanekal Nettakallappa Guruswamy was from Ballari, not Bengaluru. But it was only after his family – like Dr Rajkumar's family, they belonged to the toddy-tapping Ediga caste – moved here in Guruswamy's youth that their fortunes took off. As the oldest of six siblings, Guruswamy was inducted into the heat and dust of excise auction halls when he was only 18. And a good thing, too, for Guruswamy's father would pass unexpectedly in 1928, when Guruswamy was only 26.

In the decades that followed, Guruswamy's business went into overdrive, turning him into a wealthy, influential figure, as recognizable by the large solitaire on his finger, the immaculately tied white kachche panche, the closed-collar coat, the large white turban and the Mont Blanc pen in his pocket as by the long black Cadillac that was his steed of choice. Indulging his passions for horse riding, horse racing (although he never himself placed a single bet) and shikar – his grandson K.N. Hari Kumar, in his recent memoir about his grandparents, recalls a room full of hunting trophies, including tiger, gaur and bear heads, stag antlers and elephant tusks – to the fullest, he seemed to want or need nothing more. Joy reigned on the domestic front as well – not having children of their own, he and his wife Kadiramma had adopted the son of Guruswamy's brother, Anjanappa, naming him Nettakallappa after his grandfather.

Nothing in this picture would suggest what was to come in 1948, when Guruswamy decided, seemingly on a whim, to risk both fortune and reputation on a venture that no one in Mysore State had tried before. Notwithstanding the fact that several Kannada newspapers he had supported had folded up, he decided he would start what the city had been missing – a first-class English daily. A space had just come up for sale on 16, South Parade, which was just right for the newspaper's offices. It had most recently housed a popular dance hall called Funnel's, but now that the Raj had waltzed out, the Irish owners were looking for buyers.

On Wednesday, 16 June 1948, after much last-minute panic – the inexperience of everyone involved in the enterprise had ensured that the original printing press picked had messed up the production, and a Kannada press had to be persuaded to render its services at short notice – an eight-page tabloid, costing 1 anna a pop, was ushered into life with a small tea party at, as the invitation had it, 'the residence of *Deccan Herald*'. A few months later, it was followed by the launch of its equally iconic sister publication in Kannada, *Prajavani*.

Guruswamy's biggest triumph was the recruiting of *Deccan Herald*'s first editor, the legendary Pothan Joseph, who had also been the founding editor of the Pakistani broadsheet *Dawn*, the editor of the *Hindustan Times* and a very popular columnist (his column, 'Over a Cup of Tea', ran for over half a century!).

Both *Deccan Herald* and *Prajavani* would take their own sweet time to turn a profit, but Guruswamy never faltered. Today, it is his three grandsons who continue to bring news of their hometown to nostalgic Bengalureans all over the world from 75, MG Road.

'I know this story well! Whenever we visited Bangalore (once every two years) from Orissa, where my dad worked in HAL, we stayed at my aunt's place in NR Colony. The Nettakallappa Circle was close by, and Guruswamy's mansion too. My dad used to point to it and say they were distantly related to us. Thank you – your piece brought back old memories of my childhood.'

— T.N. HARI, EXECUTIVE CHAIRMAN - STEER WORLD, AUTHOR AND GROWTH ADVISER

•

'Nice! Do you know Hari Kumar gatecrashed my wedding? Back in the day, Mukunda (my then boyfriend) and I were good friends with Hari Kumar, the infamous T.G. Vaidyanathan (film critic, cricket writer and academic) and a few others. When Mukunda and I got married, we had a small, simple reception, just for family, at the Brindavan Hotel on MG Road. But these friends came anyway – Hari Kumar just strolled over from the *Deccan Herald* office, haha.'

— RENU MUKUNDA, SOCIAL DEVELOPMENT SPECIALIST AND WIFE OF AUTHOR MUKUNDA RAO

35

LESLIE COLEMAN WAS BORN ON 16 JUNE 1878

A Canadian Crop Doctor in Bengaluru

In the early '50s, a 72-year-old Canadian crop scientist called Dr Leslie Coleman came to Bangalore on a private visit. He had last seen the city in 1934, when India was still under British rule. But the chief minister of Karnataka at the time, Kengal Hanumanthiah, got wind of Coleman's arrival and organized a grand public reception in his honour. Spontaneously, at short notice, thousands of ragi and groundnut farmers from Ramanagaram and sugarcane farmers from Mandya travelled to Bangalore to attend the reception – they wanted to express their gratitude and respect to the exceptional scientist who, during his two decades of service as the first director of the Department of Agriculture of the erstwhile kingdom of Mysore, had contributed so much to protecting their livelihoods.

Although we have been plagued these past weeks by extraordinary climate events, including the uncharacteristic humidity in our own city, India will be focusing today – 4 June, counting day of the Lok Sabha Elections 2024 – only on its political climate. To offer a smidgen of respite on the eve of World Environment Day, let us focus instead on two remarkable Canadians who arrived in Bangalore over a century ago and transformed the lives of Mysore's farmers.

It all began (as did the Indian National Congress) with British civil servant and political reformist Allan Octavian Hume. Miffed that the government focused more on agricultural revenue than on improving agricultural efficiency across India, he proposed the setting up of a dedicated Department of Agriculture, which was rejected. In 1879, following the devastating famine of 1876–78, Hume lashed out against the government, and was fired for his pains. In 1889, with famine looming again, the government finally decided to act on Hume's proposal – for a start, English agricultural chemist J.A. Voelcker was tasked with generating a report on improvements required in Indian agriculture.

As usual, Mysore was ahead of the game. Tipu Sultan's passion for horticulture had been carried forward by Commissioner Mark Cubbon, who founded the Agri-horticultural Society in 1839 to educate farmers and introduce superior varieties of cotton, sugarcane and tobacco into the soil of Mysore. In 1881, Maharaja Chamarajendra Wadiyar set up agricultural banks to finance farmers, and in 1888, instituted an Agricultural and Industrial Exhibition as part of the Dasara festivities, to stimulate growth across both sectors. Following the recommendations of the Voelcker report, Mysore went global, bringing in experts from across the world to whet its agricultural efficiency.

The first to arrive, in 1899, was German-Canadian chemist and agricultural scientist Adolf Lehmann. Setting up his office and laboratory on the 30 acres of land that Queen Regent Kempananjammanni had donated to the Experimental Agricultural Station at Hebbal, he established rigorous processes for soil fertility experiments and pest control, and improved the process of turning sugarcane juice into sugar. In 1907, feeling the lack of a 'plant protection' expert, he invited his fellow Canadian, a 29-year-old entomologist, mycologist and plant pathologist, Leslie Coleman, then working in Berlin, to come to Mysore on a five-year contract.

For reasons unclear, Lehmann's own contract was not renewed in 1908, leaving young Coleman with far more responsibilities than he had signed up for. He must have discharged them well; in 1913, the Mysore government offered him a permanent position as the first director of its Department of Agriculture. He would continue to serve in that position for over 20 productive years, going well beyond his brief into areas like agricultural policy, education, community outreach, and mechanization, including designing the efficient and inexpensive 'Mysore plough' to replace the wooden one then in vogue.

On then-diwan Sir M. Visvesvaraya's urging, Coleman set up the Hebbal Agricultural School (today part of the University of Agricultural Sciences [UAS], on the same campus) in 1913, and served as its first principal. His discovery that the so-called 'Bordeaux Mixture' worked very well to protect young areca trees against a major fungal disease, and his measures to prevent rot disease in coffee plants, saved the livelihoods of tens of thousands of Mysore farmers. He also played a key role in the setting up of the Mysore Sugar Factory, the first joint-stock private company in India, working with sugarcane farmers to ensure their participation.

As a tribute to this remarkable scientist, the annual Coleman Memorial Lecture is hosted by UAS on his birthday – 16 June – each year. In 2023, Leslie Coleman's India papers were donated by his family to the city where he spent so much of his working life and contributed so much to; they are now held in the archives of the National Centre for Biological Sciences.

'Lovely! Nice to know that one of Bangalore's true Mannina Magas (sons of the soil) was not Kannadiga but Canadiga.'

— DR SUNITHA SASTRY, BANGALOREAN NOW SETTLED IN THE SAN FRANCISCO BAY AREA

•

'Always a pleasure to discover that the efforts and talent of a foreigner from a faraway land are contained in the areca nuts in our post-lunch paan and our morning cup of coffee.'

— VENKATESH REDDY, AVID READER, RUNNER AND EDUCATOR FROM HYDERABAD

•

'No statue or road name in Bangalore for an individual who had such an impact on people's livelihoods? The survival of thousands of farmer-households can be attributed to his efforts, but no memorial?'

— M.D. RAO, READER FROM BANGALORE

36

WORLD WAR I, DURING WHICH DAKOTA AIRCRAFT WERE EXTENSIVELY USED, ENDED ON 15 AUGUST 1945

The Sundarams: Bangalore's First Couple of Aviation

2024 marks 50 years of the passing of the last maharaja of Mysore. In his memory, here's a story about Captain and Usha Sundaram, the 'high-flying' couple in whose capable hands the aviation-loving monarch, and the leaders of a newly independent nation, put their trust – and their lives.

Flying isn't all the Sundarams are known for, however. In 1959, they founded the Blue Cross of India (BCI), the much-respected animal welfare charity, from their home in Chennai. In 1964, they launched the first sterilization programme for street dogs in the world, and in 1996, persuaded the Chennai Corporation to relinquish the inhuman catch-and-kill programme and adopt BCI's Animal Birth Control-Anti Rabies (ABC-AR) programme instead. Other cities, including Bangalore, followed suit. In 2001, the Government of India enacted the Animal Birth Control (Dogs) Rules and made it mandatory for local bodies to implement ABC.

At a recent event celebrating the memory of Maharaja Jayachamaraja (J.C.) Wadiyar on the occasion of his 50th death anniversary, his son-in-law, Raja Chandra Urs, a meticulous archivist of his remarkable life, talked about a young couple who had rendered a rather special service to the maharaja in the late forties – they had piloted his private plane, the Mysore Dakota VT-AXX, between 1946 and 1951.

How the maharaja came to own a Dakota is a fascinating tale, part of the genesis story of aviation in Bangalore, in which J.C. played a very significant role. It includes the story of why Hindustan Aeronautics Limited (HAL) came to be set up in the city in 1940, the part it played in the establishment of the Aeronautical Engineering Department at the Indian Institute of Science in 1942, and the natural fallout of these two events – during World War II, with HAL being handed over to the US Army Air Forces for the duration of the war, Bangalore became one of the most reputed aircraft tinkering shops in the east. In 1945, the Americans returned home, leaving behind several war-surplus Dakotas. It was one of those Dakotas, newly refurbished and converted into a shiny 21-seater passenger aircraft, that J.C. snapped up for himself in 1946.

Now that there was a plane, a pilot had naturally to be found. The one J.C. handpicked, Capt V. Sundaram, was something of a rock star. In 1935, when he was only 19, he had become a licensed pilot. In 1937, he became the first Indian to get a commercial pilot's licence. Over the next few years, he flew extensively across the country, served as instructor at the venerable Madras Flying Club (estd 1929), trained British and American pilots, and, according to an unconfirmed report, took the first aerial photograph of the Taj Mahal. In 1945, he joined Tata Airlines (estd 1932, later Air India), an airmail carrier set up by J.R.D. Tata that had grown into a full-fledged passenger airline. In 1946, he moved to Bangalore to become J.C.'s personal pilot.

Somewhere along the way, Capt Sundaram also found a wife, the lovely Usha Krishnamurthy, who was only 17 when they were married in 1941. Two years after the couple had moved to Bangalore, J.C., now fascinated by aviation, bought up 200 acres of land to the north of the city for an aerodrome. He handed it over to the government of the new, democratic Mysore State soon after, on the condition that it only be used to set up a flying school; in December 1948, the Government Flying Training School came up at the Jakkur Aerodrome. The first graduate of that school, who was also independent India's first woman pilot, was Usha Sundaram.

The late '40s were frenetic years in India, as the new government, especially Deputy Prime Minister Sardar Vallabhbhai Patel, toiled to integrate nearly 600 princely states into the Indian Union. There was a lot of flying around the country to be done, and J.C. generously donated his Mysore Dakota to the cause. Through 1948 and 1949, the Sundarams – with Usha first playing hostess and later co-pilot – flew the Iron Man of India some 1,00,000 miles, standing by as he masterfully stitched the country together. In 1950, once the Herculean task had been accomplished, Usha Sundaram became Prime Minister Nehru's personal pilot, and remained so until she retired from professional flying in 1952 to raise her three children.

There's one last flying story to be told about the Sundarams – in 1951, tasked with purchasing the trendy de Havilland Dove for the Government of Madras, they travelled to England by ship and then flew the Dove from London to Bombay in 27 hours, setting a record flight-time for piston-engine aircraft that is yet to be surpassed.

'Thank you for the write-up about my parents, Usha and Capt V. Sundaram. From 1946–51, we lived in No. 3, St Mark's Road, adjoining Bishop Cottons (I am a proud Josephite, however!) and right opposite Cash Pharmacy. That was the home that Sardar Patel and his daughter Maniben visited on 24 February 1947.'

— S(UNDARAM) CHINNY KRISHNA, 80, ANIMAL ACTIVIST AND CO-FOUNDER, BLUE CROSS OF INDIA

•

'Lovely piece! I studied aircraft maintenance engineering in Chennai, so the names Madras Flying Club and Jakkur are very familiar and dear to me.'

— RAM MOHAN, HONORARY CONSUL-GENERAL OF INDIA IN THE GAMBIA

•

'Very nice. My dad, an Air Force aspirant, got a Flying Scholarship in 1942–43 to train under Gp Capt Tyndale-Biscoe, chief instructor at Meenambakam. Sundaram was also an instructor there at the time.'

— ARUN SWAMINATHAN, PROFESSOR AND DESIGN CHAIR AT R.V. COLLEGE OF ARCHITECTURE

•

'Fascinating! I feel very connected to the Dakota, as this noisy, rattly, bus-like aircraft was the only hopper flight from Guwahati to Kolkata and to other parts of the North-East.'

— VIJAYLAKSHMI NAGARAJ, AUTHOR, STORYTELLER AND ARMY WIFE WHO GREW UP IN THE NORTH-EAST

•

'Wow, that is some story! I live a stone's throw away from Jakkur Aerodrome and had no idea. On another note, perhaps it was the abandoned Dakotas that led to the word 'Dakota,' in Bangalore at least, being associated with a rundown vehicle or anything in a poorly maintained condition.'

— DR UMASHANKAR, PATHOLOGIST

37

VANAMAHOTSAVA, THE OFFICIALLY MANDATED TREE-PLANTING WEEK, RUNS FROM JULY 1 TO 7 EVERY YEAR

A Legacy of Tree-Love in Bengaluru

'There's nothing to see in Bangalore. What can one show visitors other than Lalbagh and Cubbon Park?'

Taking what one has for granted is not a foible peculiar to Bangaloreans – it is a common human failing. But if we only stepped back for a moment to pause and reflect, we would realize just how fortunate we are to live in a city that boasts not one, but *two* large public parks, both over 150 years old, at its heart. That kind of thing doesn't happen by chance – the city's still extensive tree cover is the result of an unbeatable combination, over centuries, of political will, citizen vigilance, horticultural talent, corporate investment, official attention, legal rulings, and a deeply ingrained love for trees and gardens that cuts across social and economic classes. Seriously, why would you want to show your visitors *anything* apart from Lalbagh and Cubbon Park?

In a recent talk, celebrated Bangalore wildlife filmmaker Amoghavarsha J.S., best known for the national award-winning documentary *Wild Karnataka* and the beloved 2022 Kannada docudrama *Gandhada Gudi*, a paean to Karnataka's stunning landscapes and wild denizens, starring the late Puneeth Rajkumar, spoke eloquently of his new quest – finding a template for uniquely 'Indian' wildlife and nature films that do not follow 'the Planet Earth model'.

'In Indian thought and belief,' he explained, 'Nature, whether we are talking trees or birds or leopards or snakes, is not separate from humans – it is part of everyday culture, tradition, religion and human activity. Our wildlife films should reflect that. We have the largest number of people of any country, but we also have the world's largest population of tigers and Asian elephants sharing space with them – that isn't easy to achieve.'

That's a thought to chew on in the week of Vanamahotsava, India's annual tree-planting and environmental awareness festival. Decades before the world went into its collective flap about climate change, before UNESCO mandated 22 April as Earth Day in 1970 and the UN established 5 June as World Environment Day in 1974, India, in 1950, had set aside an entire week – 1 to 7 July– to celebrate and raise awareness about the environment, centred around a specific activity – tree planting, to achieve a specific goal – increasing the country's forest cover.

The first 'Tree-planting Week' was held between 20 and 27 July 1947, a fortnight before India's independence. It was initiated by the renowned civil servant, historian and botanist from Punjab, M.S. Randhawa, who would play a significant role in the Green Revolution, which modernized Indian agriculture in the '60s. The idea captured the imagination of leaders like Nehru and Gandhi; three years later, the then Union minister for food and agriculture,

K.M. Munshi, a committed environmentalist in his own right, moved it to the first week of July, a time of rejuvenation for both Man and Nature as the Indian monsoon roars in, and christened the festival Vanamahotsava.

Our own elevated city, built on unyielding granite hills at a great distance from a river, has had a deep engagement with trees and gardens, from centuries before the official memo. In the sixteenth century, city founder Kempegowda I, who built an ingenious system of 'cascading lakes' – man-made water bodies interlinked by canals that deployed the hills' natural inclines to flow from one to the other, thus ensuring that no water was wasted – established dozens of thotas, including Kempu Thota, the precursor to Hyder Ali's Lalbagh. In the eighteenth century, Hyder Ali persuaded large numbers of the green-fingered Tigalas to move from their native Tamil lands to his city to coax flowers and fruits from the red earth. His son, Tipu Sultan, an enthusiastic planter of trees himself, imported exotic species from all over the world.

British Commissioner Sir Mark Cubbon, after whom the Park is named, established the Agri-horticultural Society in 1839 and handed Lalbagh

to them; renowned British botanists like Cleghorn, New and Cameron turned it, by the end of the nineteenth century, into a world-class botanical garden. In 1907, Maharaja Nalvadi Krishnaraja Wadiyar convinced German horticulturist Gustav Krumbiegel to move to Bangalore, his mandate to green the city's avenues with local and exotic species, with Lalbagh serving as nursery. In the '50s, in neighbouring Magadi, unlettered and poverty-stricken Saalumarada Thimmakka, now 112, planted and nurtured 384 banyan trees along a 5-km stretch of highway, of her own volition.

To this day, despite the traffic, few announcements raise Bangalorean hackles as intensely as those about trees having to be cut so that a street may be widened. That's a legacy that's hard to beat.

'Thank you for this piece. We need to start taking our tree-planting weeks and months seriously. I have been thinking a lot about how and where to plant fruit trees for future generations of people and animals, and your piece has provided the necessary boost. As an aside, I believe the Green Revolution was unnecessary, and destroyed Punjab and the Punjabi farmer, but that's a different debate.'

— JASJEET KAUR, WHO LOVES BANGALORE'S HISTORY, ITS PEOPLE AND ITS OLD NEIGHBOURHOODS

•

'Enjoyed reading about greenery in Bangalore. I remember a cartoon that came out in *Koravanji* (a Kannada humour magazine my dad founded) in the '50s, when the new extension of Jayanagar was coming up, referring to Vanamahotsava (forest festival) as 'ona mahotsava' (barren festival), because of all the trees that were felled to build it.'

— M. SHIVAKUMAR, FOUNDER—EDITOR OF KANNADA WEEKLY HUMOUR MAGAZINE, *APARANJI*

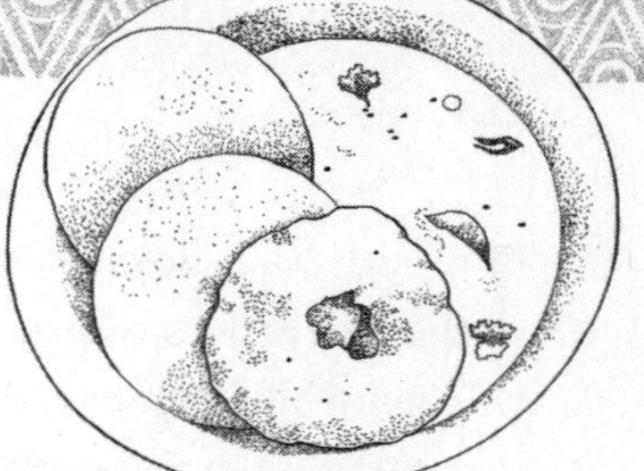

38

A Century of Tiffin in Bengaluru

2024 is a momentous year for tiffin in Bangalore – it was the year the city's iconic Mavalli Tiffin Rooms, better known as MTR, turned hundred. For a restaurant to not only survive for over a century, but also continue to be loved, in a city known for the alacrity with which it embraces new tastes, trends and experiences, is stupendous.

Since 2013, MTR has also been serving nostalgia packaged as food from its international branches to customers in Singapore, Dubai, Kuala Lumpur, London, Kathmandu, Seattle, Bellevue, and, in its centenary year, Mississauga.

I have frequented MTR's flagship outlet on Lalbagh Main Road for close to half a century, and have many memories of cooling my heels for long hours in the waiting room before finally being ushered into the hallowed halls for Sunday breakfast. Today, however, after 20 years of ferrying school students through the same halls for a delicious MTR lunch at the end of a Bangalore history tour, I have earned the right to call ahead, let the manager know we are coming and be assured of being seated as soon as we arrive. For an old Bangalorean, there are few privileges more enviable.

In end-2023, loyal patrons of the New Krishna Bhavan (NKB) savoured the last orders of green masala idlis and Mangaluru buns to be served at this beloved 70-year-old Malleswaram fixture. On 6 December, the shutters came down permanently on NKB ('we have no branches') and a delicious bit of the city's history.

To abide for seven decades in an industry where competition is fierce, labour itinerant, wastage rampant, product shelf life fleeting (think coconut chutney), profit margins paper-thin and consumer tastes capricious is a feat in itself – one would be hard-pressed to imagine (m)any of today's top eateries enjoying anything close to that kind of lifespan. But to resist the temptation to transform or tweak a perfectly good thing in the quest to 'trend' demands a different kind of mettle, which NKB, and so many other Bengaluru classics like it, have quietly displayed over the decades.

Take the restaurant in the unpretentious building on Lalbagh Road, still dishing out delectable Karnataka Brahmin food to hordes of eager patrons 100 years after talented Udupi cook Parameshwara Maiya opened an idli-and-coffee mess called the Brahmin Coffee Club on Lalbagh Fort Road in 1924. The mess moved to its current home in 1960, after Yagnappa Maiya, who had managed it after his brother passed in 1929, returned from a business trip to Europe, impressed by the standards of hygiene European restaurants insisted upon. With a brand-new name – Mavalli Tiffin Rooms – and a spanking clean kitchen that visitors were invited to walk through, MTR captured Bengaluru's imagination.

Through the years, while it continued to do what it did best, MTR demonstrated great business smarts, inventing the rava idli (thank you, MTR!) during the rice rationing of World War II, diversifying into the instant foods and masalas business to ensure a livelihood for its employees during the Emergency of the 1970s, and being part of the vanguard that brought soft-serve ice-cream machines into India in the 1990s. In 2022, it opened its first branch outside South-East Asia and the Middle East, in London.

There's also Udupi Sri Krishna Bhavan (after which NKB was presumably named) on Balepete Main Road, which will hit its own century in 2026. (Actually, Rama Holla started 'Udupi Hotel', which later became USKB, as far back as 1902; but the family that runs it reckons its age from 1926, when H.V. Janardhaniah, Holla's nephew, moved the restaurant to its current premises.) With only one other branch on Gandhi Bazaar Main Road, USKB has also stuck to the knitting, dispensing the same delicious masaal *dose* and badam halwa for decades.

Less than 200 metres away is Vidyarthi Bhavan (VB), so named because it was originally set up by Venkataramana Ural in 1943 to cater to the needs of the students of two other iconic Bengaluru institutions – the National High School (founded in 1917) and Acharya Pathashala (founded in 1935). While VB's waiters, who balance up to ten plates of its legendary masaal *dose* on a single arm, are a hit on social media 80 years on, the taste of its *dose* and the number of benches in the always-packed restaurant, have remained unchanged.

The NKB-shaped hole in Malleswaram's heart will have to be filled, if only partially, by the local favourite in the city's Benne Masale Wars, the Central Tiffin Room (CTR). The current management has CTR's founder as Ramakrishna Holla, and its founding date as 1952. That makes CTR, or Shri Sagar, as it was renamed in the 1990s, a year older than NKB, but the crowds that surge through its concertina wooden doors seven days a week reassure us that it will not be closing anytime soon. Phew.

October~November~December

African Tulip

Spathodea campanulata,
'Uchhe kai' buds brimful of water;
Above, bats and barbets in the dense green gloom,
Below, red earth stippled with coral bloom.

39

THE BATTLE OF BALTIMORE, WHERE CONGREVE ROCKETS, ADAPTED FROM TIPU'S ROCKETS, WERE USED BY THE BRITISH AGAINST THE AMERICANS, WAS FOUGHT DURING 12–14 SEPTEMBER 1812

Tipu Sultan and His Roaring Rockets

The next day, however, the Mysore troops again took possession of the ground, and as it was absolutely necessary to expel them, two columns were detached at sunset for the purpose (...) The second column, under Colonel Wellesley, on advancing into the tope, was at once attacked in the darkness of night by a tremendous tire of musketry and rockets. The men, floundering about amidst the trees and the water-courses, at last broke, and fell back in disorder, some being killed and a few taken prisoners. In the confusion Colonel Wellesley was himself struck on the knee by a spent ball, and narrowly escaped falling into the hands of the enemy.

– *Description of the Battle of Sultanpet Tope, fought in April 1799, from* Seringapatam, *by Constance E. Parsons, published in 1931*

Given that nammooru is still staggering around in a post-Deepavali fugue (all resolutions about clean eating and productive activity having fallen by the wayside in the face of never-ending chahaa-and-pakoda weather), what better way to legitimize the mood than by staying with pataakis, rockets in particular? Except, this time, we are talking eighteenth-century Mysorean rockets, those compact little missiles of death and destruction that so tormented the enemies of Mysore.

In their superficial design (and erratic flight patterns!), Mysore rockets were similar to their Deepavali counterparts (and to other rocket missiles used elsewhere in the world). Fundamentally, a rocket comprised a cylindrical tube, packed with explosive and closed off at one end, attached to a long, slim shaft that stabilized its flight and increased its range. What put Mysore rockets so far ahead of their contemporaries was the material used to fashion the cylinder – while Europe favoured paper and wood, ours were crafted out of soft iron, making them the first of their kind in the world. Casing the explosive in iron ensured greater internal pressure build-up, leading to higher 'bursting strength'. Since it also took longer for an iron cylinder to reach bursting point, the rocket could travel further before it exploded; Mysore rockets had a range of close to a kilometre!

As far back as the 1780s, when Hyder Ali ruled the roost in these parts, the Mysore Army had a full-fledged rocket corps, comprising some 1,200 men. This would only grow under his successor, Tipu Sultan, the first in the world to deploy iron-cased rockets in a military situation. On Tipu's watch, wheeled rocket launchers, each capable of carrying several rockets poised for flight, their angles of launch having been calculated in advance, were also designed. With the added advantage of mobility, the launchers created absolute mayhem in enemy ranks, for not one but several rockets were wont to fall out of the sky with no warning, from all directions, twirling, spitting fire, bouncing off the ground and heading out again in unpredictable directions, with the long bamboo staves they were attached to wreaking their own significant injuries. Another Mysorean innovation was to attach the deadly cylinders to swords – it made the whole less stable, but oh, the lacerations those little devils inflicted on the enemy!

Mysore rockets were used very effectively in the Third and Fourth Anglo-Mysore Wars, even though both, sadly, were eventually won by the British. Impressed despite themselves with the technology, London's Royal Woolwich Arsenal undertook a research programme on military rockets, based on the Mysore model, in 1801, soon after Tipu had been safely put away in his grave. In 1807, William Congreve, son of the commandant of the arsenal, and a soldier and inventor in his own right, published a tract on rocket systems and demonstrated solid-fuel rockets that were an improvement on the Mysore ones.

'Congreve rockets' played a huge part not only in the Napoleonic Wars but also in the Battle of Baltimore, fought in 1814 between American and British forces. That famous victory inspired American poet Francis Scott Key, who had watched the bombardment with trepidation, to compose what is today the national anthem of the US.

The next time you listen to 'The Star-Spangled Banner', the American national anthem, and hear the words 'the rocket's red glare', know that Key was referring to Congreve rockets, which were inspired by Mysore rockets, which were first developed in the eighteenth-century lanes around Bangalore's City Market. Awed locals referred to the area as Taramandal Pete (Constellation Town), after. . .yes, the Deepavali-type sparkles and explosions that were always lighting up the sky above it!

Well before the phrase 'Rocket Boys' was used to name a 2022 Hindi web series, a young English soldier called Bayly had inscribed it in his journal. The date was 22 April 1799, twelve days before the final battle of the Fourth Anglo-Mysore War, and the British encampment outside the Srirangapatna Fort was under heavy fire from Mysore rocketeers. 'No hail could be thicker,' wrote Bayly. 'Every illumination of blue lights was accompanied by a shower of rockets, causing death, wounds and dreadful lacerations from the 20 ft–long bamboos invariably attached to them. So pestered were we with the rocket boys that there was no moving without danger from the destructive missiles.' Alas, all those rockets would not stop the unrelenting British advance and their eventual victory on 4 May 1799.

40

RICHARD SANKEY DIED ON 11 NOVEMBER 1908

The Creative Genius of Lieutenant General Sankey

I spent 10 happy years as a student of the Stella Maris High School, located just beyond the southern boundary of the beautiful 37-acre Sankey Tank. But it was only during Ganesh Chaturthi that the tank came into sharp focus – like most people who lived in and around Malleswaram, my family went there to 'let go' of our Ganesha after the celebrations. It always rained on the night of the visarjane, the mud around the tank slipped and squelched under our bare feet, the crush of vehicles outside was tremendous and the bare-bodied young men who waded out into the dark water with our idols were always hustling, but the sound of the bells and the fragrance of the incense and the flickering of the lamps on the hundreds of thalis by the water as each family bent into their last goodbyes to the darling kadubu-loving god made it an exhilarating experience.

Few Kannadigas would have reason to be acquainted with County Tipperary in faraway Ireland if not for a delightful Kannada parody of a chartbusting British music hall song – 'It's a Long Way to Tipperary. . . (to the sweetest girl I know)' – a favourite with British soldiers during World War I. The Kannada version – 'Namma Tippaarhalli balu doora ... aadre alloul nam Basavi' (It's a long way to our Tippaarhalli ... but that's where my Basavi is) – was composed by the beloved Kannada poet, playwright, punster and overall creative genius T.P. Kailasam, who first heard the song as a student of geology in England.

Fewer Kannadigas – and Bangaloreans – however, are aware that it was a man from the self-same County Tipperary who designed some of this city's most iconic buildings and spaces and reservoirs. This man, another genius with an interest in geology (his collection of prehistoric plant fossils from Nagpur lies somewhere in the bowels of the British Museum) was Sir Richard Hieram Sankey.

It wasn't engineering that was on Sankey's mind, however, when, as a young lad of 16, he first mounted the steps of Croydon's East India Company Military Seminary, an institution whose stated mission was to train young officers to serve in the Company's private army in India. Following in the proud military tradition of his mother's family, he simply wanted to be a soldier. But his natural bent towards the mechanical and the artistic – the boy was a talented painter – was soon noticed, and he won his first commission with the Madras Sappers. After a brief period of training in military engineering, he proceeded to India in 1848, only 19, to take up his duties.

After a meandering journey through various positions in Mercara, Nagpur and Madras, Sankey was called up to Calcutta in 1857 to serve as undersecretary with the PWD. Soon after, though, with the rumblings among Indian soldiers in Bengal finally exploding in Meerut into the great 'Mutiny', the 28-year-old rode out to do his part in quelling it, as captain of the Calcutta Cavalry Volunteers. He acquitted himself very honourably for his side, both as engineer and soldier, constructing defensive works – entrenchments, causeways, roads, bridges – across the Ganga and the Yamuna, and playing a key role in vital campaigns responsible for breaking the Siege of Lucknow. For his 'great and successful exertions', Sankey was recommended by his commander (sadly unsuccessfully) for the Victoria Cross.

In 1861, we got Sankey to ourselves, as part of the engineering corps of Mysore, whence he proceeded to employ both sides of his fine brain for the benefit of Bangalore Cantonment. His systematic survey of the old tanks in the city led him to design a reservoir to supplement the growing city's insatiable water needs, but that tank, the only landmark in the city that bears his name, apart from Sankey Road, would not be completed until 1882, five years after he had moved on from here.

Elevated to chief engineer in 1864, Sankey celebrated by designing not only the lovely Attara Kacheri, the building that now houses the High Court, but also the St Andrew's Kirk on Cubbon Road, Gothic flourishes, stained glass and all. When the viceroy, Lord Mayo, was assassinated in Port Blair in 1872, Sankey designed the Mayo Hall building as a memorial, and, in parallel, designed the stately two-storeyed Government Museum on Kasturba Road, to house the second oldest museum in south India.

We've saved the best for last, though. It was Richard Hieram Sankey who, once the Attara Kacheri was completed in 1868, proceeded to design the sprawling 'grounds' behind it, and give to this city the priceless gift of Cubbon Park.

After his 13-year stint as chief engineer of Mysore, Sankey moved on to serve in the Madras PWD, designing the seaside city's famous Marina and redoing its botanical gardens. Returning to his native Tipperary after his retirement in 1883, he took on his most onerous appointment yet – chairman of Ireland's Board of Works. His favourite part of the demanding job, as can be imagined, was the care of two large parks in Dublin, which he unfailingly made time to visit at least once a week.

In one of those parks – Phoenix Park – a simple stone slab, half-hidden by the grass amid a circle of trees, attests that it was this aesthetically minded engineer who planted them in 1894. If you happen to visit and wish to pay your respects to the creative genius who gave us Cubbon Park, ask for Sankey's Wood, and someone will guide you there.

THE FOUNDATION STONE OF THE KRISHNA RAO PAVILION OF THE KRISHNA RAO PARK WAS LAID ON 11 NOVEMBER 1940

Mapping Basavanagudi's Square Central Park

At the four corners of the square park in Basavanagudi's centre, which you will read about in this piece, are four circles – Tagore Circle, Madhava Rao Circle, Arumugam Circle and Nettakallappa Circle. Everyone knows who Tagore was, but what of the other eminences? The first, B.S. Madhava Rao (the B in his name stands for Bangalore) was a mathematician and theoretical physicist (yes, the circle is not named after Diwan Madhava Rao, as many people believe!) who worked with Nobel Laureates Max Born and C.V. Raman to solve problems in field theory at the Indian Institute of Science. He was also professor of mathematics, and later principal, at Central College. To know more about Dr Armugam and K. Nettakallappa, go to the end of this piece.

One of the great pleasures of growing up in the twentieth century was poring over large atlases and fold-out maps at the dining table, and discovering cities and towns with exotic names that you had no hope of ever visiting, but complete creative freedom to conjure up, in any fashion you desired, in your head. That joy is denied to us in the age of Google Maps, when you can see, at a click, that Woolloomooloo and Woonsocket are just regular old towns, with not much to differentiate them from any other. And with Google Street View now in India, we are all in great danger of zooming further and further in, and entirely losing sight of the big picture.

That's what makes this is a good time to take a zoomed-out view – on Google Maps, if you must – at the street-grid pattern of one of the oldest Bengaluru neighbourhoods, Basavanagudi. Set up on a war footing in the aftermath of the plague epidemic that swept through Bengaluru in the mid- to late-1890s, Basavanagudi (literally, Basava's Temple), named for the giant monolithic Nandi that, from its shrine on a hill, presided over the new suburb's western end, was designed very differently from its slightly older neighbour, Chamarajpet, a neat, compact grid of (long) east–west and (short) north–south streets.

For one thing, the houses in Basavanagudi were set much further apart – the plague had brought home sound lessons on the dangers of overcrowding and the benefits of good ventilation. For another, in what was perhaps a Europe-inspired deviation from convention, Basavanagudi was built around a large central square with circles at its vertices – going clockwise from the north-western vertex, they are Tagore Circle, Madhava Rao Circle, Armugam Circle and Nettakallappa Circle – from which diagonal roads radiated. Since 1941, that 23-acre 'square' has been beloved to Basavanagudi residents as the lush, tree-filled M.N. Krishna Rao Park.

The man who would in the future be hailed as Rajakarya Prasakta Diwan Bahadur Sir M.N. Krishna Rao was only in his early twenties when the blueprint for Basavanagudi was being drawn up, but already a rising star in the finance department of the Mysore government. Accordingly, when the government offered plots in the new extension to its employees, the young man snapped one up, and had his home all built and ready by November 1907. Only the third house to come up in Basavanagudi, the stately 115-year-old building, built on a 19,500 sq. ft plot, has sustained generations of Rao's descendants, and still stands on the Kanakapura Road, very close to the park that carries his name.

Over the next two decades, Krishna Rao's rise continued unabated. When Sir Mirza Ismail was appointed diwan of Mysore in 1926, he had Rao, who was famous (and often infamous) for his unshakeable integrity, as his finance minister. When Sir Mirza travelled to England in 1930 as the maharaja's representative at the first Round Table Conference, it was Krishna Rao who filled in as acting diwan.

It wasn't the many achievements of its renowned resident, however, that prompted Basavangudi to name its erstwhile public square after him. It was a mark of gratitude for the man, who, contending that there were too few spaces in the city for women and children, donated the princely sum of 20,000 rupees for the square to be turned into a park exclusively for them, and another 15,000 rupees for

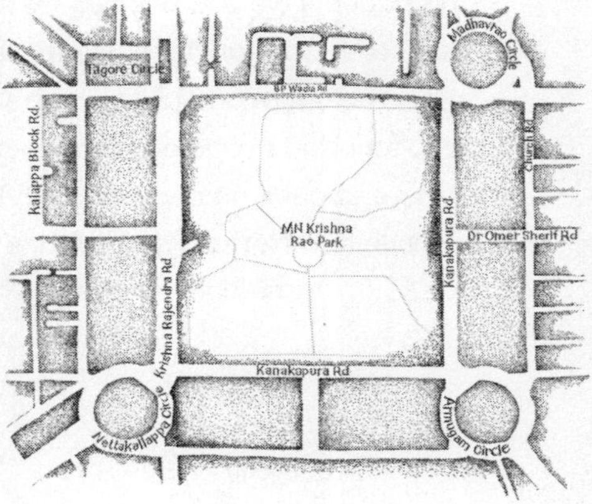

the construction of the pavilion at the centre of it. Today, the park is open to all ages and genders, and the Krishna Rao Pavilion, which once hosted all manner of cultural programmes, serves as a public library.

'My husband's family were long-time Basavanagudi residents. My cousin is married to Krishna Rao's grandson and they still live in the house that he built there. It has now been designated a heritage house.'

— ANURADHA, OLD BANGALOREAN WHO NOW LIVES IN THE US

Right. As promised in the intro to this column, let's now go on to Dr Arumugam Mudaliar and Rao Saheb K. Nettakallappa! A most well-regarded doctor, known as much for his conservative, commonsensical treatment as for his compassion, Dr Arumugam served as the superintendent of the Victoria Hospital for several years. Among his patients were luminaries like Krishnaraja Wadiyar IV and writer Masti Venkatesh Iyengar. As for K. Nettakallappa, he was a wealthy liquor baron, grain merchant and philanthropist. It was his eldest son, K.N. Guruswamy, who founded Bangalore's home-grown newspaper, *Deccan Herald.* Read more about it on page 137. (PS: The road that connects Dr Arumugam Circle to K. Nettakallappa Circle is called Madhava Rao Road, and this time, it is the diwan who is being commemorated.)

42

MIRZA ISMAIL WAS BORN ON 24 OCTOBER 1883

The Cleverest Man in India

Two monsoons provide it with an annual rainfall of 35 inches, which keeps it green throughout the year, except in the months of March and April when the grass dries up. But then Nature compensates Bangalore in other ways. The flowering trees in their gorgeous colours – the blue and mauve jacaranda, the pink and red cassias, the yellow peltophorums, the pink lagerstroemias, the plumerias, and the gold mohur, its whole top crowned with a mass of red flowers. These are the most beautiful among them – and there are other trees, like the honge and the rain tree, which put on their fresh green leaves at the driest time of the year. All these trees make the summer delightful, especially to the tree lover.

– Sir Mirza Ismail, describing his hometown
in his 1954 memoir, My Public Life

To be hailed as 'one of the cleverest men in India' by a peer, the much-respected diwan of Travancore, Sir C.P. Ramaswami Iyer, is honour enough. To also serve as prime minister to three different kingdoms – Mysore, Jaipur, Hyderabad – be knighted, and be considered a treasured friend by a Nobel Prize–winner (Sir C.V. Raman) and a king (Krishnaraja Wadiyar IV) marks one as belonging to a whole different league. But then, Mirza Ismail, grandson of the hero of a previous chapter (page 89), the Persian horse trader Agha Aly Asker, was a whole different kind of man.

There is no gainsaying that as scion of a well-known and influential family, Mirza had a considerable head start. Like other Bangalore Cantonment boys of his station, he was enrolled at St Patrick's School, and may have continued along that well-beaten track if his early accomplishments hadn't got him hand-picked to be tutored along with the minor king Nalvadi Krishnaraja Wadiyar at the school for royals in Mysore. The two boys, separated in age by only a few months, would go on to become fast friends who were rarely apart for the rest of their lives.

One would hazard that having the king as classmate would lead one quite naturally to a career in administration, but after passing out of Bangalore's Central College in 1904, Mirza joined the police force instead. That little detour was nipped in the bud by the maharaja himself – the very next year, he appointed Mirza as his private secretary. And thus it continued, until that colossus of an engineer–statesman, Sir M. Visvesvaraya, who had mentored Mirza over the years, recommended him for the diwanship in 1926. Nalvadi joyfully acquiesced, and the sight of the young diwan astride his horse (but of course he was on a horse!), poking his fine nose into everything and resolving people's complaints in double-quick time grew to be one that struck terror into the hearts of errant officials.

Like his mentor, Mirza Ismail believed in the dictum 'Industrialize or perish'. He was instrumental in clearing all hurdles to the setting up of Hindustan Aircraft (now Aeronautics) Limited in Bangalore in 1940, apart from initiating the kingdom's rural electrification programme and setting up factories to manufacture sugar, paper, cement, steel, fertilizer and electric bulbs across the state (including the Elgin Flour Mills on Hosur Road and the Government Porcelain Factory in Malleswaram). 'Mysoreans,' he would proclaim proudly in an address on All India Radio in 1938, 'wash themselves with Mysore soap, dry themselves with Mysore towels, clothe themselves in Mysore silk, ride Mysore horses, eat the abundant Mysore food, drink Mysore coffee with Mysore sugar, equip their houses with Mysore furniture, light them with Mysore lamps and write their letters on Mysore paper.'

Yet Mirza was equally an aesthete – he believed it was 'obligatory for the administration' to create beautiful urban spaces that the poor, particularly, could enjoy at no expense. His fascination with fountains and gardens ensured that work on Mysore's Brindavan Gardens began the very year after he took office. Concerned that his fellow Bangaloreans didn't have their own 'fairy fountain', he had one installed in Cubbon Park, opposite the bust of Chamarajendra Wadiyar; it still plays on occasion. To him are credited the signature decorative lamp posts in Lalbagh and the now-dilapidated Oval opposite the City Market, as well as the iconic Bangalore Town Hall.

Here's something to mourn, though – for all the contributions he made to this city and the country, there is not a street in his hometown named after this beloved son.

When Sir Mirza resigned from the position of diwan of Mysore in 1941, he became prime minister of Jaipur (1942–46) and brought it into the industrial age; a grateful city named its main thoroughfare Mirza Ismail Road. A committed anti-Partitionist, he served as prime minister to the Nizam of Hyderabad during the tumultuous years between 1946 and 1948, negotiating a stand-still agreement with the Union of India to buy time for the Nizam to come around. When the Nizam got aggressive after Gandhiji's assassination, Sir Mirza quit in disgust and retired from public life. On his death in 1959, Nobel Laureate Sir C.V. Raman wrote his obituary. 'For many years, in fair weather as well as in foul,' it said, 'Sir Mirza Ismail remained the truest of friends to me, ever ready to give support and advice. He leaves behind him a memory which will be treasured and cherished by all who have known him.'

43

THE CENTRAL OBSERVATORY, BANGALORE, WAS INAUGURATED ON 1 NOVEMBER 1867

A Century and a Half of Weather Forecasting

When we returned home to Bangalore in 2004 after a dozen years of living elsewhere, my husband and I felt the deep love we had always harboured for our hometown return with unprecedented force. We channelled that energy into becoming evangelists for the city – I wrote a city guide for tourists (it was called *Ticket Bengaluru*, and was beautifully produced by Stark Publications; sadly, it is now out of print), and Arun started BangaloreWalks, the city's first heritage walks company. Whether the walks would find resonance was anyone's guess (they did; the company is still going strong), but what was never in doubt was the killer advantage that Bangalore bestowed on a company like ours – unlike in other Indian cities, we had perfect walking weather through the year.

We have been having an extended run of wet, grey days in the city, and the citizenry's patience, as it scans the weather forecast, is wearing thin. Never mind that we are well-insulated from the pralaya-like conditions in Mumbai and Ahmedabad, and the freak 40°C temperatures across Europe and China – as everyone knows, you aren't truly Bengalurean unless you dial up the whinge when the weather is anything but perfect.

Each monsoon, the burden of a billion hopes in our still largely agricultural and rain-dependent economy falls on the hapless shoulders of the Indian Meteorological Department (IMD), which had its origins in a treatise on the Indian summer monsoon published by English astronomer Edmond Halley (yup, he who discovered the famous comet) as far back as 1686. (Needless to say, sailors, scholars and poets in these parts had known of and tracked the monsoon winds for millennia, and leveraged it for both commerce and romance, but Halley's treatise was the first formal, scientific introduction of it to the Europeans.) The barometer had been invented a few decades earlier, in 1643, by Evangelista Torricelli, but it was only once the mercury thermometer was invented in 1714 by Gabriel Fahrenheit that weather observatories were good to go.

In 1784, the British East India Company set up the Asiatic Society in Calcutta to further the cause of 'oriental research'. As one of its first activities, the Society established the Calcutta Observatory in 1785. In 1789, Madras-based amateur astronomer William Petrie gifted his measuring instruments to the government, enabling them to set up the Madras Observatory in 1792. The Colaba Observatory in Bombay would follow in 1826. Four more decades passed before our landlocked town at the centre of the southern peninsula saw similar action.

The Central Observatory, Bangalore, began operations on 1 November 1867. Belying its grandiose name, its offices were housed in a thatched shed on the grounds of the Bowring Hospital in today's Shivajinagar and boasted nothing more than a few thermometers to record temperature. Starting 14 July 1868, the city's temperature was faithfully recorded three times a day, at 1000, 1600 and 2200 hours. In 1875, following a devastating cyclone in Calcutta in 1864 and terrible famines in 1866 and 1871 due to the failure of the monsoons, the British government decided to combine all the regional met offices into one, and established the IMD.

In the same year that the IMD was established in Calcutta, Bangalore's premier institution of higher education (which then had a grand total of 43 students) changed its name from Central High School to Central College and became the nucleus of what is today the Bangalore University. In 1882, the college got one of its most celebrated principals, Dr John Cook. Apart from introducing mathematics into the curriculum (his own subject was physics), Dr Cook was deeply interested in the activities of the Central Observatory. By 1892, not only had the observatory moved to the grounds of Central College, it also had John Cook as its first official director. In 1893, Dr Cook even succeeded in persuading the Mysore government to build an exclusive observatory building on the campus.

In 1894, the observatories at Bangalore, Mysore, Hassan and Chitradurga were merged to form the Mysore State Met Department, with Dr Cook as the first meteorologist to the government of Mysore. Today, as an integral part of the IMD, Bengaluru's state-of-the-art Meteorological Centre continues to function out of the historic Central College campus on Palace Road, aided by a new outpost at the Kempegowda International Airport.

Right, back to whining about the weather now!

'With Bangalore's weather being so changeable – the joke is that we have four seasons in the course of a day – it feels like the Met Department is often unable to keep pace. Maybe, at least in Bangalore, we should call the science "whither forecasting".'

— MANOHAR D. RAO, PROFESSIONAL BRIDGE PLAYER AND TEACHER

•

'Very interesting. I must point out, though, that IMD has grown immensely and is not restricted to KIAL and Central College. It has myriad weather stations all over the state and analyses data from these, along with data from satellites using supercomputers, to forecast regional weather. Perhaps that deserves a separate article from you.'

— DR B.R. PAI, FORMER DIRECTOR, NATIONAL AEROSPACE LABORATORIES

44

THE VERY FIRST BASELINE FOR THE GREAT TRIGONOMETRICAL SURVEY OF INDIA WAS DRAWN OVER TWO MONTHS, STARTING 14 OCTOBER 1800

The Men Who Mapped the Mysore Country

Considering that more British and Indian lives were lost in the process of surveying India in the nineteenth century than in most wars fought in the same period, an appropriate Indian prayer for those formidable gentlemen would have been 'Survey janaaha sukhinobhavantu'. This column talks about three of the men who kicked off and led the process in our neck of the woods, and although it is way, way too short (600 words) to introduce even one of them, I hope this brief snapshot of their insane, path-breaking adventures will intrigue you enough to follow their lives, and their well-documented journeys, in your own time.

In February 2023, the Museum of Art & Photography (MAP), with its collection of over 60,000 pieces of Indian art, photography and textiles, opened in an edgy new building on Kasturba Road, a wonderful new addition to Bengaluru's burgeoning museumscape.

The link between MAP and the subject of today's column is somewhat tenuous, but the acronym works as a good opening to a discussion of the first scientifically conducted surveys, and the maps that resulted from them, of the Bangalore–Mysore region. Three geniuses, leading three pioneering surveys at the turn of the nineteenth century, were involved – Dr Francis Buchanan conducted the agricultural survey, Lt Col William Lambton the trigonometrical survey, and Col Colin Mackenzie the so-called Mysore Survey.

The fourth son of the chief of Clan Buchanan, Scotsman Francis Buchanan had little hope of inheriting either land or title. He chose medicine to earn a living, graduating in 1783 from the University of Edinburgh, where he also studied botany under John Hope, among the first in Britain to teach Carl Linnaeus's system of botanical classification. After serving many years as a doctor on merchant navy ships, Buchanan joined the medical services of the Bengal Presidency in 1794.

In 1799, after the fall of Tipu Sultan in the Fourth Anglo-Mysore War, Buchanan was tasked with surveying the newly acquired territories of the East India Company. In 1807, he published his groundbreaking magnum opus, *A Journey from Madras through the Countries of Mysore, Canara and Malabar*, investigating and documenting the 'agriculture, arts, commerce, religion, manners, customs, natural and civil history, and antiquities' of the region.

William Lambton came from humble origins, but his talent for mathematics won him a place in a reputed school, where he studied under surveyor and mathematician Dr Charles Hutton, famous for calculating the density of the earth. In 1781, Lambton travelled with his regiment to America, where his surveying skills soon saw him put to work measuring land for the American settlers. The loss of an eye saw him appointed to a desk job with plenty of leisure time; he used it to teach himself advanced mathematics, which would serve him well in later years.

In 1796, he came to India as part of a regiment under Lord Arthur Wellesley. Following the British victory in the Fourth Anglo-Mysore War, where he demonstrated his ability to navigate accurately by the stars in unmapped country, he asked to be allowed to undertake a survey of the new territory. Permission was granted, and in 1800, Lambton began the Great Trigonometrical Survey (GTS), a 110-year-long exercise hailed as one of the world's greatest scientific endeavours, which resulted in near-perfect maps of the Indian subcontinent.

The baseline of the first triangle that kicked off the GTS was 7.5 miles (around 21 km) long, took 57 days to complete, and was drawn in Bangalore in 1800, between what is today HSR Layout and the Ramamurthy Nagar underpass on the ORR. Lambton continued working on the GTS until January 1823, when he died with his boots on at Hinganghat, Maharashtra.

Colin Mackenzie arrived in India in 1783 to join the Madras Army, which stormed Tipu's Seringapatam in the Fourth Anglo-Mysore War. Between 1799 and 1810, he led the Mysore Survey to establish the boundaries of the state, and produced the first maps of the region, along with illustrations of the landscape and copious notes on archaeological landmarks. In 1815, in recognition of his services, he was appointed the first surveyor general of India, but remains far better known for his eponymous collection of thousands of manuscripts, epigraphs, coins and paintings, all of which are a crucial source for the study of Indian history.

'Lovely! A few years ago, I wrote a piece for a Kannada newspaper on Francis Buchanan's observations about my town, Sidlaghatta (located 63 km north of Bangalore), in his tome, *A Journey from Madras...* that you mention. He refers to it as "Silagutta", which must have been how it was referred to in that time – even today, in parts of Chikkaballapura and Kolar, and in the dialect spoken by the Muslims here, it is still Silagutta. There was no trace then, apparently, of the silkworm-rearing industry that is our mainstay now – Buchanan talks about locals growing vegetables in small farms and the weaving industry that flourished here.

On another note, Kannada writer Gajanana Sharma has recently written a book – *Prameya* – about the Great Trigonometrical Survey, in the historical fiction genre. It is 500 pages long, but it is a wonderful book, and talks about the travails and triumphs of Col Lambton, George Everest, Andrew Waugh, William Johnson and others. Do read it when you find the time.'

— MALLIKARJUNA D.G., WRITER, JOURNALIST AND SAHITYA AKADEMI AWARDEE FOR TRAVEL WRITING IN KANNADA

45

KEMPEGOWDA INTERNATIONAL AIRPORT'S TERMINAL 2 OPENED ON 22 NOVEMBER 2023

How Bengaluru Airport Got Royally Gamed

There is a new trend in Bangalore these days – board game cafés. As someone who grew up playing board games endlessly through long summer vacations, I am tempted to see this as a validation of my childhood, of how downtime with friends and family ought to be spent. If I step back from the personal, I can see it as the collective longing of a digitally overwhelmed generation to get back to a more tactile, analog way of building community. But perhaps it is only another distraction for a new FOMO-ridden world of experience junkies of all ages, another novelty to try out and post about on Instagram before moving on to the next one. (This last unequivocally indicates my own evolution into a curmudgeonly aunty who is cynical about everything – and everyone – in the world. Oh well, it happens to the best of us.)

Time was when summer vacations, for anyone who grew up in Bengaluru, meant a house full of outstation cousins who had descended on you because you happened to live in such a cool city. They meant weekends at Cubbon Park, matinee shows of 'English' films in a Cantonment theatre, ice-cream treats at Lakeview or Chit Chat, and afternoons playing endless games of carrom or Monopoly or Ludo or 'Donkey' or, if you had grandparents around, chowka bara or alagulimane/pallanguzhi.

It is traditional board games like these last – but with a royal twist! – that the newly opened Terminal 2 of the Kempegowda International Airport celebrates in four specially designed floor mosaics on its Departures side. The mosaics are inspired by drawings commissioned by Krishnaraja Wadiyar III, or Mummadi Krishnaraja, the longest-ruling monarch of the Wadiyar dynasty, for one of his many treatises on board games – no, seriously – written circa the 1850s.

Mummadi's reign began auspiciously enough; at the tender age of six, after Tipu Sultan's death in 1799 CE, he was escorted to his hereditary throne by none other than Arthur Wellesley, the future Duke of Wellington. Until 1810, when he turned 16, he ruled under the regency of his grandmother, the formidable Maharani Lakshmi Ammani. In 1831, however, he was controversially dismissed by the East India Company, after a series of popular uprisings erupted across his kingdom. He never again regained his throne, but parleyed successfully with Queen Victoria, before his death in 1868, to secure the throne for his infant grandson, the great Chamarajendra Wadiyar X.

The decades in the political wilderness may have broken a lesser man, but our Mummadi, a polyglot who spoke Kannada, English, Sanskrit, Tamil, Telugu and Urdu with ease, poured himself into writing – he was the author of several Kannada works, most prominently the *Sritattvanidhi*, which, among many other things, included illustrations of 122 hatha yoga postures, more detailed than in any other pre–twentieth century text. He also spent time mastering the veena, patronizing talented writers who collectively developed a new style of Kannada prose, artists who not only created giant murals but also illuminated manuscripts, and artistes who developed and perfected the traditional theatre form of Yakshagana.

The king also spent an inordinate amount of time locked up inside the Krishna temple in the Mysore Palace, playing board games (with Krishna himself, it was believed), and created new and fascinating versions of old ones, including Kreeda Patra, a pre-medieval Indian card game that the Mughals had adopted and knew as Ganjifa. The Mysore version of Ganjifa included 13 complex games developed by Mummadi, and featured hand-painted circular cards with mythological, astronomical and astrological themes.

Chaturanga, or chess, was another huge passion, and Mummadi is credited with being among the first known people in the world to crack the Knight's Tour, a ninth-century puzzle that involves a knight starting at any square on the chessboard and moving to the remaining 63 squares without ever repeating a square. Mummadi's version of the solution, which he had painted on a silk handkerchief in 1851, is now a prized item in the collection of American chess

collector, Jon Crumiller. In fact, several other board games that Mummadi had produced in rosewood, ivory inlay, metal inlay, or as lithographs and paintings, and gave away as gifts, now form part of private and museum collections across the globe, including the V&A in London and the Smithsonian in Washington, and often come up for sale at the world's top auction houses.

To this day, in esoteric international colloquiums on board games, Mummadi Krishnaraja is hailed as Magister Ludi, Master of the Game.

'Wow! How come we don't know of these wonderful things? Mummadi cracked the Knight's Tour – wow! Thank you for introducing me to my own city. You should consider compiling all your columns into a book.'

— SANJAY ANANDARAM, CO-FOUNDER OF THE NON-PROFIT, NETWORK OF INDIAN CULTURAL ENTERPRISES (NICE), MENTOR AND ADVISER

'So, so many interesting facts! And so nicely threaded together! Reading about board games painted on silk reminded me of similar ones I have seen, made by artisans in the Channapatna area, I think. During the pandemic, we had taken a call to buy all our Rotary prizes and gifts from the Karnataka Arts and Crafts Council, and some of those prizes were board games painted on silk. Delighted to discover that a maharaja started the trend.'

— SHARADA SHENOY, PART OF THE ROTARY FAMILY

46

HAIFA DAY IS CELEBRATED ON 23 SEPTEMBER EACH YEAR

A Bit of Palestine in the Heart of Bengaluru

What possible connection could Haifa, the 3,000-year-old port city perched on the slopes of Mount Carmel in northern Israel, have with the relatively young metropolis of Bangalore, perched on a high granite plateau in India's southern peninsula? Here's one I discovered while researching this piece – they are the IT capitals of their respective countries. But there is another, deeper connection, going back over a century, to World War I..

In May 2024, as Israel dialled up the offensive in Rafah, the government of Spain made global news by denying permission to the *Marianne Danica*, a Danish ship carrying a shipment from India, to dock at its south-eastern port of Cartagena. The denial was based expressly on the *Marianne*'s cargo – 27 tonnes of explosives – bound for the northern Israeli port city of Haifa. 'This will be a consistent policy with any ship carrying arms to Israel that wants to call at Spanish ports,' confirmed Spain's foreign minister, Jose Manuel Albares. 'The Middle East does not need more weapons; it needs more peace.'

Things were somewhat different a little over a century ago. From 1914 to 1918, as the world reeled under a brutal war that took a staggering nine million lives, Indian ships headed for the Middle East, particularly the Sinai Peninsula and Palestine, were welcomed precisely because of their cargo – Indian soldiers. Drawn not just from the British-Indian Imperial Army but also from Indian princely states, these soldiers had arrived to support the Allied war effort, leaving behind homes and families for a theatre of war that spanned the unfamiliar terrain and hostile weather conditions of Europe, Africa and the Middle East.

In September 1918, towards the fag end of The Great War, one such ship, also headed, like the *Marianne*, for Haifa, carried part of a contingent that had first set out from Bangalore on 13 October 1914. Originally raised from what was left of Tipu Sultan's forces after his defeat in the Fourth Anglo-Mysore War of 1799, the Mysore Lancers were an elite cavalry regiment that bore the mythical two-headed bird called the gandabherunda on their regimental insignia. Fighting as part of the 15th (Imperial Service) Cavalry Brigade, which also included the Jodhpur Lancers and the Hyderabad Lancers, they were handed a daunting brief: capture the port of Haifa so that British ships could land fresh supplies to replenish dangerously depleted stores.

Since 19 September, British infantry divisions had done a fine job of attacking the Ottoman front line. On 22 September, after other divisions had tried and failed to capture Haifa, it was the 15th Cavalry's turn to attempt the near-impossible. On one side, on the lower slopes of Mount Carmel, were well-entrenched German and Austrian artillery divisions, using the advantage of elevation to rain down machine-gun fire on anyone attempting to access the defile between the hills leading to Haifa. On the other were Indian soldiers on horseback, armed with nothing but lances and swords.

At 1400 hours on 23 September, with no orders forthcoming, the Mysore and Jodhpur Lancers decided to act. The Mysore Lancers went first. Urging their horses up a horrendously steep incline out of the gunners' sight, they fell upon the startled gunners from behind, allowing the Jodhpur Lancers to race unmolested into the defile. Spearing the rearguard of the German gunners, charging Ottoman positions and roaring into Haifa, the 15th captured Haifa well before sunset.

The Battle of Haifa is now considered one of the greatest cavalry battles in history. It was also one of the last classical cavalry charges before the large-scale mechanization of war. The famous victory is commemorated each year on 23 September, Haifa Day, in both India and Israel, with soldiers and officers of the 61st Cavalry Regiment (into which the Jodhpur and Mysore Lancers were amalgamated in 1954) gathering at memorials at Bengaluru (Mysore Lancers Haifa Memorial, Munireddypalya, erected in 1920) and Delhi (Teen Murti–Haifa Chowk). In Haifa itself, history textbooks tell Israeli children the story of their city's liberation by Indian soldiers, well before Israel itself was a thing.

'Thanks for sharing this bit of our past glory. Reminded me of our visit to Haifa in 2002, and particularly to the Baha'i Terraces around the Shrine of the Bab, one of the holiest sites of the Baha'i faith. Did you know that in liberating Haifa, the Lancers also rescued Abdu'l-Baha, the spiritual head of the Baha'is – who was due to be executed by the Ottomans – and earned the eternal gratitude of his followers?'

— WG CDR (RETD) CHANDRA DUTT UPADHYAY, VR.C

•

'Wow. I wonder – if history books carried stories like these, would more children choose the Humanities and better understand how borders, loyalties and agendas shift and change over the years? That kind of understanding would perhaps help future leaders work through the issues that face us today.'

— SANGEETHA RAO, EDUCATOR

47

K.C. REDDY WAS SWORN IN AS THE FIRST CHIEF MINISTER OF KARNATAKA ON 27 OCTOBER 1947

K.C. Reddy's Long Fight for Prajaprabhutva

The Uttara Pinakini (also called Penneru and Penna) rises in the Nandi Hills near Bangalore and flows northwards through Karnataka and Andhra Pradesh before turning east near Anantpur and heading for the Bay of Bengal. On the banks of this 597 km river, in the town of Vidurashwatha, located 6 km from Gauribidanur in Chikkaballapura district, stands a memorial called the Veera Soudha, commemorating the 32 unarmed victims of a 1938 police firing that took place almost exactly 19 years after the Jallianwala Bagh massacre. In this case, however, the perpetrators were not the British, but the maharaja's government. The unprecedented scale of the tragedy turned the sleepy temple town into a leitmotif of the people's march to self-determination in the kingdom of Mysore.

Another round of assembly elections, followed by yet another peaceful transition of power, has been completed, proving that democracy in India is a living, thriving thing. Once again, as it has done so many times before in Karnataka, the Grand Old Party has registered a thumping win.

It wasn't always this way, however. The transition from hereditary monarchy to a democratically elected government wasn't an easy one to accomplish, even in a princely state as liberal and benevolent as Mysore. While Maharaja Nalvadi Krishnaraja Wadiyar, whom Gandhiji once hailed as a rajarshi, had voluntarily set up a bicameral legislature with people's representatives appointed by him, the idea of a fully elected government was difficult to digest. That anxiety was only exacerbated by the Government of India Act of 1935, which assured far greater independence in decision-making to people in British-ruled provinces.

But the Act was only the culmination of a struggle for self-determination that had formally begun with the founding of the Indian National Congress (INC) in 1885, just four years after Nalvadi ascended the throne. By the 1920s, with the addition of charismatic leaders like Mahatma Gandhi, the struggle was a real force in the provinces. Naturally, that fervour began to spill into the princely states, with people viewing their kings as oppressors no different from the British. In 1930, inspired by the call for Purna Swaraj at the 1929 Lahore Session of the INC, a young, newly minted lawyer called Kyasamballi Chengalaraya (K.C.) Reddy founded the Praja Paksha party, with the mission of installing a 'responsible government' in Mysore. In 1937, the Praja Paksha, now the Praja Samyukta Paksha, joined forces with the INC to become the Mysore Congress.

In the same year, the Indian Provincial Elections were held for the first time, sweeping the INC into power in seven of the 11 provinces. That firmly brought the crisis home to Nalvadi and his diwan, Sir Mirza Ismail, who believed implicitly that Mysore should remain a sovereign monarchy. On 25 April 1938, a large group of people who had gathered at Vidurashwatha village in Chikkaballapura district to hoist the Indian flag, flouting prohibitory orders (none but the Mysore flag could be hoisted in the kingdom), were fired upon by police. At the end of 90 rounds of firing, 32 people were dead and scores more injured. The government responded by claiming that only 10 lives had been lost.

Mysore erupted in such anger that the national leadership, including Gandhiji himself, took note, sending Sardar Vallabhbhai Patel and Acharya Kripalani to Mysore to take stock. That led to the signing of the Mirza–Patel pact, which, among other things, gave Mysore Congress leaders representation in the maharaja's reforms committee and removed all restrictions on the hoisting of the Indian flag in the kingdom. The movement towards Mysore's self-determination had begun.

AS THE STATE'S FIRST CM, K.C. REDDY HAD LAUNCHED A PARTLY SUCCESSFUL CAMPAIGN TO ERADICATE BLACK MONEY, WHICH A CARTOON IN THE KANNADA HUMOUR MAGAZINE *KORAVANJI* LIKENED TO DANCING ON THE HEAD OF THE KALINGASARPA OF LEGEND

The Indian Independence Act of 1947 gave princely states the choice to either accede to the newly created Dominion of India, or to continue as sovereign states. One of the first Indian kings to sign the Instrument of Accession, on 9 August 1947, was the 28-year-old Jayachamarajendra (J.C.) Wadiyar. Even as he sought clarity on a future course of action, K.C. Reddy launched the 'Mysore Chalo' agitation with a fiery speech to a crowd of 40,000 at Bengaluru's Subhash Nagar on 1 September, demanding responsible government. On 24 September, after an intense two weeks that left 20 people dead across the state, two of them in a protest in Malleswaram, J.C. bowed to the will of the people.

On 27 October 1947, K.C. Reddy was sworn in as the first (non-elected) chief minister of Mysore. *Vox populi, vox Dei.*

'My grandfather was involved in the Vidurashwatha firings. He was a very upright policeman with a temper to match, and was called Benki Basappa (Fiery Basappa) by anyone who had cause to fear him. Even though he was an experienced policeman and only doing his duty that day, he was traumatized ever after by how quickly the situation got out of hand at Vidurashwatha – the way he told it, he could have either ordered his men to fire on the crowd or have them killed by the angry mob of 7,000 or more, and he chose the former.

'The same man, as superintendent of prisons in Bangalore a year later, allowed Indian political prisoners a lot of leeway, bringing them my grandmother's ragi mudde and saaru for dinner so that they did not have to eat prison food. When you were an Indian putting in an honest day's work to feed your family, while serving a king or the British in the process, you lived a schizophrenic life, I guess.'

— KE, SENIOR SALES EXECUTIVE AT A LEADING IT COMPANY IN THE US

THE GROUNDBREAKING CEREMONY FOR THE CANARA UNION WAS UNDERTAKEN IN OCTOBER 1928

How Cotton Built the Canara Union

A great deal of my largely idyllic Bangalore childhood was spent in and around Malleswaram. I went to school in Vyalikaval, did my two years of pre-university at a coveted junior college at the junction of 15th Cross and 10th Main, and was often to be found at my grandmother's house on 3rd Temple Street. The Canara Union was just around the corner from my college, and we girls always stole a glance at it as we walked past, hoping to catch sight of the nation's crush, Prakash Padukone, emerging from the badminton courts. Sadly, that never happened.

On 15 May 2022, India exploded in jubilation as her men's badminton team lifted the prestigious Thomas Cup for the very first time. The overall sentiment was reminiscent of March 1980, when a handsome, lanky 25-year-old with the most amazing wristwork became the first Indian to win the All-England Championships. In Bengaluru, the celebrations then were particularly joyous in Malleswaram – the new champion, Prakash Padukone, had trained for many years at the courts of the legendary Canara Union, located on 8th Main.

The building that houses the hallowed courts, now called the Prakash Courts, was raised over a century ago, in 1919, and has a hoary history, linked inextricably to the nineteenth-century global trade in cotton, the Industrial Revolution and the American Civil War.

Circa 1860, the cotton industry in Lancashire, England, a product of the Industrial Revolution, was experiencing a boom the likes of which it had never seen before. But trouble was brewing in America, from where most of the raw cotton was imported. In 1861, America plunged into a protracted Civil War, with boycotts and blockades cutting off cotton to Lancashire.

Looking for alternatives, Lancashire's eyes naturally fell on the black, loamy soil of the cotton-growing regions of the Deccan Plateau. Around the same time, Anappa Sirur, a prosecutor for the British government in the North Kanara district of Karnataka, was looking to change his line of work, heartsick at the moral compromises he was being forced to make. He found the perfect fit with a Scottish cotton-exporting firm called P. Chrystal & Co., which was looking for someone to manage their bustling operations at the Kumta port. When Anappa retired, his unimpeachable reputation ensured that his sons were also absorbed into P. Chrystal & Co.

Soon after, looking to diversify into cotton spinning and weaving themselves, P. Chrystal tasked the older Sirur boy, Ramakrishna, with setting up two mills in Hubli, and put the younger one, Narayan, in charge of a mill they had acquired in Bangalore – the Mysore Mills, whose permanent assets were owned by the maharaja. By the turn of the century, however, with their fortunes changing, P. Chrystal decided to put their mills up for sale. It was Narayan's son, Dattatreya, not yet 30, who negotiated with the Mysore government to buy the mill in 1904.

It was a hard, hard slog for Dattatreya, aka D.N. Sirur, to turn the fading Mysore Mills (later Raja Mills; today, the Mantri Mall stands in that location) around. Things changed dramatically in 1914, when World War I broke, causing a severe shortage of manpower in Lancashire. Flush with orders, D.N. Sirur lost no time replacing his European managers with Indian ones, mostly drawn from his own community of Chitrapur Saraswat Brahmins. Scores more were employed in the mill and moved to Malleswaram, altering the demographics of the neighbourhood. In 1919, D.N. Sirur made a generous donation towards the setting up of a social and cultural centre in Malleswaram for Chitrapur Saraswats (to which community Prakash also belongs), and the Canara Union was born.

D.N. Sirur would go on to set up another mill, a state-of-the-art one this time, just a little up the road. The Minerva Mills would enjoy its own great successes, and, in 1980, 43 years after his passing, become a cause célèbre for the Indian judicial system – look up Minerva Mills Ltd and Ors vs Union of India and Ors – resulting in a landmark judgement by the Supreme Court that would serve to safeguard the Indian Constitution.

(Fun fact: Infosys co-founder Nandan Nilekani's father, Mohanrao, worked as general manager in the Mysore and Minerva mills!)

'Are you the author of the article "How Cotton Built the Canara Union", which is doing the rounds among all our Chitrapur community? It is a beautiful piece and you have captured the incidents of those days so wonderfully. With your permission, we would like to reproduce your article in the July 2022 issue of our *Canara Union Newsletter*.'

— MEERA PHILAR, HONORARY GENERAL SECRETARY, CANARA UNION

•

'Recently, at a talk I gave in Malleswaram about Malleswaram, I talked about the Canara Union and Padukone and Nilekani's father, Mohanrao, all filched from your piece in the *Hindustan Times*. The talk was well received. Thanks!'

— THE LATE VIJAY THIRUVADY, WHO USED TO LEAD EXCEPTIONAL TREE WALKS IN BANGALORE

49

CHAMARAJENDRA WADIYAR X WAS CROWNED KING ON 23 SEPTEMBER 1868

A Missionary, a Palace and the Bhagavad Gita

Bangalore owes a debt of gratitude to Rev. John Garrett who, apart from doing many wonderful things for the city, also sold his ginormous parcel of land on the outskirts of the Cantonment to the maharaja of Mysore for the grand sum of 23,000 rupees. For many Bangaloreans of my vintage, that parcel of land, the Palace Grounds, holds many fond memories of being young, cool, happy, and very drunk – beginning in 1994 and going all the way to 2012, it was where some of the world's great rock bands and musicians, including Jethro Tull, Deep Purple, Bryan Adams, Roger Waters, The Rolling Stones, Sting, Mark Knopfler, Iron Maiden, Aerosmith and Metallica, thrilled audiences 35,000-strong. These premium music acts were brought to us by a pioneering entertainment company called DNA, founded in 1986 by T. Venkat Vardhan, a young Bangalorean who also happened to be the grandson of the man who built the Vidhana Soudha (see page 227).

Dasara is almost here, and with it, the familiar frisson of excitement that accompanies the annual coming of the Nadahabba. Once again, old Bengalureans will promise themselves that they will get a 'gold pass' next year (always next year) to watch the Jumboo Savaari in Mysuru on Vijayadashami day. Once again, they will explain to the ignorant that in Karnataka, it has always been Dasara, not Dussehra, and no, it is *not* the same thing. Once again, the pomp and pageantry of the erstwhile capital of Karnataka will take centre stage as Yaduveer Wadiyar, the ceremonial maharaja of Mysuru, holds a private darbar in the Mysore Palace.

It was the much-loved Sir Mark Cubbon, who served as commissioner of Bangalore from 1834 to 1861, who first moved the capital from Mysuru to Bengaluru, thus creating two separate entities – a royal capital and an administrative capital. This was during the 50-year period from 1831 to 1881 when Mysore was administered directly by the British. By the time of the Rendition in 1881, when Mysore went back to the Wadiyars and the 18-year-old Chamarajendra X was crowned king, Bangalore had established itself as a city that even the royals could not ignore.

In fact, once Queen Victoria approved Chamarajendra as the next king of Mysore in 1866, his British guardians immediately began to scout for a place in Bangalore that could function as a royal residence when the boy visited, for his lessons with British tutors. In 1873, they zeroed in on a 454-acre parcel of land that belonged to a Rev. John Garrett. Construction began the next year, and by 1878, the somewhat incongruous (for these parts), but decidedly stately Bangalore Palace, built largely in the Georgian and Victorian style, was ready for occupation. (And that was how Chamarajendra and his successors finally came to possess something that continues to be a popular aspiration – their 'own house' in Bengaluru.)

Which brings us to the question – who was Rev. John Garrett? When he sold his land to the maharaja, Garrett was an old Bangalorean. He had already lived here for 33 years, serving as a Canarese missionary with the Wesleyan Mission since his arrival in 1840. Having worked as a printer earlier, he came with an exalted brief – to set up the first Kannada printing press in Bangalore Pettah/Pete.

Garrett was blessed with such a fine ear for language that he had soon mastered not only Kannada, but also Sanskrit, Tamil and Persian. As early as 1849, he translated and published the very first Kannada version of the Bhagavad Gita, commissioned by Sir Mark Cubbon. It was based on the very first English translation of the text – *The Bhagavat Geeta, or Dialogues of Krishna and Arjoon* (1785) – by the English orientalist and typographer Charles Wilkins, a founding member of the Asiatic Society.

Perhaps even more than preaching, the good Reverend Garrett enjoyed teaching. In 1858, he started an Anglo-Kannada school, simply called the Bangalore High School, in a shed in the Pete, with him as its first principal. That little school would grow up to become one of the city's greatest educational institutions, Central College.

(PS: The second principal of Bangalore High School was 23-year-old Benjamin Lewis Rice (more about him on page 105), who would woo and marry Garrett's daughter, Mary Sophia. Rice himself would go on to research and translate thousands of ancient Kannada inscriptions and be hailed as the father of Kannada epigraphy and Mysore's first archaeologist. He was the son of Rev. Rice, who served a rival mission – the London Missionary Society. A proper Capulet–Montague story in the heart of Bengaluru Pete!)

'If I may add something here: Actually, there was already a building on the property – John Garrett's home – when he sold it to the British government/maharaja. That building, which even the British thought was strangely designed (because of its castellated structure) for a private home, became the heart of the palace we see today. It was later expanded by Col Malleson and chief engineer of Mysore, Richard Sankey.'

— ARVIND KRISHNASWAMY, FOUNDER AND EDITOR, BENGALURU.COM

•

'Interesting. While B.L. Rice's father-in-law translated the Gita into Kannada, his father and brother had some role in translating the Bible – the Old Testament – into Canarese. These missionaries seem to have had a real flair for languages. Also, there is a church on Avenue Road – Rice Memorial Church – named after B.L. Rice's father, Rev. Benjamin Holt Rice.'

— SANTOSH KUMAR, CARD-CARRYING BANGALOREAN

•

'Loved the Capulet–Montague gratuity at the end. Inspired the limerick writer in me.'

A greedy young lassie named Garrett
Said, her dad she could no longer parrot,
She was not very nice
When she told young Rice
'That ring had better not be 18-carat!'

— RAMJEE CHANDRAN, HOST OF *THE HISTORY OF BANGALORE* PODCAST

50

RAJYOTSAVA DAY IS CELEBRATED ON 1 NOVEMBER EVERY YEAR

A Birthday History for a Beloved State

Bangalore is the capital of Karnataka, but its geographical location, less than 100 km from towns in Tamil Nadu and Andhra Pradesh, has ensured that it has always been a cosmopolitan, multilingual city. In the southern peninsula itself, it occupies a position equidistant from ports on the eastern and western coasts, which has meant that it was criss-crossed through the ages by traders and adventurers, soldiers and wayfarers. The same is true of many parts of Karnataka – through the ages, borders have been drawn and redrawn across this land, dividing and uniting Kannada speakers. And yet, through all the upheavals, a deep love for the language prevailed, and was brought to bear, post-Independence, in the creation of a new state called Karnataka. Kannadigas haven't stopped celebrating since.

The old political slogan, 'From the (Jordan) river to the (Mediterranean) sea,' which defines a geography for the Palestinian nation, is back in the world's consciousness – and on its conscience. With Karnataka's birthday around the corner, this is a good time to wonder – if we were to define Karnataka's extent similarly, what geographic markers would we use? One possible answer is proposed by the ninth-century *Kavirajamarga*, a treatise on grammar and poetry that is hailed as the earliest literary work in Kannada. Composed during the rule of Amoghavarsha, the greatest king of the Rashtrakutas, *Kavirajamarga* states unequivocally that 'Kaveri-indama Godavari-varam-irda nadada Kannada' – 'The land that lies between the Kaveri and Godavari rivers is Kannada Nadu'.

It has been some centuries since Kannada speakers occupied such a large swathe of the Deccan, but they certainly did in Amoghavarsha's time. At its height, the Rashtrakuta Empire extended well beyond the Godavari basin, to the Ganga–Yamuna doab! But Kannada's rise to prominence had begun even earlier, in the fourth century CE, with early Kannada dynasties like the Kadambas of Banavasi and the Gangas of Talakadu establishing Kannada as the language of administration. There was even a Kannada script by then – the fifth-century Halmidi Inscription, the earliest of its kind, is written in what is known as the Kadamba script (a version of the much older Brahmi script that was devised specifically to write Kannada and Telugu).

These early dynasties were followed by the mighty Chalukyas of Badami, whose greatest ruler, Pulikeshi II, built the first south Indian empire by consolidating the entire region between the Kaveri and the Narmada rivers, and ushering in a golden age in the region known today as Karnataka.

A century after Amoghavarsha, 'Adikavi' (The First Poet) Pampa would write his Kannada classics *Adi Purana* (on the life of the first Jain Tirthankara,

Rishabhanatha) and *Pampa Bharata* (a retelling of the Mahabharata), setting a literary benchmark that future generations of Kannada writers would strive relentlessly to live up to. Under the Western Chalukyas, who ruled between the tenth and twelfth centuries from Kalyana (today Basavakalyana) around Bijapur, a radical new genre of metaphysical and devotional Kannada literature – Vachana Sahitya – found patronage.

The Hoysalas, who ruled most of today's Karnataka in the eleventh and twelfth centuries, also patronized Kannada, but their sphere of influence was much smaller than the Rashtrakutas' had been. In the courts of the last great southern empire, Vijayanagara, which lasted well into the sixteenth century, Kannada was on an equal footing with Telugu, which had flourished between the twelfth and fourteenth centuries under the Kakatiyas of Warangal.

In the face of the southern expansion of the Mughals and the Marathas in the seventeenth and eighteenth centuries, and with the Asaf Jahis of Hyderabad crowding in from the east following Mughal decline, it was left to the Wadiyars of Mysore to keep the Kannada flag flying. The British takeover of Mysore following the death of Tipu Sultan in 1799 changed the dynamics – and the borders – once again. By the end of the nineteenth century, the anguish of the Kannada people, separated for too long by arbitrary lines drawn across a region that had been, for millennia, united by culture and language, could no longer be borne.

Appropriately, it was Kannada writers, articulate and aesthetic in their longing, who kick-started the movement for Ekikarana (unification). In Dharwad, the epicentre of the movement, journalist Aluru Venkata Rao made fiery speeches, and wrote his magnum opus, *Karnataka Gatha Vaibhava* (The Glory That Was Karnataka), to remind Kannadigas of their storied past. In Bangalore, the legendary novelist Anakru (A.N. Krishna Rao) wrote spirited editorials in the magazine *Kannada Nudi* to galvanize Kannadigas from all over. In 1924, at the Belgaum session of the Indian National Congress, playwright–poet Huilgol Narayana Rao composed and sang, for the first time, what would become the rousing state anthem for many years – 'Udayavaagali Namma Cheluva Kannada Nadu' (May our beautiful Kannada Nadu rise!). Finally, on 1 November 1956, the long-held aspirations of the Kannadigas were realized when the new, unified Mysore State was born.

Happy 68th, Karnataka! Shine on!

'Your mention of "Kaveri-indama Godavari-varam" was very apt. By the way, have you seen the Halmidi Shasana? I am sure you have, because of the history walks you lead – it is in the Government Museum on Kasturba Road. When I saw the inscription, it reminded me of my visit to the British Museum in London, and how it felt to lay eyes on the Rosetta Stone there. I felt bad that we haven't done a great job of preserving, displaying or describing the Halmidi Shasana in the way the Rosetta Stone has been. I guess the British were and are very good at keeping records and preserving artefacts, theirs and those of others.'

— SHANKARA SHASTRY, JP NAGAR, BANGALORE

SIR M.V.'S BIRTHDAY, 15 SEPTEMBER, IS CELEBRATED AS ENGINEERS' DAY

The Man Who Engineered a Revolution

Sir M. Visvesvaraya lived to be over a 100, but he had passed by the time I made an appearance. I could not escape his long shadow, though – it seemed there was nothing in the old Mysore state that he had not touched, built, made better. My dad and I got our engineering degrees, 34 years apart, from the University Visvesvaraya College of Engineering, an institution he had set up as the kingdom's first college of engineering in 1917. As a family, we loved hanging out at the Century Club, also founded by Sir M.V. in 1917. My aunt taught at Sri Jayachamarajendra Polytechnic, which he established in 1943. Across Karnataka, my civil engineer uncle built dams for generating electricity on the lines of the ones designed by Sir M.V. Like I said, there was no escape.

To engineers across India, September heralds the one day of the year – National Engineers' Day – when their tribe is acknowledged. For this, they have Mokshagundam Visvesvaraya (1861–1962), who was born on 15 September in a village called Muddenahalli, 60 km north-east of Bengaluru, and celebrated during his lifetime as 'one of the very ablest of India's engineers', to thank.

Knighted in 1915 by King George V, Sir M.V. was so admired in his own state that he acquired folk hero status, becoming a metaphor for extraordinary intelligence, rectitude and discipline. To this day, in Kannadiga homes, it is common to describe a bright youngster as being bestowed with 'Visvesvarayyana talay' (Visvesvaraya's brain). Legends abound about his uprightness, like the one in which Sir M.V. fetched a different pen and inkwell to help a friend fill a form, instead of using the ones he had been using for his work, because he would not use the government's resources for his personal business. And his insistence on punctuality had even ministers showing up at his door five minutes early, knowing that they would be turned away if they knocked even a minute after the appointed time.

If this aspect of his personality made him an unusual Indian, there was another, which put him in ideological conflict with his towering compatriot, Mahatma Gandhi. Even though Sir M.V. was the older by eight years (and a couple of weeks), it was he who was the more 'modern' in his approach to development; he embraced the Western industrial-capitalist model, exhorting the country to 'Industrialize or perish', while Gandhiji advocated for self-sufficient agrarian village republics. So much of Sir M.V.'s work as a civil engineer, however, was about building dams, irrigation systems and reservoirs, all of which benefited farmers, that Gandhiji had nothing but praise for him.

In a remarkable career spanning seven decades – he retired from the board of Tata Steel at the age of 95 – Sir M.V. spent only 23 years 'in harness', working for the British Indian government in Bombay Presidency. In that time, he designed an intricate irrigation system in the Deccan Plateau, gave recommendations for water supply and drainage systems in Aden (today's Yemen), and patented his design of automated weir floodgates for dams. In 1908, having opted for voluntary retirement, he travelled to Europe for a closer study of industrialized nations.

In 1909, after a successfully executed commission from the Nizam of Hyderabad to design a flood-protection system for the city had turned him into a celebrity, the Mysore diwan, V.P. Madhava Rao, invited Sir M.V. to take over as chief engineer of Mysore, which he graciously accepted. Thus, at long last, did the best-known alumnus of Bengaluru's Central College wend his way homewards.

In 1912, the then maharaja, Krishnaraja Wadiyar IV, appointed Sir M.V. diwan of Mysore. In a too-brief seven-year stint, he founded several enduring institutions, including the State Bank of Mysore, the Government Engineering College (now the University Visvesvaraya College of Engineering), the Bangalore Press (whose calendars continue to grace so many homes), the Century Club, and a whole slew of industries and factories that catapulted Mysore unequivocally into the twentieth century. In 1918, the staunch secularist and meritocrat, who believed that religion was a plague and caste inequalities were best addressed by means of education and

SIR M. VISVESVARAYA

community leadership, courted huge controversy when he resigned in a huff, in opposition to the maharaja's proposal to bring in affirmative action.

Today, in Sir M.V.'s erstwhile home on Museum Road, his descendant Satish Mokshagundam lovingly preserves, among other souvenirs, the peepal leaf-shaped medallion that was bestowed on 'Thatha' in 1955, making him the very first recipient from Karnataka of the country's highest civilian honour, the Bharat Ratna.

Sir M.V., everyone knows, was a stickler for time management. In the Sir M.V. museum, two of his timetables prove this without a doubt. Here they are:

When he was 25:

5 a.m. – 7:30 a.m. > Read Parabola [a book?] and mark useful formulae

7:30 a.m. – 9 a.m. > Private affairs

9 a.m. – 12 noon > Office work

12 noon – 12:30 p.m. > Important office work

When he was 95:

7 a.m. > Breakfast

7:30 a.m. – 12:30 p.m. > Study and work

3 p.m. – 5 p.m. > Attend to post and other correspondence

5 p.m. > Walk

8 p.m. > Dinner

9 p.m. > Newspaper reading

– SUMAA TEKUR, DESCENDANT OF SIR M.V., IN HER PIECE 'WHY EVERY KANNADIGA SHOULD BE PROUD OF SIR MV', PUBLISHED IN *DNA* (DNAINDIA.COM), IN 2010

The Silk Route: The International Story of Mysore Silk

Even in a country that has such a variety of spectacular silks to choose from, Mysore silk has held its own, for centuries. But the road to its current success, which criss-crosses the globe in surprising ways, has had its ups – sometimes literally, as when all the available silk was requisitioned for parachutes during World War II – and downs. And although more and more women are opting for cruelty-free 'Ahimsa silk' sarees, in which the silkworm is allowed to emerge from its cocoon before the broken threads are spun into a silk that is rougher than usual, most of them aren't letting go of their heirloom Mysore silks, passed down through the generations.

The birth of Krishna, celebrated with much joy across the country, is a sign that the Indian festive season has kicked into high gear. In Bangalore, it also means that it's time to pull out the silks after months of slopping about in jeans and dri-fits.

It is surprising that we don't wear silk more often, given that a whopping 70 per cent of India's raw silk, and 43 per cent of its mulberry raw silk (silk produced from the cocoons of silkworms fed on mulberry leaves) are produced in Karnataka; the Government Cocoon Market in Ramanagara on the Bangalore–Mysore highway is Asia's largest such market. Mulberry silk is the base of the famous Mysore Silk, which became the state's first GI-tagged product in 2005.

Well before it received official recognition, however, silk from Mysore was known far and wide. Way back in 1791, British officer Robert Andrews reported meeting two men who had been employed in silkworm rearing in Srirangapatna under Hyder Ali. By then, Hyder had been dead eight years. His son and heir, Tipu Sultan, so the story goes, entranced by the quality and sheen of a length of fine silk gifted to him by an ambassador from China, became determined to produce it in his own kingdom. He sent off deputations not only to China but also closer home, to Bengal, which had had a thriving silk industry for centuries, to source the best silkworms and related knowhow. Both deputations returned, years apart, with mulberry cuttings, but only the Bengal one brought back Chinese silkworm eggs, of the 'yellow bivoltine race'. In south Indian climactic conditions, the worm stopped hibernating, tweaked its genetics and diverged from every other 'race' of silkworm to morph into the 'Pure Mysore race'.

Tipu's short reign (1784–99), marked by the destructive Third and Fourth Anglo-Mysore wars, was not the best ecosystem for industry to flourish. After his death, Mysore's silk production, while it continued to survive in pockets, saw a steep decline. Hopes of a resurrection in 1866, with the opening of the Silk Filature Company in Kengeri by an Italian entrepreneur – the Italians were the pioneers of filature (silk factory) technology – during the half century when Mysore was directly administered by the British (1831–81), came to nought.

In 1893, Bombay industrialist Jamsetji Tata was on a visit to Japan, which dominated the world in silk production at the time. So impressed was he with how Japan had adapted global best practices – silk egg production from France, which used Louis Pasteur's game-changing antibacterial techniques to keep the eggs disease-free, and Italian filature technology – to create their own version of scientific sericulture that he wanted to try it in India as well. Bangalore's mild climate, and Mysore's established end-to-end silk production ecosystem, saw Jamsetji take his proposal to Seshadri Iyer, the then diwan of Mysore, in 1896. Iyer bit. By 1902, the cutting-edge, not-for-profit Tata Silk Farm, a training centre, had set up operations near Basavanagudi, under Japanese experts, and ran successfully until well after Independence.

In 1912, Krishnaraja Wadiyar IV, inspired by the flourishing silk trade in Europe, imported looms from Switzerland and set up a factory in Mysore to produce the finest silk for the use of the royal family. Post-Independence, the factory was taken over by the Mysore State Sericulture Department. In 1980, it was handed over to a Government of Karnataka enterprise called KSIC (Karnataka Silk Industries Corporation) Limited.

If you are in the market for a Mysore Silk saree today, make sure you look for the KSIC hologram stamped on it, which guarantees that it is authentic – and very, very expensive.

'It's fascinating to me that it has been men who have driven the innovation and resurrection of the silk industry. I associate silk with sarees, of course, but given its vast uses, it is no wonder that there was great interest in the fabric. On another note, on our first visit to Bangalore in the '80s, my parents, a Punjabi couple who had no experience with sarees, bought Mysore silk sarees for their daughters, who were not yet in their teens! Just goes to show that an appreciation of quality is universal.'

— JASJEET KAUR, WHO MOVED TO BANGALORE 20 YEARS AGO

•

'Thank you for sharing this article. Today, as I wore a Mysore silk (I am now taking out and wearing my old pure silks once or twice a week), I was thinking of the Mysore silk factory. My uncle was the manager there, and so we all got to have a close look at the worms, the mulberry leaves, the spinning and weaving machines, the bundled-up Mysore silk... Lovely colours, the best feel, and the shine remains for ever! Good to know the route silk took to land in Mysore – once again, we see Tata's hand and vision there!'

— VASANTHA MURTHY, 83, FORMER PRINCIPAL OF A DEGREE COLLEGE IN ANANTAPUR, WHO MOVED TO BANGALORE AFTER HER RETIREMENT

53

ONE OF KANNADA'S EARLIEST WOMEN NOVELISTS, TRIVENI, WAS BORN ON 1 SEPTEMBER 1928

The First Ladies of the Kannada Kadambari

The first official Kannada kadambari, or novel, was a translation – Ishwar Chandra Vidyasagar's *Bhrantivilasa*, translated from the Bengali by B. Venkatacharya in 1876. It would be another 23 years before the first original Kannada novel, Gulavadi Venkata Rao's *Indira Bai*, made its appearance. In the 1920s, the female voice began to emerge with Nanjanagoodu Tirumalamba, a poet, novelist, literary critic and publisher of literary magazines. But the real revolution in the woman-authored Kannada kadambari as a mainstream, popular literary form that foregrounded women's concerns would have to wait until the number of 'women who could read' hit critical mass – the 1940s.

On 1 September this year, an Instagram post by Anusha Kumar, a second-generation Indian American who had just received a PhD in clinical psychology on her late grandmother's birthday, went viral on social media. Neither she nor her mother had ever known the grandmother, wrote Anusha, for she had passed away in 1963, at the age of 34, just nine days after childbirth. The post went viral because the grandmother she was referencing was the cult Kannada novelist Triveni, many of whose books, written in the '50s, are a deep dive into the impact of family pressures, and sexual and financial exploitation in and outside marriage, on the mental health of women, long before such a thing was ever acknowledged, let alone discussed in public.

Triveni was the pen name of Mysore-born Anasuya Shankar. Her paternal uncle, the great B.M. Sri(kantaiah), was a pioneering writer and academic who set the course for the renaissance of Kannada literature in a modern, secular, accessible avatar in the early decades of the twentieth century. Her aunt, M.N. Subbamma (pen name Vani), was also a Kannada writer who would come into full flower around the same time as her niece.

Triveni's first collection of short stories *Eradu Manassu* (Two Minds) was published in 1950, when she was only 22. Over the next 12 years of her short life, while she herself struggled through successive miscarriages and resulting depression, 'Kannada's Jane Austen' would write 21 hugely popular novels (among them were *Belli Moda*, *Hannele Chiguridaaga*, *Hoovu Hannu* and *Sharapanjara*, which were posthumously made into blockbuster Kannada films by celebrated director Puttanna Kanagal), bringing women's inner lives to the forefront of Kannada literature.

Well before Triveni's searing stories, however, were the tongue-in-cheek, slice-of-life writings of Kannada's first woman humorist. Born in 1917 into a wealthy family of Mysore, T. Sunandamma's delightful writings were first published in the legendary Kannada humour monthly, *Koravanji*, in 1942. The magazine ran for 25 years, and Sunandamma, who shared space with such greats as G.P. Rajarathnam and Na Kasturi, ruled the pages as the sole female voice for most of those years, garnering legions of fans, both male and female, in the process.

M.K. Indira, best known as the writer of the Sahitya Akademi Award–winning *Phaniyamma*, the heart-wrenching true story of a child widow in an unrelentingly orthodox Karnataka village at the turn of the twentieth century, was born in the same year as Sunandamma, but would not have her first novel published until 1963, the year of Triveni's death. Indira was 45 that year; it was a chance meeting with Triveni, who had urged her to try her hand at a novel, that had led to Indira's debut. Indira would go on to write over 50 novels and become one of Karnataka's most acclaimed novelists.

Of a later vintage, but equally popular as novelists, were Dr Anupama Niranjana (b. 1934), Nalini Murthy (b. 1937) and Usha Navaratnaram (b. 1939). All of them died relatively young – Anupama at 56, Nalini at 55 and Usha at 61 – but otherwise had very different lives.

Anupama was a practising medical doctor in Bangalore who was known as much for her novels as for her popular non-fiction books on themes like childbirth and cancer. She also wrote a hugely popular series for children called 'Dinakkondu Kathe' (A Story a Day), comprising 12 volumes of 30 stories each. An electrical engineer, Nalini got her PhD at Canada's Nova Scotia Technical College, becoming the first female engineer to register with the Association of Professional Engineers (APENS) in Nova Scotia, before settling there with her family. She still found the time not only to write books demystifying science and maths for children but also heart-warming novels. Usha, fluent in French, worked as a teacher for over 30 years. Her romance novels, over 40 of them, were all the rage with women readers in the '70s and '80s, before television made couch potatoes of us all.

'Loved it! I didn't know that Puttana Kanagal's *Sharapanjara* was based on Triveni's book! I had heard of the film as a kid but watched it when I was past 50, after my mother had passed away. Watching the protagonist wither away due to mental illness brought my mother's life before my eyes and I couldn't help tearing up...'

— T.N. HARI, AUTHOR, EXECUTIVE CHAIRMAN - STEER WORLD, AUTHOR AND GROWTH ADVISER

•

'Loved reading the article, mostly because one knows and has read most of the writers you mention. Triveni, Pattabhi (Aryamba Pattabhi, Triveni's sister, who was also a novelist) and Usha were the first ones to introduce "local" romance into our Mills & Boon lives.'

— RENU MUKUNDA, SOCIAL DEVELOPMENT SPECIALIST

•

'Shared this column in my family group – and received this response from one of my uncles, Sheenu Mama: "Triveni's husband S.N. Shankar was the son of S. Narayana Rao, who lived in Nanjanagoodu. Shankar taught us English when I was a student at Mysore's Sharada Vilas College between 1969 and 1973. He was a wonderful lecturer. Nice to know that Triveni has a Nanjanagoodu connection, which is only fitting, because that was where Tirumalamba (my paternal aunt), the first novelist in Kannada, wrote most of her books!"'

— BHUMIKA K. FREELANCE JOURNALIST

54

JAYA KARNATAKA, THE MAGAZINE THAT SERVED AS THE CLARION FOR KANNADA UNIFICATION, WAS FOUNDED BY ALURU VENKATA RAO IN NOVEMBER 1922

Kannada Ekikarana: The Great Coming-Together

Q: When you are travelling abroad, how can you tell a group of Kannadigas apart from other Indian groups?
A: They are all talking to each other in English.

Thus goes a popular, self-deprecating joke by Kannadigas about Kannadigas. The point of the joke depends on who is telling it – to some, it is a critique of our lack of bhaashaabhimana, love for one's mother tongue. To others like me, it illustrates, with gentle humour, our admirable ability to blend in. As for the anxiety that the language isn't getting enough love, one has only to see how wildly popular Kannada reels and their young makers are on social media to feel reassured. And what of the online trolling by angry / hurt / entitled new settlers, who accuse the locals of harassing them because they don't speak the local language? Well, one can only hope that empathy and mutual respect will be practised by both sides, so that everyone benefits. That has always been the way of Kannada Nadu.

On no other day in the year does the Kannadiga heart swell as proudly as on the first of November, Rajyotsava Day. This was the day, back in 1956, that the aspirations of hundreds of thousands of Kannadigas came to fruition, with the state of Mysore expanding its borders to embrace neighbouring Kannada-speaking regions into itself. This 'ekikarana', or unification, had been campaigned for since the early 1900s; the sundering of the Kannada country itself, however, dated back to the sixteenth century.

The end of the vast Vijayanagara Empire in 1565 cast the Kannada-speaking regions it had once incorporated into disarray. To the south, however, the kingdom of Mysore continued to be the heartland of the Kannada people, administered as it had been by the Kannada-speaking rulers of the Wadiyar dynasty since the fourteenth century. In the latter half of the eighteenth century, Hyder Ali and Tipu Sultan expanded Mysore to include more Kannada-speaking regions, only to lose them again in the aftermath of the Fourth Anglo-Mysore war. The spoils were divvied up between the East India Company and its allies, like the Nizam of Hyderabad and the Marathas, in 1799.

In nineteenth-century British records, the six Kannada-speaking regions of the Deccan were classified as Bombay Karnataka (part of the Bombay Presidency), Hyderabad Karnataka (Nizam's territories), Madras Karnataka (Madras Presidency), Coorg, Mysore, and miscellaneous princely states like Mudhol, Jamkhandi and Savanur. Nearly two-thirds of what is today Karnataka fell outside the bounds of the kingdom of Mysore.

Following the fall of the Marathas in 1818, British officers setting up schools in erstwhile Maratha territories naturally leaned towards Marathi as the medium of instruction, only to find to their surprise that in certain districts, like Dharwad, Belgaum, North Kanara and Bijapur, it was not

Marathi but Kannada that was the lingua franca. Small wonder, then, that the earliest stirrings of rebellion against linguistic (and consequently economic) oppression began in Dharwad, with the founding, by eminent educationist R.H. Deshpande in 1890, of the Karnataka Vidyavardhaka Sangha, for the protection of Kannada and the unification of the Kannada-speaking regions.

Circa 1907, inspired by Madhusudan Das's movement for a state based on language that began in Orissa in 1895, and the rage against the 1905 Partition of Bengal, which cleft Bengali-speakers in two, Dharwad journalist Aluru Venkata Rao launched the Kannada Ekikarana Movement. He also published, in 1912, his magnum opus on the glorious history of Karnataka until the fall of Vijayanagara, *Karnataka Gatha Vaibhava*, which was instrumental in getting people to rally to the cause. One of the wonderful fallouts of the Unification Movement, championed all along by writers, was the establishment of the Kannada Sahitya Parishat in Bangalore in 1915.

The road to unification would prove to be a long, hard one, with even past allies like the Mysore administration turning against it – unkindest cut! – unwilling to take on the burden of the economically backward and arid northern regions. But public aspiration proved too strong. On 1 November 1956, Mysore was 'reorganized',

ALURU VENKATA RAO

bringing great joy to Kannadigas everywhere. Happily, Aluru Venkata Rao, then hailed as 'Kannada Kulapurohita' (the high priest of Kannada) lived to see the day. On the same date in 1973, the state adopted the name Karnataka.

To this day, the Kannada Sahitya Parishat dedicates itself to the promotion and celebration of Kannada. As for Rao, his memory lives on in a main thoroughfare in Kalasipalyam called AV Road. (It used to be called Albert Victor Road after Queen Victoria's grandson, which proved very convenient when its name was changed to Aluru Venkatarao Road – same initials!).

'Oho, this is perfect! Shall forward to all members of the Maharashtrian side of my family who go on and on annoyingly about how Belagavi belongs to Maharashtra.'

— RADHIKA SATHE MANTRI, HALF KANNADATHI ON PAPER AND FULL KANNADATHI IN SPIRIT

•

'A beautiful read on the eve of Rajyotsava Day. So full of admiration for patriots and nationalists who built us a beautiful country with such sensitivity to local populations.'

— PRAMOD AGARWAL, IMMIGRANT TECHIE, WHOSE KANNADA GETS BETTER EVERY DAY

55

KUVEMPU WAS BORN ON 11 NOVEMBER 1994

A Radical Rashtrakavi: Remembering Kuvempu

Of all the literary giants that Karnataka has produced over the years, Kuvempu is among the tallest, as beloved for his evocative prose and poetry as for the themes he concerned himself with. Both a product of colonialism and a harsh critic of it, equally influenced by Western and Indian thought, Kuvempu truly embodied the ideal he himself conceptualized – Vishwamaanava. Today, his childhood home in Kuppali, a village in the Thirthahalli taluk of Shivamogga district, has been converted into a beautiful museum called Kavimane (Poet's House). On a hillock to the south of the house is Kavishaila, a Stonehenge-inspired half-circle of megalithic rocks at the centre of which Kuvempu was laid to rest. The memorial was designed by Kuvempu's son, Poornachandra Tejaswi, a polymath who was, among other things, a brilliant novelist, painter, photographer and environmentalist, and supported entirely by the late V.G. Siddhartha, founder of the iconic Café Coffee Day chain.

There are many reasons to celebrate November, chief among which are nippy Bengaluru mornings, the glorious beginnings of the pink *Tabebuia* blossom, the lengthening afternoon shadows that herald the dark nights of Deepavali, and the fact that it is Karnataka's birthday month. Which makes it a good time to remember an extraordinary man, arguably the greatest Kannada poet of the twentieth century, who passed 29 years ago on 11 November.

Growing up in Kuppali, a small hamlet nestled in Karnataka's picturesque Malenadu region, the young Kuppali Venkatappa Puttappa (later, he would take on the pen name Kuvempu) was enthralled by the natural beauty that surrounded him. His early education in a Sanskrit school trained his ear to the cadences of that language, and exposed him to the great stories of the Ramayana and the Mahabharata. In stark contrast to that magnificence was the society around him, a feudal one riven by caste and class distinctions, blind superstition and rampant discrimination. All these early influences would fashion Kuvempu's ideas, and find moving and radical expression in his writing, establishing him as a thinker far ahead of his time.

At the Wesleyan High School in Mysore, Kuvempu came under the spell of English poets like Wordsworth and Milton. In 1929, at the age of 25, he graduated from Maharaja College, Mysore, with a major in Kannada, all set to embark on a literary and academic career.

Interestingly, Kuvempu's first book of poems – *Beginner's Muse* – was in English. A chance meeting with the Irish mystical poet James Henry Cousins changed his outlook – chiding him gently, Cousins exhorted Kuvempu to write in his mother tongue. Once that course correction had been made, there was no looking back – plays, poetry, essays, biographies, literary criticism, novels, collections of short stories, quirky stories and poems for children, translations, adaptations of English works, including Shakespeare's plays, all poured out of his prodigious pen, attacking societal evils, subverting epic stories, advocating the equality of all humankind, as Basava and the Buddha had done before him, through his conception of Vishwamaanava, the Universal Human.

In his first play, *Jalagaara* (The Sweeper), written when he was only 24, Lord Shiva appears before the eponymous low-caste protagonist to assure him that he (Shiva) and the jalagaara were no different from each other, for Shiva was a sweeper as well, one who swept away the world's injustices. In his magnum opus, the two-volume epic poem *Sri Ramayana Darshanam*, which won Kuvempu the Jnanpith Award for 1967, making him the first Kannada writer to be so honoured, Rama volunteers to undertake the Agnipravesha with Sita, so that they can each prove their fidelity to the other. In a little handbook, *Mantra Maangalya*, he lays out the framework for an alternative, meaningful wedding ceremony, devoid of Vedic ritual, that can be performed by partners of any caste or religion. Happily, several Kannadiga couples continue to opt for this secular, 'modern' ceremony.

Kuvempu's voice was, and continues to be, a towering presence in the Kannadiga discourse about social equality. His conviction that children in Karnataka should mandatorily learn Kannada alongside English significantly influenced state education policy in the 1950s. But perhaps what resonates most with Kannadigas is his deep love for the state and the Kannada language, expressed most eloquently in the Karnataka state anthem, 'Jaya Bharata Jananiya Tanujaate, Jaya He Karnataka Maate' (O daughter of Bharat, O Mother Karnataka, all hail to you!), and the poem, simply titled 'Kannada', that opens with – 'Kannada ene kunidaaduvudennede/ Kannada ene kivi nimiruvudu' (Say Kannada, and my heart dances with joy/ Say Kannada, and my ears perk up with delight). Goosebumps.

'How do you manage to capture a giant like Kuvempu in a column, and so appropriately? Delightful reading.'

— PRATEETI BALLAL, MUSICIAN, DANCER, ACADEMIC AND MEMBER OF THE CURATORIAL TEAM OF THE BANGALORE LITERATURE FESTIVAL

•

'What a superb tribute! Thanks so much for writing about Kuvempu – my wife and I got married following Mantra Maangalya!'

— RAGHAV CHAKRAVARTHY, CO-FOUNDER OF QSHALA, WHICH PROVIDES QUIZZES AS A LEARNING TOOL FOR STUDENTS GLOBALLY

•

'Wow! So informative. I never knew that Kuvempu was so radical/secular. I only knew about the poems and the Ramayana... Thanks for sharing.'

— SURESH RAMASWAMY, THIRD-GENERATION BANGALOREAN

56

THE VIDHANA SOUDHA WAS INAUGURATED ON 1 NOVEMBER 1956

The Man Who Dreamed Up the Vidhana Soudha

The night that I was born was the night the Vidhana Soudha was illuminated for the very first time. My mum missed it entirely – she was already in labour. But my dad and aunt and uncle were among the crowd that had gathered along the western boundary of Cubbon Park, which burst into spontaneous applause and a collective, awestruck 'Aaaaah!' as the thousands of yellow incandescent lamps flamed into life. 'It was you,' my dad never tired of telling me on my birthday each year. 'You brought gold to the Vidhana Soudha.'

The problem with being Bangalorean (a very different thing from 'living in Bangalore') is that many of its benefits can only be experienced, not articulated. This is partly why Bangaloreans are at such a loss when visitors demand to be shown their city's sights. In the end, putting a brave face on it, visitors are taken to 'see' Lalbagh, Cubbon Park, and the one building that is bound to draw a gasp or two, the Vidhana Soudha.

In a long-ago interview, the second chief minister of Karnataka, Kengal Hanumanthaiah, revealed that it was a similar problem that had made him nix the original plans for a new legislature building for Mysore State, which his predecessor, K.C. Reddy, had approved. It was a Soviet delegation that Hanumanthaiah was showing around the city then – that tour, also, would most likely have included Lalbagh and Cubbon Park, apart from the Attara Kacheri, the old British Public Offices (now the High Court of Karnataka), into which the Mysore legislature had moved at Independence. After the tour, the visitors asked a pertinent question – 'We have only seen British buildings – where are yours?'

Stung to the quick, Hanumanthaiah returned to his chambers and took a fresh look at the plans for the proposed two-storey building, whose foundation stone had already been laid by the then prime minister, Jawaharlal Nehru, in 1951. Dismissing it as a 'plain and simple type of American architecture', the fierce nationalist, federalist and champion of unification (of the Mumbai–Karnataka and Hyderabad–Karnataka regions with old Mysore) came to a decision – the plan would be revised; the new building would be a magnificent expression of the power of the people, a work of art worthy of Mysore's vibrant traditions, featuring local materials, architecture and craftsmanship.

Work on the new three-storeyed building, the largest of its kind with its 700x350 ft footprint and 175 ft height, began in 1952. The location was moved from the original site inside the Cubbon Park to higher ground, next to the Raj Bhavan and facing the Attara Kacheri. The design, described as Neo-Dravidian, included architectural elements from the Chalukya, Hoysala and Vijayanagara empires – columns, domes, latticed stone windows – and a soaring flight of stairs that placed the Soudha's entrance way higher than the entrance to the Attara Kacheri, which emphatically achieved its purpose of dwarfing the latter into insignificance.

Five thousand convicts were put to work on the grand edifice, with the assurance that their sentences would be commutated post its completion; 1,500 stonecutters and artisans worked tirelessly on granite quarried from Magadi and other sites around Bengaluru. Hanumanthaiah took a personal interest – it was on his say-so that the words 'Government's Work Is God's Work', and their Kannada equivalent, were emblazoned prominently over the doorway. As everyone raced against the clock to have the building ready in time for the birth of the unified Mysore State on 1 November 1956, it became clear that the Soudha had spectacularly blown its budget, going from the estimated 33 lakhs to 1.7 crores.

All hell broke loose. Hanumanthaiah's detractors launched a vicious attack, demanding an investigation, which the chief minister gladly ordered, into the 'reckless expenditure'. The naysayers weren't convinced. In the end, Hanumanthaiah resigned, on 19 August, weeks before his grand dream was realized. It fell to the interim CM, Kadidal Manjappa, to see the Soudha project through.

KENGAL HANUMANTHAIAH'S CONFLICT OF INTEREST – AS BOTH PRESIDENT OF THE MYSORE CONGRESS AND CM OF MYSORE STATE – CRITICIZED IN A CARTOON IN *KORAVANJI*

In 1957, the new Mysore government decided to erase Hanumanthaiah's words from the entrance archway and replace them with 'Satyameva Jayate'. It never happened. Today, it is in those words, often ignored by those who pass under them, that Kengal Hanumanthaiah lives on.

'While living at the sports hostel in Kanteerava Stadium back in engineering college, we used the steps of Vidhana Soudha to build our endurance, spending 1–2 hours running up and down in waves from one side to the other. Your article brought back those fond memories.'

— KOWSHIK BHAT, CONSULTANT, SAN FRANCISCO BAY AREA, WHO PLAYED HOCKEY FOR BANGALORE UNIVERSITY IN THE '90S

•

'The grandson of one of the artisans who had worked on the Vidhana Soudha did some stonecutting for us when we were constructing our house. Like his grandfather and other stonecutters in his community, he had an incredible mathematical brain – he would keep calculating the running length of stone slabs of different thicknesses, to reach uniformity for each course. It was amazing to watch.'

— JAYARAM KRISHNAN, MANAGEMENT CONSULTANT AND FOUNDER, ASPIREKEN

•

'Even today, most state capitals have British-era buildings to house their legislatures. Among them, Vidhana Soudha stands tall in its majesty. If it had the kind of long view Rashtrapati Bhavan has, imagine how much grander it would have looked!'

— SHANKARA SHASTRY, VORACIOUS READER AND KNOWLEDGE GATHERER

December~January~February

Pink Trumpet

Tabebuia avellanedae's clusters of lush
Bestow on crisp winter skies a comely blush,
And bring lovers, poets, families – moppet to matriarch –
To pink-wreathed Ringwood Circle in the heart of Cubbon Park.

57

THE ANNUAL BANGALORE LIT FEST IS HELD IN DECEMBER

A Long and Storied Literary Legacy

This column was written when I, and thousands of other book-loving Bangaloreans like me, were coming off the high of the 2022 edition of the much-loved Bangalore Lit Fest (BLF). Every BLF is special, but that one was particularly so, for my then-new book *Cubbon Park: The Green Heart of Bengaluru* had had a wonderful airing there. This year (2024), in August, another literary festival, The Book Brahma Literature Festival (BBLF), made a thumping debut – 110+ sessions, 440 writers, 18,000 visitors across three days – in the city. With the tagline 'Soul of South', BBLF is a first-of-its-kind multilingual festival whose purpose is 'to celebrate (...) the rich 2,500-year-old legacy of south Indian languages (Kannada, Tamil, Telugu, Malayalam) in shaping world literature.'

'Bangalore is the only city that has sizeable populations of native speakers (and readers, one reckons) of all four languages,' says festival director Satish Chapparike. 'BBLF could not have worked anywhere else.'

This past weekend, Bangalore came together to celebrate books and writers – of which there is an inordinate number in this city – on the lawns of The Lalit Ashok (or, as every self-respecting old Bangalorean knows it, Ashoka Hotel). The occasion was the annual Bangalore Literature Festival (BLF), an admired, admirable institution that has reached its 11th edition without ever needing to attach the name of a corporate sponsor to its own; the vibrant festival is supported entirely by a handful of citizens – Friends of BLF – in their individual capacities.

An affinity for the written word is not new to Bangalore or Karnataka. Kannada writers have been conferred the Jnanpith Award, the country's highest and oldest literary honour, no less than eight times since the prize was first instituted in 1961. A uniquely Kannada genre of popular music called Bhavageethe has, since the '70s, brought the poetry of the greatest contemporary Kannada poets to the masses.

In the early sixteenth century, when the great Krishnadevaraya ruled the Vijayanagara Empire, the saint Purandaradasa, widely considered the father of Carnatic music, composed his deeply moving devotional poetry to Vitthala within the precincts of the eponymous temple in Hampi. Writing in the twelfth century, Veerashaiva saints, most drawn from the working classes, bequeathed to Kannadigas a precious corpus of spiritual and philosophical literature, collectively called Vachana Sahitya, in language that was immediately accessible. The oldest extant Kannada poetry is credited to Adikavi Pampa, who lived and worked between 900 and 950 CE. (Prose and poetry in Kannada must have existed for centuries before Pampa, however, given that Rashtrakuta emperor Amoghavarsha wrote the earliest treatise we know of on Kannada grammar and poetics, *Kavirajamarga,* circa 850 CE.)

What of literature in English, the language of the colonizer (and the colonized)? One of the best-known English writers of pre-Independence India, whose fan base stretched from London to New York to Moscow, was the homegrown R.K. Narayan. Even before Narayan was born in 1906, however, a future Nobel Prize–winner then working out of Bangalore had had his very first book published. The book was called *The Story of the Malakand Field Force: An Episode of Frontier War* (1898). The author, a 23-year-old British military officer, was called Winston Churchill.

Not academically inclined, Churchill struggled through school, gaining admission to the Royal Military Academy, Sandhurst, only on his third attempt. In 1895, all of 21, he was commissioned as second lieutenant in a cavalry regiment called the 4th Queen's Own Hussars. Eager to see action on the ground, he used his family's considerable influence to get himself posted to Cuba, which was then engaged in a war of independence. From the front, Churchill sent despatches to the *Daily Graphic* in London, cutting his journalistic teeth in the process.

Arriving in India in October 1896, he joined his regiment at Bangalore, where he would be based until March 1899. In June 1897, hearing of an outbreak in the Swat Valley against the British Indian government by the Mohmands, a Pashtun tribe, Churchill petitioned General Bindon Blood to allow him to join the Malakand Field Force, which was fighting the rebels. Blood agreed to take Churchill on only as war correspondent, to which the latter happily acquiesced. Returning to Bangalore in October 1897, Churchill compiled his ringside experiences of the conflict into his very first book.

What started in Bangalore would go on to become a prodigious, obsessive (writing, he once said, helped to keep his 'black dog', depression, at bay) and lucrative literary career – he had had five books, including his only novel, published by 1900 itself! But Churchill would have to wait until he was 78 to receive the ultimate honour. The Nobel Prize for Literature was conferred on this polarizing Englishman in 1953, during his second term as prime minister of the UK.

'What a lovely ride from Pampa to Churchill for someone who did not grow up in Bangalore! Clearly, Karnataka is the land that ignites literary minds!'

— ANIRUDDHA ABHAYANKAR, URBAN DESIGN INNOVATOR

•

'We are such a book-loving lot as a city, which probably explains our peace-loving-ness as well.'

— ARATHI DESAI, EXPAT BANGALOREAN WRITING FROM SINGAPORE

•

'I knew about Churchill's Nobel, but not about his connection to Bangalore! Polarizing is the only way to describe him – his infamous quote on Gandhi and his decisions during World War II that caused the devastating Bengal famine are severely problematic. But he was also probably the best wartime leader the UK had. Plus, the fact that he lost the post-war elections possibly hastened our freedom. In any case, one cannot be judgemental about history.'

— SHANKARA SHASTRY, READER FROM BANGALORE

58

HYDER ALI DIED ON 7 DECEMBER 1782

A Mysore Nawab and His French Connection

We tend to think of the 'global village' as a recent phenomenon, wrought mainly by technology. But the world has always been a very connected place. As this despatch from the archives of world history reveals, happenings in eighteenth-century Mysore significantly impacted Versailles, and beyond. In the early twentieth century, with the invention of the Bangalore Torpedo (see page 93), a weapon that was used extensively in both the World Wars, our own city began to impact world affairs. It also became a verb – 'to be Bangalored' was to be blown to smithereens. (As an aside, the verb came back into popular usage at the cusp of the twenty-first century, when the call centre phenomenon first broke. 'Being Bangalored' then came to mean 'losing your job to someone in India.' Which has the same effect in the short term, I suppose, as being blown apart by a Bangalore Torpedo.)

After that weird, wonderful and very wet opening ceremony of the 33rd Paris Olympiad, La Ville-Lumiere has once again exploded into our collective consciousness as a city we simply cannot ignore. It seems a good time, therefore, to examine one of our own city's historical connections to *la belle* France – the eighteenth-century military alliance that Nawab Hyder Ali forged with the French crown. Or did it, in fact, happen the other way around?

The French East India Company (EIC) was late to the India party; it arrived in 1664, well after the British EIC (1600) and the Dutch EIC (1602). It was also dispossessed earlier than the others, reeling under the financial ruin caused by French governor Dupleix's imperial ambitions. (PS: Dupleix had raised a native sepoy infantry while in south India, of which a young Hyder Ali had been a part). Dupleix's dream was shattered by a clerk in the British EIC called Robert Clive; in 1769, the French EIC was dismissed, and its territories taken over by the French crown.

Six years before, in 1763, the Treaty of Paris had ended the Seven Years' War between the British and the French for control of North America. The British won, and the proxy battles that the two sides had fought all over the world, including in India, ceased. When the dust settled, the French, despite controlling five trading posts in India – Pondicherry, Mahe, Yanam, Karaikal and Chandernagore – thought of the subcontinent as '*l'Inde perdue*', India lost.

Things changed in 1776, when French support for the American Revolutionary War led to unexpected success against the British. Inspired, the French began seeking Indian allies to oust the British from India as well. One of the names that came up frequently in Versailles was 'Hyder-ali-can, nabab de Mayssour', who, in 1769, had famously won what we now call the First Anglo-Mysore War. Across the Atlantic, the Americans, hopeful that

British losses in India would help their own cause, were also rooting for Hyder – John Adams, John Quincy Adams and Benjamin Franklin were among those who kept track of Hyder's exploits against British Admiral Edward Hughes, Lt Gen Eyre Coote, Col Baillie and Col Munro.

In 1782, the celebrated French admiral Pierre André de Suffren arrived in India to fight on Hyder's side in the Second Anglo-Mysore War. He won five naval battles against Admiral Hughes, thus ensuring French dominance of the seas off the Coromandel Coast. The history of south India – and Mysore – might have proceeded differently from there on if not for the signing of another Treaty of Paris in 1783, which granted independence to the American colonies and brokered the so-called Peace of Paris, marking the end of British–French hostilities across the globe.

By this time, Hyder was dead from what was possibly cancer. The French summarily withdrew their support to his heir Tipu Sultan. Even though he had the upper hand in the battles at that point, Tipu was forced, in 1784, to accept the peace the EIC was offering.

But Tipu and the French were far from done. Soon after withdrawing support, Louis XVI, the king of France, sent diplomats to persuade Tipu to continue trade links with France. On his part, Tipu sent several embassies to the court of Louis XVI to request the services of French engineers (who helped build, among other things, the famous mechanical contraption called 'Tipu's Tiger'), artisans, gardeners, and manufacturers of porcelain. Well after the

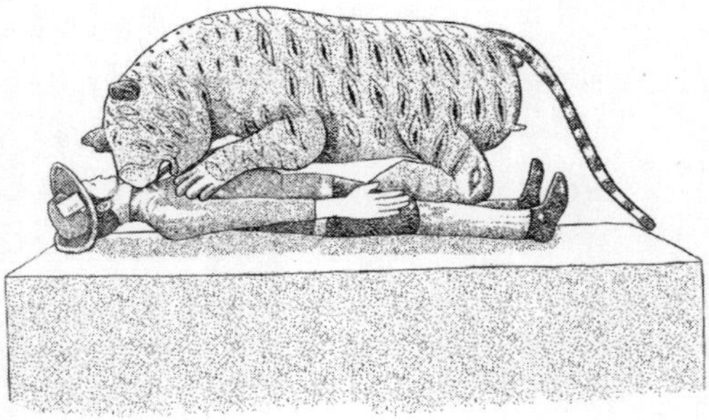

French monarchy was violently dismantled in 1789 – cue the headless Marie Antoinettes from the opening ceremony of the 2024 Olympics – Napoleon Bonaparte himself would extend a hand of friendship to Citoyen Tipu – Citizen Tipu – in 1798. Why that alliance never came to be is a story for another day.

'Nice. Only Dupleix was not foiled by Clive at all. The entire period (and Indian history in general) defies binaries. But the English thrust 'Dupleix and Clive' on us, and so it has stayed.

Dupleix was defeated by a combination of poor cash-flow management, the absence of the French Navy in Indian waters at critical moments and the malevolence of his superiors in France. Eager for glory though he was, Clive was too junior to have merited even a passing thought in the Frenchman's head.

— VENKATESH PARTHASARATHY, AUTHOR AND HISTORY ENTHUSIAST

•

'OMG! We have a play development proposal in the pipeline on exactly these events in world history! A university in Philadelphia will likely be collaborating on this. Will keep you posted.'

— VIJAY PADAKI, TRUSTEE EMERITUS OF THE BANGALORE LITTLE THEATRE FOUNDATION

•

'Great article. Never seen a piece so lucid about the French POV in India.'

— ARVIND KRISHNAN, FOUNDER, THE FULLER LIFE

59

CHAMARAJA WADIYAR X DIED ON 28 DECEMBER 1894

Maharani Vani Vilasa Sannidhana, Queen of Hearts

Many wonderful stories are told of the grit, courage and foresight of the queen regent of Mysore, Kempananjammanni Vani Vilasa. How she commissioned Asia's largest hydroelectric project at Shivanasamudra, which brought electricity to Bangalore as early as 1905. How she offered Jamsetji Tata every kind of support for his proposed institute of higher education, on the condition that he set it up in Bangalore. How she sold some of her own jewellery to help fund the building of the Krishna Raja Sagara Dam across the Kaveri, which would secure her people against devastating famines. But it was how she took charge during the plague pandemic of 1898 that elevated her to legendary status.

Never mind the year now. It was 15 August, a balmy day of no particular significance in Bangalore Cantonment, when there arrived a terse piece of news that rattled the administration. A man had died. He had travelled to Bangalore Cantonment by rail just a few days prior, from the Dharwad district of Bombay State.

None of this would have been remarkable if not for the fact that a pandemic was raging in Bombay; the man had died from that killer disease. In other words, Fortress Bangalore had been breached.

Significant though his death may have been, this column isn't about Patient Zero of the 1898 bubonic plague outbreak. It is about the woman behind the swift response to this event – the dowager queen of Mysore, Vani Vilasa Sannidhana.

The queen began life as Kempananjammanni, daughter of a noble family of Kalale (a village near Nanjangud that had historically provided military commanders to the Mysore kings). She was married at 12 to the 15-year-old maharaja, Chamaraja Wadiyar X – king only in name, for Mysore had been under the direct administration of the British Raj for almost 50 years. Mercifully, Mysore was restored to the king in 1881, and Kempananjammanni became, in both letter and spirit, Maharani Vani Vilasa Sannidhana.

While Chamaraja's stellar reign proceeded in a whirl of path-breaking initiatives – the first high school for girls, the first Representative Assembly in princely India, the sponsoring of Swami Vivekananda's famous voyage to Chicago in 1893 (which would lead serendipitously to the setting up of the Indian Institute of Science in Bangalore in 1909 – more about that on page 59) – the maharani busied herself with the care of her five children. In 1894, tragically, the 31-year-old maharaja succumbed to diphtheria. His eldest son, the 10-year-old Krishnaraja Wadiyar IV, was anointed Yuvaraja, but until he turned 18, the burden of rulership would fall to his young and inexperienced mother.

With her capable, long-serving diwan, K. Seshadri Iyer, by her side, the Queen Regent never faltered. Quickly, she created a Regency Council to advise on matters of governance. A champion of women's health and education, she oversaw the transformation of the girls' high school in Bangalore into Maharani's College and instituted several scholarships for women. By the time she handed over the reins, Mysore had over 200 schools for girls. Most gratifyingly, in 1902, two students from Maharani's College passed the Bachelor of Arts exam, becoming South Asia's first women graduates.

In 1897, rather presciently, she laid the foundation stone of a free public hospital in Bangalore to commemorate Queen Victoria's Diamond Jubilee. The Victoria Hospital would serve the city well during the three-year plague. She also, again presciently, green-lighted two new localities in Bangalore conceived of as models of town planning – Malleswaram and Basavanagudi.

With Patient Zero identified, the queen swung into action, tripling the state's healthcare expenditure and establishing more hospitals (which would prove invaluable in managing the Spanish Flu 20 years later). To assure people that their homes in the congested, insanitary Pete area, where the plague would hit hardest, were not being demolished with malicious intent, she had the Palace Fort also decongested. When people refused to leave their homes (which was the only way to contain the spread), she made personal appeals. With Malleswaram and Basavanagudi now ready to be occupied, she ensured that the rehabilitation of people from the Pete proceeded at a fast clip. The Black Death was contained – and fewer lives were lost in Bangalore than elsewhere.

Today, right next to the Victoria Hospital, the Vani Vilas Women and Children Hospital, inaugurated in 1935, honours the memory of a courageous young queen who, in a time of great crisis, took on the mantle without flinching, stepped up to the plate, and gave her all.

Maharani Vani Vilasa's regency (1894–1902) was a most eventful one. In February 1897, during the wedding celebrations of her daughter, a rogue spark set off an inferno, destroying the marriage mantap and large sections of the original Mysore palace, which had been built of wood. Recovering quickly, the maharani commissioned celebrated British architect Henry Irwin, who also designed the Viceregal Lodge in Shimla and the Chennai Central Railway Station, to build the family a brand-new palace within the same sixteenth-century fort where so many generations of the Wadiyars had lived. Completed in 1912, the new palace, Amba Vilas, better known simply as Mysore Palace, today receives over six million visitors each year.

60

REV. KITTEL DIED ON 18 DECEMBER 1903

A German Priest on MG Road

In the hyper-nationalist age that we are living through, not just in India but across the globe, an examination of our histories and the cross-cultural currents that shaped them is often all the reality check we need to alter our perspectives. Kannadigas understand this well – our state and its capital have benefited greatly from administrators, entrepreneurs, bureaucrats, musicians, sportspeople and even litterateurs who did not have Kannada as their mother tongue; this awareness is perhaps what has traditionally made us so accepting of (respectful) outsiders. But even among the legions of non-Kannadigas who have contributed to our language, culture or history in some way, there are some who stand taller than the others. Among them, no debate, is Rev. Ferdinand Kittel.

Which luminaries a city chooses to honour with full-size statues on its main avenues can tell you a thing or two about that city and its people. Who are they, then, that watch over Bangalore from their respective pedestals? Among others, local heroes like Kempegowda I, founder of the city; Chamarajendra Wadiyar, visionary king who, before his tragic death at 31, not only instituted the Kingdom of Mysore's first representative assembly but also sponsored Swami Vivekananda's legendary visit to the Chicago Parliament of Religions in 1893; Basavanna, celebrated twelfth-century poet–saint and social reformer of the Lingayat tradition, and Dr Rajkumar, beloved thespian and evergreen symbol of Kannada pride, apart from assorted pan-national rock stars like Mahatma Gandhi, Dr B.R. Ambedkar, Jawaharlal Nehru and Swami Vivekananda himself.

Expectedly, the erstwhile British Cantonment – specifically Cubbon Park – features some inherited pedestal-toppers – Queen Victoria, her son Edward VII, and old Mark Cubbon.

And what of the city's marquee boulevard, MG Road? Three eminences grace this 2 km–long ridge that, for a century and a half, played host to British balls, banquets and bacchanalia. At its western end is the aforesaid once-empress of India, looking down her imperial nose at the smaller figure of Mahatma Gandhi in the park opposite (the irony of her still lording it over a street named after him is inescapable, but the scene is so 'adjust-maadi' in its essence that you can't help loving it, either). The third, a lesser-known, less-noticed personage, stands opposite the Mayo Hall.

When I was in high school, one of our Kannada lessons was about a great Kannada scholar who, in 1894, put together one of the very first, and certainly best-known, Kannada–English dictionaries. To our young minds, that someone could compose an *original* dictionary was a thing of wonder in itself (weren't dictionaries born from other dictionaries?). But the fact that this famous lexicon – popularly referred to as *Kittel Nighantu* – was compiled by a German missionary whose native language was neither of the two was frankly astounding. His name, we learnt, was Ferdinand Kittel.

Arriving in India in 1853 at the age of 21 as an ordained priest with the Basel Mission, Kittel was posted straight to Dharwad to begin the task of converting the 'heathens'. Intuiting that a knowledge of the local language would be an invaluable asset in this endeavour, young Ferdinand – already a polyglot, being fluent in Hebrew, Greek and Latin, apart from English – began to earnestly swot it up. A smart thing in hindsight, for he would end up living and working in Karnataka for the next 39 years!

When he first started writing in Kannada, however, Kittel wasn't thinking of dictionaries. One of his earliest works, more in keeping with his brief, was *Kathamale,* a collection of poems on the life of Jesus. But so entranced was he by the language that he quickly moved to more 'secular' work – editing, in the main, an ancient text on Kannada grammar – *Shabdamanidarpana* – and one on prosody – *Chhandombudhi* – that had hitherto only existed as palm-leaf manuscripts, thereby performing a great service to the language and its speakers.

Kittel's crowning achievement and greatest legacy, however, remains the *Nighantu* – a unique combination of lexicon, thesaurus and handbook of literary allusions featuring 70,000 entries, sourced first-hand from every corner of Karnataka, across a whopping 1,758 pages.

Most fitting, then, that the Reverend is part of the MG Road trinity, standing as a symbol neither of imperialism nor peace, but of a large-hearted respect for and celebration of the other. A symbol, in other words, of the city itself.

Even though his name is the most recognized, Kittel wasn't the only, or even the first, German missionary to spend a lifetime in the service of the Kannada language. Seventeen years before Kittel, 25-year-old Hermann Moegling, also of the Basel Mission, had arrived at the ancient port city of Mangalore in Karnataka.

Moegling is best known as the founder–publisher of the first-ever Kannada newspaper, *Mangaluru Samachara*, whose first edition, with a print run of 7,850 copies, came out on 1 July 1843 (today, 1 July is celebrated as Kannada Press Day). But he was also insanely productive otherwise, not only writing much-acclaimed Kannada poetry and a history of Coorg but also compiling, editing and producing, for the very first time, ancient and classical works of Kannada literature in printed form. The series, called 'Bibliotheca Carnataca', included, among other works, Lakshmisha's *Jaimini Bharata* (a version of the Mahabharata), *Dasarapadagalu* (devotional compositions by Purandaradasa and Kanakadasa) and *Shivasharanara Vachanagalu* (metaphysical poetry by Basavanna and others).

HAL WAS FOUNDED ON 22 DECEMBER 1940; AERO INDIA IS HELD IN FEBRUARY EACH YEAR

The Genesis of Bangalore's Soaring Success

In the mid-1950s, a German aeronautical engineer called Kurt Waldemar Tank moved to India as director of the Madras Institute of Technology (where one of his students was A.P.J. Abdul Kalam). A few years later, he joined Hindustan Aeronautics Limited in Bangalore, and helped design India's first military aircraft, the Marut fighter–bomber.

The Marut, which was to be developed according to the specifications (twin-engine configuration, Mach 1.5 speed) provided by the Indian Air Force (IAF), first flew in 1961, but it never attained supersonic speeds. The Indian government rejected Rolls-Royce's offer to design a better engine, the IAF allegedly did not cooperate with Tank, and it is said that the project was mismanaged. In 1967, once the first Marut had been delivered to the IAF (the planes were retired in 1985), Kurt Tank quit HAL and moved back to Germany.

Here's a bit of eye-popping trivia, though: Herr Tank was also the celebrated designer of the Fw 190 (Shrike), the dreaded German Luftwaffe's most reliable single-seat fighter during World War II!

Bengaluru is looking up! Literally. Or will be, when the thrilling flypasts and flying displays of the 14th edition of Asia's largest air show, Aero India, begin in the skies above the Yelahanka Air Force Station. The pièce de résistance at the 2023 'India Pavilion'? A full-scale LCA-Tejas – the highly agile, fourth-generation supersonic fighter jet that other countries have been eyeing for their own air forces – that was designed and built right here in Bengaluru.

When it received its final operational clearance in 2019, Tejas propelled India into the very elite club of countries that have developed their own advanced fighter jet. Small wonder, then, that it is Tejas that is at the heart of the Aero India logo.

There is a lot that is meta about that. The reason the Ministry of Defence chose Bengaluru as the venue for Aero India way back in 1996 was because this city had long been the country's aviation and aerospace hub. The reason Tejas was developed here was for the same reason; both collaborators on the project – the Aeronautical Development Agency (ADA) and the Aircraft Research and Design Centre of Hindustan Aeronautics Limited (HAL) – are based here. The reason HAL is based here is – ah, thereby hangs a tale.

Cut to the year 1939. Fifty-six-year-old Bombay businessman, dreamer and nationalist Seth Walchand Hirachand Doshi, who had built up a huge business empire with interests in construction (HCC, still among India's largest construction firms), sugar and confectionery (Walchandnagar Industries and Ravalgaon, both still doing brisk business), and shipping (the company he founded is acknowledged as the very first swadeshi shipping company), from scratch, was smarting from the rejection his proposal for an automobile manufacturing firm had received from the government. A chance meeting with American tycoon William D. Pawley, who had interests in aviation in China and the US, got him dreaming again. One of Pawley's companies assembled US Navy fighter–bombers at the Huangzhou Airbase for the Chinese Air Force, to help them carry out raids against Japan – instantly inspired, the Seth asked Pawley if he would help him set up India's first aircraft factory.

Pawley bit, as scouting began for a suitable location. Many princely states – Baroda, Bhavnagar, Gwalior and Mysore – were appealed to for support, but none but Mysore, with its savvy, progressive diwan, Mirza Ismail, was forthcoming. Around September 1940, after consulting with the British Resident and the newly installed maharaja, 21-year-old Jayachamaraja Wadiyar, Sir Mirza made the Seth an offer he could not refuse – if Walchand agreed to set up his aircraft factory in Bangalore, the government would not only provide 300 acres of land free of cost, and electricity and water at concessional rates, but also make a generous investment in return for a stake in the company. In December, with Pawley installed as president, Hindustan Aircraft Limited began operations.

Things moved very quickly after that. With the threat of Imperial Japan looming, the British government bought a one-third stake in HAL in April 1941, seeing it as a strategic imperative. By April 1942, they had bought out the Seth, so that they could exercise full control. Mysore refused to sell her stake, but recognizing that trained manpower would be required to keep the factory going, urged the Indian Institute of Science (IISc) to consider opening an Aeronautical Engineering Department, which they did in December 1942, with the pioneering Dr V.M. Ghatage from HAL as its head.

In 1943, HAL was handed over to the US Army Air Forces (USAAF) for the duration of the war, and became the centre for major overhaul and repair of every kind of American military aircraft. By 1945, when control reverted to the Indian government, HAL had become one of the most reputed aircraft tinkering shops in the east, and a steady stream of aeronautical engineers had begun to make their way out of IISc.

The rest is history.

'My husband Rajan's family was very closely associated with the Walchand Hirachand family. Walchand's nephew Vinod Doshi, who headed Premier Automobiles (also part of the Walchand Group), and my father-in-law were college buddies in Mumbai.'

— MADHURI BHENDE, READER FROM PUNE

•

'I remember chairing a session at Aero India years ago. It was a panel on national security. I was invited to do it because I was one of the first women to write about the LCA-Tejas.'

— DR VEENA RAVIKUMAR, POLITICAL AND STRATEGIC AFFAIRS COMMENTATOR

62

BANGALORE TURF CLUB WAS CONCEIVED IN DECEMBER 1920

Cheetahs and Horses: A Fine Bangalore Menagerie

The house where I grew up was very close to the Race Course. When we drove past on race days, there was always a crush of people going in and out of the gates, and crossing the road in the most disorderly fashion. My parents always looked disapproving, muttering 'Betting' under their breaths but offering no other explanation. That did not deter me from eagerly consuming the sports pages of the *Deccan Herald* each morning, particularly the horse-racing news. I loved the names of the horses – Excalibur, Sweet Memories, Excellent Lass, Shamrock, Elusive Pimpernel. I knew that legendary horse trainer Rashid Byramji's horses won most of the races, and that Aslam Kader and Vasant Shinde were champion jockeys. But what tickled me the most was the byline that accompanied the stories: 'by our Racing Correspondent'. I always imagined a hapless reporter, gasping as he galloped around the track with the horses, desperately taking notes as he ran.

That cheetahs were once plentiful in India is easily established – dozens of paintings record them being captured from the wilds of Rajputana during the sixteenth and seventeenth centuries. Emperor Akbar famously had a thousand cheetahs of his own, and used them for coursing (i.e., hunting using animals that hunt by sight, rather than scent) blackbuck and gazelle. The royal cheetahs wore jewelled collars and rode in palanquins, their blindfolds keeping them calm until the hunt began.

Akbar's successor, Jahangir, more famous for his opium addiction and his very capable queen than any political achievements, nevertheless had one great victory – he was the first to successfully breed cheetahs in captivity, in 1613. (The feat would only be repeated three centuries later, in 1956, by the Philadelphia Zoo.) Be that as it may, by the time our feline-loving Tipu Sultan came along, the cheetah population had been severely compromised – he owned merely 16 fine specimens, one of which he gifted to King George III, in 1799. In 1947, Maharaja Ramanuj Pratap Singh Deo of Koriya (in today's Chhattisgarh) reportedly shot the last three Asiatic cheetahs dead.

What was the cheetah doing in the years between Tipu and Singh Deo? In 1930, so the legend goes, one of them was attacking the young, well-muscled Chinna Reddy of village Rangavaram in present-day Tiruvallur, as he kept nightly vigil over his banana plantation. Reddy fought back bravely with his trusty sickle and chased the cheetah away. A few years later, Wimco Limited immortalized the incident on its iconic 'Cheeta Fight' matchboxes.

In our own city, in the first decades of the 1800s, according to *Bengalurina Itihasa* (1986), an acclaimed history of Bangalore by Ba Na Sundara Rao, cheetahs were apparently fighting each other, or British army officers, in a sporting arena located somewhere between Domlur and Austin Town, while bloodthirsty members of the audience bet on their favourites!

Meanwhile, as early as 1752, the official rules of horse racing were formulated by the members of England's Jockey Club in Newmarket, Suffolk. Madras, the British HQ in the south, had its own racecourse by 1777. Bangalore's weather, perfect for the breeding and maintenance of fine Persian steeds, had ensured that there was a surfeit of horses here – from the 1830s onwards, the Mysore cavalry stabled theirs at Kalasipalyam, and the horse-mad commissioner, Sir Mark Cubbon, had over 60 of his own on the grounds of his residence (today's Raj Bhavan) by the time he retired in 1861.

As the cheetahs dwindled in the city, horse racing came to the fore. Naturally, Bangalore's first racecourse – one of the shorter ones at a mile and two furlongs, but more challenging because of the uneven terrain – came up in the largely abandoned cheetah fight arena.

In 1858, the administration passed from the East India Company to the British crown. The military personnel streaming into Bangalore Cantonment needed new barracks, and the racecourse was the ideal location to build them. Scouting began immediately for a new racecourse location. One near Lalbagh was considered, and speedily rejected because it was low-lying (a sensible decision, as recent flooding events have proved). Finally, officials picked a piece of land at the western end of the Cantonment, in the High Grounds.

In March 1921, at a meeting of the stewards of the Bangalore racecourse, the official rules for a new club called the Bangalore Race Club were passed. By May, duly rechristened, the Bangalore Turf Club was inaugurated. A century later, it functions from the same location.

As for the old cheetah fight arena, no vestige remains of it save the name of a street – Old Racecourse Road – in Victoria Layout.

'It's really tragic to read about how we lost our cheetahs in the first place. Also, OMG, I totally remember the green-and-yellow Cheeta Fight matchbox – didn't know there was a story to it!'

— ARATHI DESAI, BANGALOREAN SETTLED IN SINGAPORE

63

R.K. BALIGA WAS BORN ON 29 DECEMBER

The Dazzling 20/20 Vision of Ram Krishna Baliga

When I began studying computer science and engineering at the University Visvesvaraya College of Engineering in 1988, it was still a new and shiny course – Bangalore University had introduced it only in 1982, which meant that only three batches had graduated by the time I came in. For our all-important final year 'Project'. two of my batchmates and I landed a gig at a company called Wipro Infosystems. Personally, I was thrilled – my project-mates were girls who were among the brightest in my batch (which meant I wouldn't have to do very much), we had a sweet young (male) mentor at Wipro and, most importantly, their office was on MG Road, very close to the iconic Gangaram's Book Bureau. Looking back now, I realize what a historic thing it was to be in on the action in the early years of Wipro and IT in Bangalore, and wish I had paid more attention (and swiped a couple of floppy disks as souvenirs).

In March 1976, almost half a century ago, the *Times of India* reported that a newly formed organization called the Karnataka State Electronics Development Corporation Limited (KEONICS) foresaw an 'electronics decade' for the state. With an authorized capital of one crore rupees, the report said, KEONICS aimed at making Karnataka the 'electronics state' of the country.

No one really questioned that claim – at that time, riding on the back of Bharat Electronics Limited (BEL), established in Bangalore as far back as 1954, Karnataka already accounted for 30 per cent of India's total electronics production and a whopping 90 per cent of professional electronics equipment. But few reckoned how wholly the state, and more specifically its capital, Bengaluru, would redeem that pledge. Except for the man who dreamed it up, the first chairman and managing director of KEONICS, Ram Krishna Baliga.

In the year of India's Independence, having completed his K-12 education in his hometown, Mangalore boy Bantwal Ram Krishna Baliga headed to the hallowed College of Engineering, Guindy, for a degree in electrical engineering. A Madras Government Merit Scholarship brought him to Bangalore's Indian Institute of Science (IISc) for a master's in power engineering, which he followed up with a doctoral programme in the same institution. In 1953, an assignment with General Electric (GE) took him to the US, where he would spend three years, moving from GE to Westinghouse Electric before sailing back to India to work at Tata Iron and Steel, Jamshedpur, and Union Carbide, Kolkata. In 1960, Baliga moved back to his home state to teach at our homegrown MIT, the Manipal Institute of Technology, where he set up the department of electrical engineering. He then moved back to Bangalore to join BEL, where he would work for the next 15 years.

Short stints in Paris and Japan, apart from his experiences in the US, had convinced Baliga that what Bangalore needed to kick up the electronics tempo was a 'hi-tech cluster' like California's Silicon Valley, in which the government supported and enabled private entrepreneurs. When he shared his dream with fellow Rotarian G.V.K. Rao, the then chief secretary of Karnataka, in 1975, Rao advised him to come up with a 'white paper' to present to the then chief minister, Devaraj Urs.

Charged, Baliga drew up an audacious plan, identifying 332 acres, 20 km south of Bangalore city, around the villages of Konappana Agrahara and Doddathoguru, for his cluster. 'I see the area between Bangalore and Hosur bubbling with activity,' he said excitedly to Rao. The idea was met with scepticism by almost all concerned, but Urs decided to bite. In months, KEONICS was set up, with Baliga as its chief. In 1978, Baliga's dream, Electronics City, became a reality. The 1981 KEONICS *Annual Report* confirms that Baliga's instinct had been on point – the response from industry had been most encouraging.

Other developments were happening apace. In 1980, a new company called Wipro Information Technology Limited, seeing opportunity in the vacuum left by the unceremonious ouster of IBM from the country in 1977, opened their first office in Bangalore and began developing mini-computers in collaboration with IISc. In 1981, seven engineers with stars in their eyes founded a company called Infosys Technologies in Pune. In 1983, encouraged by the industry-friendly policies of KEONICS, they moved their corporate headquarters to Bangalore.

In 1984, a year before Texas Instruments chose Bangalore to set up India's first software design centre, R.K. Baliga moved on from KEONICS.

In 1988, only 58, the visionary technocrat succumbed to diabetes-related problems, entirely missing the spectacular rise of Electronics City – and the morphing of Garden City to Silicon City – in the wake of India's economic liberalization of 1991.

'Extraordinary foresight! We should celebrate the achievements of people like R.K. Baliga. Naming a prominent circle or street in the area after him would be a good start.'

— G. KUMAR NAIK, RETIRED IAS OFFICER, CURRENTLY MP FROM RAICHUR CONSTITUENCY

•

'Both my parents worked in BEL, so Baliga was a name we heard often at home. Although credit must be given to Chief Minister S.M. Krishna for Bangalore's IT boom, such visionaries as R.K. Baliga, who actually conceived of it and made it happen, should not be forgotten.'

— SHAINI V., SENIOR SECONDARY SCHOOL TEACHER

•

'I did not know this backstory at all! This offers much-needed perspective to the younger generation on Bangalore's journey to becoming India's IT capital. It is unimaginable for me that there was an electronics company in Bangalore as early as 1954. You have goaded me to learn more about the past of my own city, Chennai.'

— HARI RAM NARAYANAN, AUTHOR AND SOFTWARE EXECUTIVE, CHENNAI

64

CHRISTMAS

In Bengaluru, the Ghosts of Christmases Past Linger

My first alma mater, where I studied from Class 1 to 10, was the Stella Maris Girls' High School in Vyalikaval. It was a missionary school, run by the Sisters of Charity, but a more secular school would be hard to find. Most of our teachers were Hindu, the student body was made up of that wonderful mix of Christian, Muslim, Hindu and Jain kids drawn from across the socio-economic spectrum that only missionary schools seem to be able to gather, and Catechism was mandatory only for the Catholic girls; the rest of us were taught 'moral science'. And yet, despite that liberal atmosphere, or perhaps because of it, we knelt, voluntarily, at the grotto of Mother Mary before an exam, longed to be allowed into the convent's hushed, high-ceilinged chapel, and looked forward most eagerly to Christmas and the annual Nativity play. In the '70s, in the circles that I moved in, those were not Christian things, just Bangalore things.

In less than a week, it will be Christmas, the season when the erstwhile Bangalore Cantonment comes into its own. Once again, the old Cantonment churches will draw legions of the faithful to midnight mass to celebrate the birth of the Christ-child, as they have done for well-nigh 200 years. In missionary-run schools in the Cantonment and beyond, children of all religions will sing Christmas carols, partaking joyfully in an old, time-honoured Bangalore tradition.

Which begs the question, how old? The records of the St Thomas Christians, or the Syrian Christians, attest that Christianity was introduced to the subcontinent, specifically Kerala, by 'Doubting' Thomas, one of the 12 hand-picked apostles of Jesus himself, who sailed to the Malabar coast in 52 CE. Remarkably, Christianity would take another 1,500 years to make landfall in neighbouring Karnataka. That happened when Goan Catholics migrated down the coast to Dakshina Kannada (South Canara) in three waves, from the sixteenth century onwards.

The first wave of refugees came in 1560, fleeing the Goan Inquisition imposed by the Portuguese, who persecuted 'New Christians' (mostly Hindus who had been forcibly converted) suspected to be secretly worshipping their old gods. The second came between 1570 and 1575, when a pan-Asian alliance – comprising, among others, the Sultanate of Bijapur and the Sultanate of Aceh (in present-day Indonesia) – launched a combined assault against the Portuguese in Goa. The third wave arrived in 1683, during the Maratha–Portuguese War, which broke out after the death of Chhatrapati Shivaji.

Well before this, however, Christianity had ventured inland. In 1649, an Italian Jesuit called Leonardo Cinnami established the Mysore Mission in Srirangapatna, the then capital of the Wadiyars of Mysore, opening the doors to a rocky relationship between the Wadiyar court and the Christians.

In 1763, Hyder Ali, who had established himself as de facto ruler of Mysore, captured Mangalore, which put him in the crosshairs of a formidable new enemy in the peninsula, the British. The latter took Mangalore in 1767, and hung on to it until 1784, when Hyder's son, Tipu Sultan, won it back. Furious with the Mangalorean Catholics, who he believed had aided the British during the war, Tipu captured 60,000 of them, marched them to Srirangapatna, converted them to Islam and kept them in captivity for over 15 years, until his defeat and death in May 1799.

With the throne of Mysore occupied by a new Wadiyar king, whose actions had to be approved by a British Resident, peace returned to the Christians. By 1803, Bengaluru had got its first thatched-roof chapel, in an area that the British called Blackpally (today's Shivajinagar). Set up by the French Catholic missionary Jean-Antoine Dubois, affectionately referred to as Dodda Swami-avaru, it was a chapel to the Virgin Mary. In 1813, it was expanded with British help to become the Church of the Purification of Our Lady. Today, further enhanced, it stands on the same location, as the St Mary's Basilica. Taking inspiration from Abbe Dubois, who adopted the local garb, Mother Mary is always draped in a saree here.

By 1807, a year after the maharaja of Mysore had granted 900 acres to the east of Bengaluru Pete for the construction of a British Cantonment, Bengaluru's first Protestant church, the Drummers' Chapel (later the Fort Church), came up next to Tipu's Summer Palace for the use of the British troops. Today, the Vani Vilas Hospital (Obstetrics and Gynaecology) stands in its place. In 1808, a brand-new garrison church – the St Mark's Cathedral – was commissioned at the western end of South Parade (MG Road) in the heart of the Cantonment.

Enough with the history, folks – get out there and have yourself a very merry Bengaluru Christmas! 'Tis the season!

'I loved reading that children of all religions in Bangalore sing Christmas carols! And that Mother Mary is dressed in a saree! What bothers me, though – and it happened a lot in ancient times and continues to happen – is the messing around with people and their faith, and the imposition of a different belief system. What happens externally – religious things – are not important, what is important is what lives in our hearts. What is important is that we love one another. That, of course, is the true Christmas message.'

— MIRELLA ZIJP, WRITING IN FROM THE NETHERLANDS

•

'The 60,000 Mangaloreans – I'm glad you mention them. Not because it reads as a criticism of Tipu – it doesn't – but because it lays out the privations of war. It's like Hemingway said in his introduction to the anthology of war stories – *Men at War* – that he edited: *The Germans are not successful because they are supermen. They are simply practical professionals in war*. . .'

— RAMJEE CHANDRAN, HOST OF *THE HISTORY OF BANGALORE* PODCAST

65

THE NEW YEAR – AND BEER!

Here's to a Happy, Hoppy New Year!

Peco's, Black Cadillac, NASA, Guzzler's Inn, Windsor, White Horse – if these names spark instant recognition and deep nostalgia, you were probably partying in Bangalore in the '80s and '90s, swigging crisp, cold, cheap draught beer and grooving to rock anthems, thanking your stars that you lived in a city so sophisticated that no one batted an eyelid if a group of college girls walked into a pub in the middle of the afternoon and ordered a round. You probably sniggered a little at those poor sods from Madras who took the Friday overnight bus to Bangalore and, freed from the tyranny of TASMAC for 48 hours, went a bit overboard. And you probably cannot believe your luck that a good three decades later, your city, with over 70 microbreweries (and new largest-in-Asia ones opening all the time), is still way ahead of the rest of the country at the barley-hops game. Cheers to that!

On 31 December, as Bengalureans ring out the old year and ring in the new, thousands of sweating pitchers of this metropolis' favourite tipple will be joyfully quaffed by its citizenry. While sophisticated palates will debate the merits of a Chocolate Coffee Stout versus a Basmati Blonde, others will lean on the crisp, comforting predictability of the world-famous local lager. Regardless, each will be participating in a century-old city tradition.

Beer is no stranger to India – the Vedas mention a beer-like drink called sura, and tribal societies have brewed, for millennia, some form of rice beer. European-style beer, however, came to India only in the eighteenth century, imported from England to wet the grateful throats of East India Company (EIC) employees wilting in a tropical climate most unsuitable for brewing it.

It was the Bow Brewery, in London's East End, that first cornered the Indian market in the 1780s. Its shrewd proprietor, George Hodgson, leveraged his small brewery's proximity to the EIC docks as an enticement, apart from extending a generous line of credit. Hodgson's brewery was famous for a dark, working-class beer called porter, but his fortunes really turned when he added another lighter beer – October beer – to his offerings. The six-month-long, sea-tossed journey to a warmer clime worked on October beer in ways no one had anticipated – by the time it reached Indian shores, it had matured into a drink that EIC officers took to with relish. That was the genesis of the beer we know today as IPA – India Pale Ale.

Hodgson's son (as sons will) changed the Bow Brewery's business practices when he took over, cutting off credit to the EIC. It didn't go down well – the EIC turned to Allsopp's brewery in Burton-on-Trent, a beer-brewing region that was suffering from the Napoleonic blockades of the European markets, for a customized version of October beer. Perhaps it was the water of the River Trent that made the difference, or the fact that it was more 'hoppy' and had a higher alcohol content, but Allsopp's IPA became the toast of the EIC's top brass in India.

Around 1830, the first Indian brewery came up in Kasauli in Himachal Pradesh. It was set up by – hold your breath – Edward Abraham Dyer, the father of the more infamous Colonel Dyer, 'the butcher of Jallianwala Bagh', and produced Asia's first beer brand, Lion, still in production and today the signature beer brand of Sri Lanka. (Fun fact: Dyer Breweries, incorporated in 1885, has been Mohan Meakin Breweries since 1967.) By 1882, there were 12 breweries in British India, including two in south India.

In 1915, Scotsman Thomas Leishman combined five south Indian breweries – the Castle Brewery (founded in 1857), Nilgiri Breweries (1857), Bangalore Brewing Company (1885), British Brewing Corp (1903) and BBB Brewery Company Limited (1913) – to form United Breweries (now UB). Draught bullocks pulled hogsheads of freshly brewed lager (now you know why it's called draught beer!) from the brewery (which was located where UB City stands now) to pubs that had naturally sprung up around the brewery, in the erstwhile British cantonment.

In 1946, a 22-year-old prodigy from Karnataka called Vittal Mallya began buying up UB stock. The very next year, he became UB's first Indian director, and soon after, its chairman. In 1950, UB came home for good to Bengaluru.

Today, one of the city's best-known microbreweries offers a ragi-based ale they call 'Namma Beeru' – our beer. The state's Kuruba community may have a quibble with that. To them, Namma Beeru would probably bring to mind their beloved deity, Lord Beereshwara, to whom a temple stands right by the Mallya Hospital, a stone's throw away from where the city's most famous brewery once stood.

'G and I are on vacation, and currently drinking Lion beer in Sri Lanka! Thank you for that deliciously frothy tidbit of trivia!'

— DIPTI RAO, DGM, PRESTIGE CENTRE FOR THE PERFORMING ARTS

•

'Really enjoyed this piece. An article by a writer I admire on the local history of my favourite drink in a city I love. And no, I did not know that fun fact about "draught" beer!'

— ARVIND KRISHNAN, BANGALORE ENTREPRENEUR

•

'Great read. You should know that I contribute in my small way to the story of Bangalore beer. I have a "nano" brewery at home (most people do not know that beer can be brewed at home) where I make small batches of craft beer and teach others how to brew as well.'

— THE LATE DR KISHORE NAYAK, FORMER DEAN AT THE BANGALORE INSTITUTE OF DENTAL SCIENCES

66

THE FIRST BANGALORE PRESS CALENDAR IN ENGLISH CAME OUT IN JANUARY 1921, THE FIRST KANNADA ONE IN 1936

The Bangalore Press and Its Iconic Calendar

Who would have thought that a maharaja who was ranked among the world's wealthiest individuals and hailed as the second richest Indian (his personal fortune in the 1930s was assessed at 57, 901 crore rupees) would be so cut up about the cost of printing the invitations for his own wedding that it would rankle even 12 years later? Who could have imagined what the fallout of that recollection would be? But kings, as we know, are not regular people.

It's the fourth day of the new year, which means that in hundreds of thousands of Bangalore homes, the annual ritual of hanging up a fresh red-and-black calendar from The Bangalore Press has been completed to everyone's satisfaction. What many of the calendar's loyalists perhaps do not realize is that this tradition is over a century old – the first calendar was published in 1921!

The story of how The Bangalore Press came to be is probably apocryphal but very plausible. In the year 1912, a dozen years after Maharaja Krishnarajendra Wadiyar IV was married to Pratapa Kumari Ammanni, he happened to mention to his newly appointed diwan, Mokshagundam Visvesvaraya (Sir M.V.), how expensive the wedding invitations had been to print, joking that he could have used the money to set up a printing press instead. That was it. Sir M.V. decided that princely Mysore would have its own printing press, and got to work on turning the idea into reality.

The British government, as expected, was less than enthusiastic. Concerned that the press would be used to print anti-colonial propaganda, they refused to support the idea financially. The state itself could not afford it. Not to be daunted, Sir M.V. set up a public limited company – The Bangalore Printing and Publishing Company – with 18 eminent personalities, including the philanthropist–administrator Sir K.P. Puttanna Chetty and the polymath–polyglot scholar C. Hayavadana Rao, and established The Bangalore Press on the premises of the State Bank of Mysore on Kempegowda Road, in 1916 (which makes it one of India's oldest existing companies).

With such stalwarts as its founding fathers, the press was bound to go places. The first calendar, published in 1921, was a runaway success, in part due to its clean design, but mostly because it was the first complete 'Indian' calendar in English. In consultation with Hindu and Muslim astrologers, archbishops and Jain religious leaders, the calendar listed auspicious times and important festival and other dates for all religions, apart from lunar and solar months, full moon and new moon nights, sunrise and moonrise times, and more. All this, in addition to general holidays, bank holidays and restricted holidays, among others!

The calendar's designer, Bengaluru Puttaiah, was quite a legend himself. In 1912, Puttaiah was sent off to London for a course in printing technology by his employers, the British-run Government Press (the building in which this press was housed was set up in 1871 – over 130 years later, the heritage structure was knocked down to make way for the Vikasa Soudha). In 1915, the Bengaluru boy did his city proud by topping the list of candidates taking the typography exam for the UK and the colonies. Naturally, Sir M.V. co-opted him for the calendar design project.

Puttaiah's design looked very much like the current one, except that the floral border was green instead of red (the red was adopted in 1960). But the really unique thing about it was that it was a 'vertical' calendar – weeks are arranged vertically, instead of the more common horizontal convention.

The first Kannada calendar from The Bangalore Press was published in 1936 – it was Jnanpith award–winner Masti Venkatesh Iyengar, then a senior copywriter at the press, who pushed for it, offering the press the rights to all his future works in return – a great bargain for the latter, as it turned out!

Today, The Bangalore Press prints over 18 lakh calendars each year, and is valued at a staggering 200 crore rupees. To its fans in India and across the world – nostalgic NRIs who visit over Christmas pick up a calendar or ten – it continues to be a priceless, beloved link to their past.

'Happy new year! What an interesting and informative article about the Bangalore Press calendar! It was nice to remember all the great souls of yesteryear. Incidentally, we are currently visiting our daughters in the US, and my husband has already requested my sister to reserve copies of the calendar for us so that we have it ready to put up when we return, haha.'

— BRINDA RAO, FREELANCE WRITER IN KANNADA AND ENGLISH-TO-KANNADA TRANSLATOR

•

'That red, white and black calendar always takes a prominent spot in my parents' home. Since that one cannot be touched, I tried replacing an SBI calendar in our kitchen with a nice Audobon calendar I had brought with me, and got thoroughly ticked off by my mom, who squealed, "How will I know the bank holidays without it?" Bangaloreans and their calendars!'

— RUPA KRISHNAN, BANGALOREAN SETTLED IN CALIFORNIA

•

'My yearly must-have is two Bangalore Press calendars – one the tabletop version on which I keep track of milk and newspaper delivery, and a wall calendar for putting down my children's exam dates. Had no idea there was such a wonderful history to it!'

— MALATHI N.S., CHARTERED ACCOUNTANT

67

RAI BAHADUR ARCOT NARRAINSWAMY MUDALIAR RECEIVED HIS TITLE IN THE DELHI DURBAR HELD IN JANUARY 1877

The Vegetable Seller Who Built the Attara Kacheri

Time was when there were seven (as far as I knew) single-screen movie theatres in the Bangalore Cantonment – Galaxy, Symphony, Rex, Blumoon, Bludiamond, Lido and Plaza. All of them only played English-language films, and the biggest Sunday treat for my sister and me was to be taken to watch a matinee show at one of them. A few years later, we were thrilled to discover that two of my brother's best friends in school belonged to the family that part-owned the Plaza. The land on which the Plaza stood had first been acquired, they told me, by an ancestor who had overseen the construction of the beautiful neoclassical nineteenth-century structure called the Attara Kacheri, which stands opposite the Vidhana Soudha. Sadly, I never watched a movie for free at the Plaza – mum would not allow me to exploit connections in that way – but I did get to be good friends with both boys, and remain so to this day.

In 2014, one of Bangalore Cantonment's iconic landmarks, the 78-year-old Plaza Theatre, bowed out, to make room for the Plaza Metro Station. With it went the heady aroma of fresh popcorn that wafted daily out of its lobby to evening shoppers (and loafers!) on MG Road, signalling the imminent intermission of the matinee show.

To nostalgic Bangaloreans, this was a tragedy, a slice of their youth crushed under the juggernaut of progress. In truth, it was only one more of the many transitions the site had been through over the last 200 years. Our focus today is The Bangalore Agency, the establishment that preceded the Plaza, and its proprietor, the Right Honourable Dharmaratnakara Rai Bahadur Arcot Narrainswamy Mudaliar.

That's a right mouthful, but the Rao Bahadur didn't start out that way. As a boy, he was plain old Narrainswamy from the town of Arcot in the Madras Presidency. In 1837, his father, Muniappa Mudaliar, who had migrated to Bangalore in search of work, died unexpectedly, leaving the 10-year-old behind as primary breadwinner. A dozen years of doing all manner of odd jobs later, Narrain's hereditary trading instincts kicked in. Noticing that vegetables – including 'English' ones like peas, potatoes, carrots and cauliflower – were plentifully and cheaply available in cool, misty Bangalore, while Madras was starved of them, Narrain set himself up as a travelling salesman, soon getting a sweet two-way supply line going – selling Bangalore veggies in Madras and Madras salt in Bangalore.

In time, the trade grew and flourished, allowing Narrain to open a little supermarket at Cavalry Road, and then a branch at the Infantry Road Barracks, to service the needs of the British military. His list of clients was impressive, and in 1859, grew to include the maharaja of Mysore, Krishnaraja

Wadiyar III – himself. A grateful Narrain lost no time in renaming his store 'Mysore Hall'.

The real windfall was yet to come, however. In the early 1860s, the commissioner of Bangalore, Lord Bowring, contracted the construction firm, Wallace & Co., to build the city a spanking new set of Public Offices, which had been designed by the chief engineer of Mysore, Major General Richard Sankey. Learning on the barracks grapevine that the firm meant to subcontract, Narrain partnered with the banker Bansilal Ramrathan to launch a bid, and won! By the time the vision of loveliness called the Attara Kacheri (today the High Court of Karnataka) opened its doors in 1868, Narrain had become a very wealthy man. Soon he had diversified into real estate, auctioneering, livestock and banking, with all business being conducted from new premises at 19, South Parade (today's MG Road). That establishment was The Bangalore Agency.

Still in his early forties, the 'Merchant Prince of Bangalore' now had the time and space to focus on the things he really wanted to do. His readings of the works of the great Tamil saints had made him deeply philosophical, and he was keen to use his wealth for social reform and formal education, which he himself had been denied. Realizing that there were no schools in the Cantonment for 'native' children, whether boys or girls, he began by setting up a free English primary school in 1873. Other initiatives followed fast on its heels – schools for girls, orphanages, choultries, even a technical school for civil engineering.

At the magnificent Delhi Durbar of 1877, the viceroy of India, Lord Lytton, conferred on Narrain the title of Rai Bahadur. In 1894, an appreciative Chamaraja Wadiyar X honoured him with the title 'Dharmaratnakara'.

Today, the over 15 RBANM (you know what the initials stand for now!) educational institutions in the Ulsoor area celebrate the legacy of this prince turned philanthropist.

Lord Bowring's New Public Offices soon came to be known as the Attara Kacheri, which translates to 'Eighteen Departments'. That name was originally given to the system of administration used by Mughal emperor Aurangzeb, which was adopted by the Mysore king Chikka Devaraja Wadiyar after he bought Bengaluru from the Mughals for three lakh rupees in 1684. Among the 18 administrative departments were the treasury, the cavalry, the infantry, the police, the postal department, the department of sandalwood and the Huzur office (which dealt with the payment of salaries of secretariat staff, courts, heads of government departments, and others). The same system was carried on by the British when they took over the direct administration of Mysore between 1831 and 1881. Today, even though the business conducted inside it only relates to the dispensing of justice, the skinny, low-slung beauty decked out in 'Pompeiian red' is still often referred to as Attara Kacheri.

68

SOPHIA'S HIGH SCHOOL WAS FOUNDED JANUARY 1949

Girls Getting Schooled: A Bengaluru Story

Well before the phrase 'getting schooled' took on the morally superior and low-key aggressive vibe of 'teaching someone a lesson' that it has today, it simply meant what it said – 'being formally educated.' That privilege was accorded to the young female population of our always progressive city rather early, thanks to the efforts of Christian missionaries and the liberal policies of the maharajas. If the London Missionary Society founded the Canarese Girls' School in the Pete in 1840, Krishnaraja Wadiyar III established the Old Vani Vilas Girls' School in the City Market Area in 1868. By 1902, there were 235 public schools for girls in the kingdom, with a combined enrolment of 12,500 students. In 1906, two students of the Maharani's College, Mysore – Rukminiyamma and Srirangamma – created history by becoming the first women in south India to be awarded a BA degree.

On 3 August 2024, the city's venerable Sophia High School celebrated its 75th birthday with much fanfare. For the legions of girls who have passed through its portals since it was founded, less than two years after India became independent, the anniversary served as an occasion for an outpouring of nostalgia and gratitude for their alma mater.

Old as it is, however, Sophia's is by no means the oldest girls' school in Bangalore. That honour belongs to a Canarese (Kannada) girls' school on Mission Road that predates Sophia's by, hold your breath, over one hundred years.

The impetus towards modern institutional education for girls (and boys) in India was provided, in many ways, by the British Charter Act of 1813, which, among other things, extended the East India Company's (EIC) rule for 20 years, granted permission to Christian missionaries to travel to India to promote 'moral and religious improvements', and sanctioned a sum of 1,00,000 rupees annually for the education of Indians. Unfortunately, that funding lay unused for two decades, stymied by bitter unresolved debates between the Orientalists (who wanted to use it to promote traditional education in classical Sanskrit and Persian to Indians) and the faction led by the governor's councillor, Thomas Babington Macaulay, which believed Western education in English was where it was at.

In 1833, the EIC's 20-year-charter came up for renewal and was granted, but the debates continued unabated. In February 1835, Macaulay's impassioned 'Minute on Education', a paper in which he argued in favour of English education for Indians, and the support he received from the then governor general of India, Sir William Bentinck, gave victory to the latter faction. As quickly as March 1835, the English Education Act made English the official language of India and the language of higher education.

Meanwhile, on the missionary front, the first Wesleyan Mission in India had been established in Madras as early as 1817; by 1821, Rev. Elijah Hoole had not only set up a branch in the Bangalore Cantonment but also applied to the Government of Madras for permission to set up a school for the local population. While Macaulay and his ilk wanted to teach Indians English to create a sympathetic workforce that could help the British administer the country, the missionaries were doing the opposite – mastering Indian languages to be able to deliver sermons, translate the Bible, compose hymns and build bonds with local communities. Missionaries in Bangalore Cantonment and Pettah were also keenly reading Kannada, Tamil and Telugu literature, and translating both religious and secular texts from those languages into English.

Both Macaulay and the missionaries, however, were also keen to bring modern ideas and education – including maths, geography, literature and the sciences – to Indians. To this end, the Wesleyan Mission set up, for the first time, printing presses in regional languages, to print vernacular Bibles, original research work on culture and customs, and, of course, school textbooks.

Which brings us back to the question of the oldest school for girls in Bangalore. Never mind that the Wesleyans got here first, it was the London Missionary Society (LMS) that beat them, and the Cantonment, to it. Well before 1855, when the Wesleyan Tamil Girls School (known since 1905 as the Goodwill Girls' High School, and located on Promenade Road), came up, Mrs Sewell and Mrs Rice (wife of Rev. Benjamin Rice and mother of the great Kannada epigraphist B.L. Rice), had, in 1840, set up the Canarese Girls School in the Pettah.

Once the Wesleyans and the LMS merged in 1920, that school came to be called the United Mission School; post 1947, it was christened the Mitralaya

Girls School. To this day, 184 years after it was first founded, Mitralaya, like Goodwill, continues to educate and empower the girls of Bangalore.

'I teach a course on social movement; for any movement to become social, it has to be first awakened by its social history. Your articles offer great insights into that aspect of Bangalore and Karnataka's history. For a reader like me, who is new to the city and the "ethnic other", they are very illuminating.'

— DEVANJAN KHUNTIA, ALLIANCE UNIVERSITY

•

'What a lovely slice of educational history – the first school for girls in Bangalore set up in 1840! Now that is very early in the whole process of social reform emphasizing women's rights in India. I suspect the lead in this wider female emancipation, however, was taken by the Bengal and Bombay presidencies. Of the four major socio-religious reform institutions of the nineteenth century – Brahmo Samaj, Paramhansa Mandali, Satyashodhak Samaj (founded by Jyotiba Phule in Pune) and Prarthana Samaj – three were from Maharashtra. My maternal grandmother, who grew up in Bombay, was among the very first Indian women who went to the UK for a medical degree. It would be intriguing to unearth how the women's reform movements evolved in the old Mysore state, especially Bangalore. A future column of yours?'

— JAYENDRA NAYAK, FORMER CEO AND CHAIRMAN, AXIS BANK

69

THE 125TH BIRTHDAY OF CHAMARAJPET WAS CELEBRATED ON 28 JANUARY 2017

Bengaluru Urban: A New Extension Called Chamarajpet

I have never needed much dental work – lucky me! – but my older sister got braces put in when she was in high school. And because mum could not leave me behind for the long hours my sister would spend on the dentist's chair, I got to spend a large chunk of my vacation, one long-ago summer, hanging around the Government Dental Hospital in Chamarajpet. Once she was done, we would all walk over to the Victoria Hospital next door, where my uncle was the head of the Department of Medicine, to be taken out for lunch and ice cream. Sometimes, because both my sister and I had notoriously poor eyesight, we would also do a pitstop at the Minto Eye Hospital down the road for a check-up. Until I was much older, that was all Chamarajpet would mean to me – hospitals – but without any of the sting.

In January 2017, a rather unusual anniversary was marked with much fanfare in the heart of Bangalore. It was the 125th birthday of one of the city's oldest planned residential 'extensions' – the venerable Chamarajpet. Given that it had been named after Chamaraja Wadiyar X, and that several of its residents were descendants of the original families that had settled there in the 1890s, the current Mysore royals, including Maharaja Yaduveer Chamaraja (yup, another Chamaraja) Wadiyar, graced the event. As they proceeded to the Kote Venkataramana Swamy Temple (built by one of their predecessors in the seventeenth century) to perform the pujas that would kick off the celebrations, they waved and beamed at the crowds lining the streets, from a golden chariot. It was all very yesterday once more.

Except it wasn't. Not entirely. For Chamarajpet still retains a considerable amount of its old-world charm. Somehow, the sweeping changes that have blasted through sections of the city, rendering them unrecognizable even to people who grew up there in the '70s, have more or less spared this particular five-Mains-nine-Crosses (non-Bangaloreans may have a bit of trouble deciphering that!) rectangular street grid that was meticulously laid out in 1892.

To no one's surprise, this pioneering initiative, like so many others, was the brainchild of Mysore's longest-serving diwan, K. Seshadri Iyer, who also commissioned Asia's largest hydroelectric project at Shivanasamudra, the Victoria Hospital, and the Glass House at Lalbagh, apart from urging his king, Nalvadi Krishnaraja Wadiyar, to donate 370 acres of prime land in Bangalore to a certain J.N. Tata to set up a premier institute of scientific research in 1909 (today, it is the Indian Institute of Science).

Iyer had his reasons for setting up a new extension. For one, the narrow streets of the City (Pete) had grown too congested and insanitary to hold its burgeoning population (up from 62,000 to 80,000 in the 1880s alone!), and cholera outbreaks were a constant concern. Worse, on the other side of the tracks, the British-administered Cantonment was expanding and flourishing like the green bay tree. The situation called for decisive action. Some 150 acres of land to the west of the Pete were quickly acquired, and close to 1,000 plots – most of them in the somewhat odd size of 30x108 ft – were marked out for sale. Specific clusters were reserved for specific castes and religions, for the cosmopolitan Pete abounded with Muslims (settlers from Hyder and Tipu's reign in the eighteenth century), Christians (from the time of the British occupation in the nineteenth century), and traders and weavers and makers of all persuasions who had come in when the Pete was first built by Kempegowda in the sixteenth century.

Chamarajpet's northernmost 'Main' was named Albert Victor Road (AV Road) after the grandson of Queen Victoria, who had, during his tour of India in 1889, laid the foundation stone of the Lalbagh Glass House, less than 3 km away. Today, it continues to be AV Road, except it now honours Aluru Venkata Rao of the Kannada Unification Movement (see page 219).

By the mid-1890s, the new extension was entirely ready for occupation, but not many were excited. The residents of the Pete didn't quite fancy living out in the 'wilds'. It was only when the plague swept through Bangalore in

1898 that things changed. By the turn of the century, with every plot sold, most built on and occupied, and close to 5,000 residents, Chamarajpet was on its way.

Tipu Sultan's Summer Palace, a popular tourist destination in Chamarajpet, has a rather melancholy history. When Tipu's father, Hyder Ali, first took over as ruler of Mysore in 1761, he realized how important the seventeenth-century Bengaluru Fort was, given its strategic location between the British stronghold of Madras and his own capital of Srirangapatna. He made it one of his first tasks, therefore, to repair and strengthen the fort. Twenty years later, Hyder began the construction of a palace inside the fort. Tragically, he died the very next year. Tipu completed the building in 1791, just before Lord Cornwallis's forces attacked and breached the Bengaluru Fort and claimed the palace for themselves. The British returned the palace to Tipu in 1792, as per the treaty signed after their victory in the Third Anglo-Mysore War, but he swore he would not occupy it until he had destroyed the British. Sadly, that never came to be – Tipu was killed in the heat of battle during the Fourth Anglo-Mysore War in May 1799.

70

THE ANNUAL AVAREKAI MELA IS HELD IN JANUARY

The Enduring Romance of the Humble Avarekai

I would not swear to it, but if memory serves, this essay, when it was published in the *Hindustan Times* Bangalore edition, got more excited responses than any other. One attentive reader sent me a link to a review of Toast & Tonic, rock-star chef Manu Chandra's lovely, cosy restaurant on Wood Street in Ashok Nagar. One of the dishes mentioned in the review was 'Warm Asparagus, Avarekai and Green Beans Salad.' Now, Chandra has always been innovative, but his inclusion of avarekai in a fine-dining restaurant menu reveals why he is also super successful – he 'gets' his market.

Whether it costs upwards of 400 bucks in an upscale bistro or less than 100 bucks on the street, however, you may count me out of the avarekai party. I am both Kannadiga and Bangalorean, but I do not care for the bean. (Yes, I am aware I have just committed social suicide. Goodbye, cruel world.)

Come winter, and the 'sogadu' (a Kannada word variously and appropriately translated as quintessence, fragrance, the condition of being addicted to a taste, and 'something remembered') of the humble flat bean called avarekai (avarekalu / avarebele) takes over the Kannadiga soul.

In a time-honoured Bengaluru tradition, people have thronged the markets over the last few weeks to buy up quantities of avarekai. In a parallel tradition, nostalgic outpourings about the communal shelling of the bean in the family kitchen and recipes for the various beloved dishes that showcase it – avarekalu usli, huli, rotti, uppittu, bisibelebath, and the grande dame, hitikidbele (avarekalu with the sheath around each bean sloughed off, leaving only the tenderest inner bean) saaru – have been enthusiastically traded.

In Karnataka, we are used to thinking of avarekalu as 'our bean', and with good reason. The name of the state's capital, according to an apocryphal tale of generosity featuring the people of this town, was originally Bendakaalooru, or 'the town of boiled beans' (for beans, read avarekai). In addition, Karnataka accounts for a staggering 90 per cent of the country's production of the bean. Fortunately, through careful stewarding by common people through the centuries, the domestic market is proportionately gargantuan.

A recent effort in the same tradition that has given the bean – and those who grow it – a huge leg-up in Bengaluru is the annual Avarekai Mela (which has seen more than 20 editions to date), founded by Geetha Shivakumar of Sri Vasavi Condiments, VV Puram. The store has been around since 1995, but it was only when Geetha noticed the plight of the avarekai farmers from Magadi, who, at the end of each day of selling their beans at the Sajjan Rao Circle, simply dumped the unsold stock into the gutters (avarekai, especially the skinned variety, has a short shelf life – deep fry it, however, and it turns into a delicious, protein-rich snack that keeps well for up to a year), that she decided to do something about it. A festival hero-ing the bean, at which people would not only be able to buy the raw produce but also enjoy a mind-boggling variety of dishes made from it seemed like a good idea.

Geetha's intuition was right on the button. From the very year of its inception, the mela has been an unqualified success, and is now one of the most awaited events on Bengaluru's cultural calendar.

Which is all wonderful, but still leaves us with two important questions: Where did avarekai come from, originally? And, more importantly, what is the avarekai's English name? In the nineteenth century, English botanist Robert Sweet, often described as the first practical botanist, changed the genus of the avarekai plant from *Dolichos* (Linnaeus's classification) to *Lablab* (in the early Proto-Indo–European tongue, 'lab' meant a blade, or something that hung down loosely, and the scimitar-shaped hanging pod of the avarekai might have inspired Sweet). He clearly believed the avarekai was special – he classified it as the only species in the Lablab genus, and gave it the botanical name *Lablab purpureus.* The common English name for avarekai, however, is – never be stumped again! – hyacinth bean (perhaps the efflorescence reminded people of the hyacinth flower: one variety of the bean has purple pods and blooms).

As for where avarekai came from, after a debate spanning centuries, botanists agree that although archaeological evidence clearly shows that it has been in India for at least 2,000 years, its original home base was eastern Africa, specifically Ethiopia. Within India itself, scientific and linguistic evidence indicates that it was the Dravidian peoples who introduced it into human diets and the rest of the country. Yup, always knew it was ours!

Oho, loved reading this! Never knew anything about this kaalu except that it is so, so delicious. Have got my northie family used to eating akki tari uppittu with avarebele and hitikidbele saaru. Off to share your article with other avare-devotees now!

— RADHIKA SATHE MANTRI, EDUCATOR AND LIBRARIAN

•

This is definitely a Bangalore love story – my robust and extensive clinical testing has shown that you need to be Bangalore-born and / or -bred, to love this bean in the way a Bangalorean would – so mad about it that we can eat it at every meal during the season. Some of my cousins born outside of Bangalore do not like it, which I find STAGGERING and CONTEMPTIBLE (the hyacinth bean does elicit the strongest of emotions).

— PRIYA NARAYAN, BANGALOREAN LIVING IN LONDON

•

My fave bean! Just made avarekai akki rotti last night, which my kids love. And the hidikavare [same as hitikidbele] is also a huge favourite, which my mom makes every year during the season and sends to us here in freezing Virginia.

— REKHA RAGHURAM, BANGALOREAN LIVING IN HERNDON, VIRGINIA

71

BANGALORE'S ROHAN BOPANNA BECAME WORLD NO. 1 IN MEN'S DOUBLES IN TENNIS IN JANUARY 2024

Why Bangaloreans Have Always Been Good Sports

I have never played a sport at any level, leave alone competitively. I'm not proud of it, but I'm not ashamed of it either – it's just who I am. I don't even watch much sport. But what I do, with much joy, is read about sportspeople. I seek out their backstories, follow their journeys, cheer their wins, worry about their injuries, stalk my favourites on Instagram. . . When a sportsperson also happens to be Bangalorean, my level of engagement, in the language of my city's tech bros, is 100x. And that can get pretty exhausting, especially when there are so many of them (Bangalore sportspeople, I mean, not techies, although the Lord knows there are far too many of those as well).

PS: Entire sporting disciplines, and champion sportspeople from Bangalore, have been left out of this column. Mea culpa, but it is the tyranny of the word limit that is the real culprit.

Last week, sports fans in India exploded with joy when Rohan Bopanna was crowned men's doubles World No. 1 at the Australian Open, making him, at almost 44, the oldest player ever to hold that coveted position. Back home, Bengaluru preened at the success of its homegrown lad, but with practised flair; the city is used to its boys and girls doing rather well in the global sporting arena.

Strangely, Bengaluru's vibrant sporting culture is not acknowledged as much as its podium-finish performances in other races, including IT, biotech, education, aerospace, microbreweries and start-up unicorns. But the city has always had a strong leaning towards sport, partly because of a fortuitous coming together of several different factors – its clement year-round weather, which renders any kind of al fresco activity a pleasure; its undulating topography, which creates just the kind of challenges amateur runners, cyclists, hikers and climbing enthusiasts love; and its history as a town beloved of the Wadiyar kings who straddled the Indo-British divide with ease and grace, patronizing cricket, tennis and wrestling with equal enthusiasm.

The British, who ruled Mysore between 1831 and 1881, also played a role. In the Bangalore Cantonment, established in 1806, strong, fleet horses were much in demand by the cavalry, but the small local breeds did not make the cut. Enter, circa 1824, a canny 16-year-old from Shiraz, Iran, called Agha Aly Asker, with a contingent of his horse-trading family's finest specimens in tow. Asker's horses soon became the toast of the Cantonment. With no wars to worry about, British thoughts soon turned to sport that used horses – polo, racing and the annual hunt – kick-starting the city's involvement in organized sport.

Two centuries after Aly Asker first arrived here, his descendant, Bengalurean Fouaad Mirza, continues to carry the equestrian torch – he won two silver medals at the 2018 Asian Games, and was the only Indian to qualify for any equestrian event at Tokyo 2020.

Golf, believed to have been invented by the Scots, was the other sport to make an early appearance in the Cantonment – the Bangalore Golf Course (estd 1876) was only the third golf course in the country. Today, the shining star in the Indian golfing firmament is young Bengalurean Aditi Ashok, who finished fourth at Tokyo 2020.

Of the city's passion for cricket, and the roll call of stellar cricketers it has produced or nurtured over the years – Vishy, Prasanna, Chandra, Kirmani, Binny, Dravid, Kumble, Srinath, Prasad, Shantha Rangaswamy – little needs to be said. Beginning life in 1933 as the Mysore Cricket Association, the KSCA is today one of the best-organized state cricket associations in the country, and its home ground, the Chinnaswamy Stadium, has witnessed more thrilling feats than there is space to enumerate here. The Mysore State Lawn Tennis Association (today the Karnataka State Lawn Tennis Association), on whose courts Mahesh Bhupathi and Bopanna himself have trained, was also established around the same time.

In 1974, the National Institute of Sports (now the Sports Authority of India), chose to set up its Southern Centre, meant to cater to the entire region, at the Sri Kanteerava Stadium in the city. In 1980, Bengalurean Prakash Padukone was crowned World No. 1 in badminton; in the same decade, sprinter Ashwini Nachappa (who on two occasions outran the great P.T. Usha) and heptathlete Reeth Abraham brought the city's focus firmly to athletics.

Bengalurean engagement with sport, whether as players, audiences, patrons, coaches, enablers, or administrators, continues to grow, aided in large part by its beloved champion sportspersons, who invest time, money and talent in their own training centres of sporting excellence across the city. Win-win all round!

'Less glamorous sports too – ball badminton, kabaddi, basketball, and hockey, both men's and women's, for a start. There may be a book there for you.'

— SURESH MENON, AUTHOR, CRICKET WRITER, AND A FORMER EDITOR, *NEW INDIAN EXPRESS*

•

'Great piece, but did I miss the hockey references? We have a number of Olympians from the city.'

— KOWSHIK BHAT, WHO PLAYED HOCKEY FOR BANGALORE UNIVERSITY IN THE '90S

•

'Sporty read indeed! Too hard to cover everyone and everything in a column, I suppose. We also have Nisha Millet in swimming, Pankaj Advani in billiards, so many Bangalore champs!'

— VIDYA MANI, CO-FOUNDER OF AN INDEPENDENT CHILDREN'S BOOKSTORE IN SOUTH BANGALORE

•

'Your column reminded me of reading about Churchill playing polo in the Parade Ground on MG Road in the 1890s, and hunting for the best horse breeds.'

— SUMANTH NAIK, BANGALORE ENTHUSIAST AND OCCASIONAL TOUR GUIDE

72

MAHASHIVARATRI IS USUALLY CELEBRATED IN FEBRUARY

Mallapura to Malleswaram: A Temple Tale

When it comes to divine families, my own family is partial to Shiva's. Gowri–Ganesha Habba is a very big deal, as is Shivaratri – the first one is about feasting, the second about fasting. As a child, I looked forward as much to the second, for its thrilling subversiveness – no one badgering me to take my nose out of a book and come to lunch, a 'head bath' at sunset, and uppittu for dinner (instead of breakfast) at my grandmother's house. But although my grandmother lived only 50 m away from the Kadu Malleshwara temple, we never joined the very long lines there on Shivaratri night. Instead, we visited – and still do – a small but popular shrine a few metres away, attached to a community hall that my grandparents built in the '60s. That made it dearer to us, of course, but also, as the patrons' grandchildren, we got to skip the queues.

Just around the time when the mild Bengaluru winter is turning into the mild (although you wouldn't think it, given how much everyone complains) Bengaluru summer, Shiva-worshipping Bengalureans feel their spirits quicken as they get ready for Mahashivaratri, the annual festival of austerity and reflection. This year, as per usual, these devotees will array themselves in long, patient lines outside temples to their favourite deity, waiting their turn for a one-on-one communion. And while there are many popular shrines in the city, traditionalists and old Bengalureans will swear by the centuries-old majesty of the temple on the hill dedicated to Shiva-in-the-forest, Kaadu Malleshwara.

It was the temple that lent its name to the neighbourhood around it, Malleswaram. In 1898, as the plague swept through the congested, insanitary Bengaluru Pete, two new and modern extensions were set up on a war footing for the rehabilitation of the survivors. One of them was Malleswaram; the other, which also took its name from the main shrine in the area, was Basavanagudi. Over three decades later, the very specific 'old Mysore' vibe of these two neighbourhoods would inspire master storyteller R.K. Narayan to pinch off bits from their names to create the beloved fictional universe of Malgudi.

The main architects of 1898 Malleswaram were two remarkable gentlemen. One of them was V.P. Madhava Rao, who had earned his laurels as headmaster of the school for Mysore's royals. Having then been inducted into the administration, he was serving as the kingdom's inspector general of police when the plague hit. In double-quick time, he was appointed plague commissioner, and did so well in the tough role that he went on to garner other plum appointments, receiving in 1906 the ultimate honour of the diwanship of Mysore. The other was Standish Lee, an Indian-born engineer of Scottish extraction, then serving as Mysore's sanitary engineer. It was Lee who designed the extension of Malleswaram, divvying up the 291 acres of land to the north of Bengaluru Pete into plots of different sizes, which he then grouped into enclaves for specific communities – Brahmins, Lingayats, Mohammedans, native Christians. He also made sure to carve out spaces for a school, a market and a park. We are not sure if Lee also named the new extension, but it seems logical that whoever did took their cue from the temple.

In 1909, however, a Malleswaram archaeologist called N. Narasimhachar discovered, on a boulder within the temple complex, an inscription dated 14 November 1669, which recorded the endowment of the village of Medaraningahalli to 'Mallapura's Mallikarjuna Temple' by the then ruler of Bengaluru, Ekoji Bhosale. (A brief aside: Ekoji I, or Venkoji, was the step-brother of the Great Maratha, Shivaji. In 1664, Venkoji inherited the jagir of Bengaluru from his father, Shahaji. In 1673, defeating the Nayaka of Madurai who had invaded Thanjavur, he crowned himself king, becoming progenitor of the Thanjavur Bhosale dynasty.) That inscription – go and check it out sometime – makes it clear that a town called Mallapura predated Rao and Lee's Malleswaram by over two centuries. Unfortunately, the temple itself is difficult to date, so we may never know whether it was the deity that inspired the name of the seventeenth-century town or if it was the other way around. Suffice it to say that the temple, around which such long lines of devotees snake each Shivaratri night, has a reasonably hoary history.

PS: Madhava Rao, who was so instrumental in setting up Malleswaram, was descended from the Thanjavur Marathi Brahmin community, which emigrated to and settled in that city following its conquest by Ekoji!

'Very interesting! It also reads extremely well, despite the prune and nip, tuck and trim you must have done to keep it within word limits. The information density is very high in this one, but it is still very pleasant to read. Turns out I know so very little of this chapter in the history of Bangalore, despite having grown up in Malleswaram.'

— SRIRANG MANOHAR, PROFESSOR, UNIVERSITY OF TWENTE, THE NETHERLANDS

•

'I may have actually visited this temple only once or twice in my entire life, but I never missed the Shivaratri jaatre (fair) outside it, or the teru (chariot procession) that was taken out the morning after. My favourite part was throwing the banana into the chariot.'

— KEERTHI ESWARAIAH, BANGALOREAN FROM PENNSYLVANIA

73

C.V. RAMAN DISCOVERED THE RAMAN EFFECT ON 28 FEBRUARY 1928; THE DAY IS CELEBRATED AS NATIONAL SCIENCE DAY IN INDIA

An Accountant Who Won the Physics Nobel

Even though he died the year I was born, I have encountered C.V. Raman, serendipitously, at various points in my life. The first I heard of him was when I was seven – both parents of one of my best friends in school worked at the Raman Research Institute (RRI). His home, I discovered when I was 16, was just around the corner from my pre-university college. In the early '90s, my father-in-law-to-be, a scientist himself, spoke admiringly of a polymath called Rad (Raman's son, Venkataraman Radhakrishnan), who was then director of the RRI. Over a decade later, the late Vijay Thiruvady, Bangalore's wonderful raconteur of tree lore, told me that his own grandfather, the great K.V. Krishnan, had been Raman's unacknowledged collaborator in the discovery of the Raman Effect. More recently, in the course of a translation project, I came upon a beautifully poignant poem by Kannada poet K.S. Nisar Ahmed, called 'Raman Satta Suddi' (The News of [C.V.] Raman's Death). Yup, Raman was 45 when he first came to live in Bangalore, but he certainly made – and is still making – his presence felt.

On 14 March 1988, Larry Shaw, the legendary technical curator of San Francisco's science, tech and arts museum, the Exploratorium, led the celebrations of the very first Pi Day (3.14 – or 14 March in American) at the museum. Given the cool coincidence that the mathematical constant Pi (the ratio of a circle's circumference to its diameter) and pie (apple, cherry, pizza – all of which are usually circular in shape) were homophones, the idea caught on; the day continues to be observed by the scientific community by eating plenty of the latter.

What does Pi Day have to do with Bangalore? Not much, but since 14 March is also associated with two of the world's most renowned physicists (Einstein was born, Hawking died), this day seemed like a good time to talk about our own colossus in that department, Sir Chandrasekhara Venkata Raman. (He has his own Day, by the way – the day he discovered the optical phenomenon known as the Raman Effect – 28 February 1928 – has been celebrated as National Science Day since 1986.)

Precocious from childhood, Raman topped his bachelor's degree exam at the University of Madras at age 16, winning gold medals in physics and English (and casually publishing a scientific paper on the side). In another year, he had got his master's degree, and was looking to continue his research in England when a most unexpected obstacle stopped him in his tracks – a physical examination had his doctor conclude that he would 'die of tuberculosis' if he went to England.

Bummed, but not entirely, Raman took the exam for the Indian Finance Service instead, and, ho-hum, topped it. Posted to Calcutta as assistant accountant general, the 19-year-old was not only conscientious with his work but also got enthusiastically involved with India's first scientific research institute, the Indian Association for the Cultivation of Sciences

(IACS). His work at the IACS – whether it was mentoring PhD students or publishing papers in the scientific journal *Nature* – won him the position of the first Palit professor of physics at the University of Calcutta. Resigning a little reluctantly from the civil service, where the salary was much better, Raman accepted. The rest is history.

In 1924, he was elected as a Fellow of the Royal Society (FRS). In 1926, he became the first editor of his new baby, the *Indian Journal of Physics.* In 1928, he discovered the Raman Effect, which explained why the sea looked blue (nope, not because it reflects the colour of the sky). In 1930, he became the first Asian to win a Nobel Prize in any field of science.

And finally, Bangalore. Invited to our fair city in 1933 to take over as the first Indian director of the Indian Institute of Science in Malleswaram, Raman accepted with alacrity, setting up a department of physics there soon afterwards. Only three years later, accused of being entirely biased towards physics, and that too at the expense of the other sciences, he was forced to step down from the directorship, but continued to head the Institute's department of physics until Independence. In 1948, retiring from the IISc, he walked into his own institute of scientific research next door, the Raman Research Institute, where he served as director until his death in 1970.

WHILE RAMAN HOLDS FORTH ON THE REFRACTION OF LIGHT, A STUDENT KEENLY WATCHES THE REFRACTION FROM THE DIAMOND EAR-STUD OF HIS COMELY CLASSMATE

In 1954, Prime Minister Jawaharlal Nehru conferred the first-ever Bharat Ratna, the country's highest civilian honour, on Sir C.V. Raman.

PS: So confident was the recently knighted Raman of winning the Nobel in 1930 that he set sail for Stockholm with Lady Raman well before the official announcement, contending that he would miss the award ceremony if he waited around for confirmation!

'Fascinating! Such a Sheldon Cooper–type character (is that mildly blasphemous?)! These geniuses just HAVE to graduate at 16, top every exam there is and make us feel awful about ourselves! Imagine booking tickets for Stockholm even before the Nobel announcement!'

— MADHUCHANDA BHATTACHARYA, HEAD, TECHNICAL COMMUNICATIONS, TATA CONSULTANCY SERVICES

•

'My father was the architect of the Raman Research Institute (RRI) in the '70s. It wasn't Raman who was my dad's client, though, it was his son, Rad (Venkataraman Radhakrishnan), a brilliant astrophysicist who had taken over as director of RRI in 1972. Actually, Raman's family was full of genius scientists – among his nephews, he counted Sivaramakrishna Chandrasekhar, who received many honours for his work on liquid crystals, S. Ramaseshan, who became director of IISc in 1981, S. Pancharatnam, who did pioneering work in the field of optics, and Subrahmanyan Chandrasekhar, who also won the Physics Nobel in 1983!'

— NARESH NARASIMHAN, PRINCIPAL ARCHITECT, VENKATARAMANAN ASSOCIATES

Books and the Ooru: A Valentine's Day Love Story

Fifteen years ago, when I first met Thomas Abraham, the sharp, genial managing director of Hachette India, I had just published my first book with Hachette. That book would eventually become an eight-part series – Taranauts, India's first complete fantasy-adventure series for children in English – that was loved not only by young readers but also by Thomas himself. Ever since that first meeting, he has never tired of telling me how unusual Bangalore is as an Indian city when it comes to books and reading, simply going by one metric that publishers keep a keen eye on – how many bookstores does a city have, and how many new ones are opening up, confident that they will be able to recover their investment? On both counts, says Thomas, Bangalore consistently tops the charts.

In February 2024, Bengaluru hosted a series of events around the launch of a new book that describes the warm relationship shared by two of her most famous citizens – the homegrown infotech pioneer N.R. Narayana Murthy and his bestselling-author wife Sudha Murty. As she has in past interviews, Sudha reiterated that what had first drawn her to 'Murthy' was how voraciously – and eclectically – he read.

Mr Murthy grew up in Sidlaghatta, a raw silk–producing and silkworm-rearing hub an hour away from Bengaluru, Mrs Murthy in faraway Shiggaon, then part of the cultural and literary hub of Dharwad. But there is something very Bengalurean about the fact that it was books that brought the two together.

For reading books (in cafés, club reading rooms, libraries, or public parks), talking books (at book launches, author talks, book clubs and the wonderful annual Bangalore Lit Fest), and browsing in bookstores (as part of weekend family outings, couple dates, staycations, or me-time afternoons) are all bona fide Bengaluru occupations. While both boutique bookstores and large chains struggle to stay afloat across the country in the face of deep discounting by online behemoths and a decline in the reading habit among customers, in Bangalore, independent bookstores (think English bookstores Atta Galatta and Champaca, Kannada–English bookstores Bahuroopi, Ankita Pustaka and Harivu Books, and children's bookstores Lightroom and Funky Rainbow) continue to blossom.

It all began in 1905, over a century before a 2017 survey of consumer book-buying behaviour across India declared Bengaluru India's 'best-read city'. That was the year that C.H. Higginbotham opened the city's first English bookstore in the heart of the British Cantonment. The stately 1897 building on posh South Parade (today's MG Road), still stands, and

Higginbothams is still in business. In 1945, bibliophile lawyer K.B.K. Rao relocated from Kurnool to Bengaluru and set up Select Book Shop in a garage on Museum Road. In 1977, Rao's son K.K.S. Murthy (now 94), took over, moving the shop to an alley off Brigade Road, from where it has continued to delight seekers of rare and antiquarian books.

The coming of the unified state of Mysore in 1956, the result of a movement spearheaded by Kannada litterateurs, brought Kannada publishing firmly into the spotlight. In 1960, the first major Kannada publishing house and bookstore – Navakarnataka Publications – made its entry. In 1965, the legendary Bangalore Book Bureau (BBB) opened in the busy hub of the erstwhile City, near Kapali theatre in Gandhinagar. Through the last decades of the twentieth century and beyond, it was the generous and erudite Mr Shanbhag's legendary Premier Book Shop (estd 1971, closed 2009); Gangaram's Book Bureau (BBB's Cantonment-side cousin, estd 1975), presided over by the genial Atmaram Gangaram on MG Road; the lovely Venkatesh and Guru Prasad's Nagasri Book House in Jayanagar (estd 1976); and Sapna Book House (estd 1967), which Mumbai railway-porter-turned-entrepreneur Suresh Shah first set up in a tiny space in Gandhinagar, that became Bengaluru's go-to booksellers.

While Premier is now only a fond memory, Gangaram's lives on in a smaller avatar, and Nagasri has carried gamely on,* Sapna has exploded – it is one of the largest bookstores in India today, both in terms of sales volume and square footage, and the largest publisher of Kannada books.

*Sadly, four months after this column was published, Nagasri closed down permanently. 'The only reason we are closing,' said Venkatesh in an article published in the *New Indian Express* in June 2024, 'is our age. It's always good to end on a strong, happy note, so we decided it's time to stop.'

Perhaps the sweetest Bengaluru book story, however, is that of the impecunious 19-year-old engineering student from the small town of Rangasamudra outside Mysore. Looking to earn some money on the side, young Mayi Gowda began selling second-hand books on the MG Road footpath, very close to the venerable Higginbothams. Today, his three bookstores on Church Street, all called Blossom Book House, are Bengaluru landmarks.

Heart-warmingly, Mayi's protégé Krishna Gowda's excellent bookstore, Bookworm, also flourishes alongside Blossom, on the very same street.

'Bangalore truly has an amazing history of reading. I've visited barely half these bookstores! I shall use this article as a guide to take me around.'

— REENA PURI, EDITOR-IN-CHIEF, AMAR CHITRA KATHA

•

'Absolutely enjoyed it. When I was a kid, my long-time wish was to own a bookshop even if it was in my parents' garage, and read all the books before selling them. That wish continues to linger on somewhere.'

— SREELATA MENON, CHILDREN'S AUTHOR

(Author's note: *I wanted to be a salesgirl in Gangaram's for the same reason!)*

•

'Love this! Bangalore's love affair with books reads like a Mills and Boon novel!'

— SHAINI V., HIGH-SCHOOL HISTORY TEACHER

75

Dating the City: An Epigraphical Quest

If every city had a word that captures its essential spirit, what is Bangalore's? Many would agree that 'cool', which contains in itself a sense of young, smart, trendy, quirky, and easy-going, is a hot contender, and not just because of the city's much-envied climate. How did a city that isn't particularly young (official accounts date its founding to 1537 CE, which makes it a dozen years shy of 500 at this point) achieve this exalted status?

As the columns in this book have revealed, Bangalore's story is made up of hundreds of apparently unrelated stories that feed into each other (or don't!) in surprising and delightful ways. Each contains within itself the seeds of the city's enduring coolness. But that isn't the end of the story, or even its beginning. In 2017, a few years after 24-year-old Bangalorean Nikhil Kamath upped the cool game with Zerodha, new archaeological evidence pushed the age of the city back by several centuries. It seems that as Bangalore gets older, Bangalore gets younger. Benjamin Button, anyone?

KITTAYYA HERO STONE

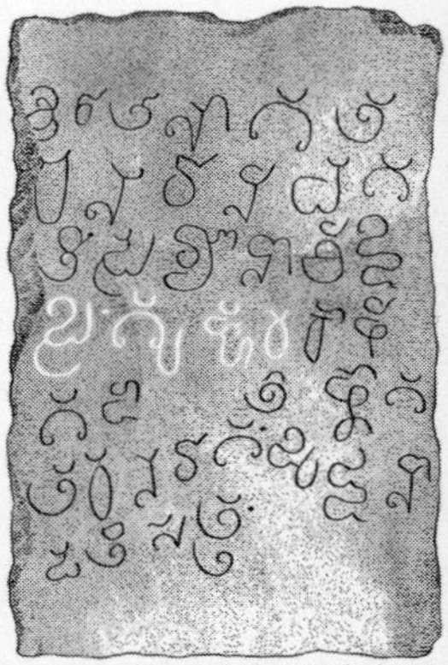

BEGUR EPIGRAPH WITH 'BENGALURU' HIGHLIGHTED

How old is Bengaluru? With the Republic Day Flower Show at Lalbagh (on until 26 January) choosing the history of the city as its theme for this year (2023), this is a timely question. Very few Bengalureans would be able to answer this question instantly, or with any conviction, however. Not because the information is not easily available, but simply because not many Bengalureans concern themselves with details of local history.

The few who are interested in such things will hazard that the city was founded by Kempegowda I 'at some point in the sixteenth century'. Popular history would agree – the 'official' town of Bengaluru, i.e., the one enclosed within a double-walled mud fort to the south of the erstwhile Dharmambudhi Tank (today's Kempegowda Bus Station), was indeed raised by Kempegowda I in 1537 CE.

Is Bengaluru 14 years shy of her 500th birthday, then? That is already a hoary age for a city to be, but a popular legend – in which the Hoysala king, Veera Ballala II, names an existing settlement Bendakaalooru ('the town of boiled beans') to honour the generous spirit of one of its citizens, who shared her frugal meal of boiled beans with him – pushes back its origins by some 350 years, to the twelfth century.

It would have been easy to dismiss this story as fiction (although oral tradition is considered a legitimate source for interpreting history), if not for a mammoth exercise undertaken by Benjamin Lewis Rice, the director of the Mysore Archaeological Department between 1886 and 1906. Intrigued by ancient stone and copperplate epigraphs he encountered in 1873 while on tours across the state as the inspector of education, Rice began to have them translated, putting together a massive 12-volume series, *Epigraphia Carnatica* (*EC*), containing translations of over 9,000 epigraphs, the oldest from the third century! Of them, 1,500 were recorded in a roughly 8,000 sq. km area covering Bengaluru Urban, Bengaluru Rural and Ramanagaram, of which 175 epigraphs lay within the boundaries of Bengaluru.

One of them, from the walls of the Someshwara Temple in Madivala, dated 1247 CE, confirmed at least part of the Bendakaalooru legend. Whether boiled beans had any part to play in the christening is moot, but the Tamil inscription from the Chola period, asserting that a certain Pemmattaiyar of Veppur (Begur) 'granted some lands below the big tank of Vengalur (Tamil for Bengaluru) to the god Sembasuram' confirmed that a town by that name had definitely existed around Ballala's time.

But it was another epigraph that Rice discovered in a temple in Begur (off today's infamous Silk Board Junction) that was the zinger – the ninth-century inscription mentioned a town called Bengaluru in the vicinity. The age of the city had been pushed back again, by another couple of centuries!

In 2017, a Bengaluru computer engineer called P.L. Udaya Kumar, inspired by a talk on epigraphy he had attended, began trying to trace the 175 Bengaluru inscriptions in the *EC*. To his horror, he discovered that at least 100 were entirely missing, and decided that something had to be done. Since January 2021, as honorary director of The Mythic Society's 3D Digital Conservation Project, Udaya is on an extended sabbatical from work, pairing his skills with state-of-the-art technology to conserve priceless epigraphs for posterity.

The conservation project hit pay dirt when Udaya's team discovered a hitherto undocumented epigraph from 750 CE in Hebbal, recording that when the Rattavadis (Rashtrakutas) attacked the town of Hebbala, a brave hero called Kittayya saved the day. That proves that at least one neighbourhood of Bengaluru was around 1,300 years ago!

As for the age of Bengaluru itself, watch this space.

Acknowledgements

It doesn't happen often, but there are times when I wish I had grown up in another city. Just so that one day, when I was almost grown up, I could have stepped out of a train or a bus, prickly with trepidation, shivering a little in the unaccustomed chill, fully prepared to hate this new, unfamiliar town that I was moving into. And proceeding, with indecent alacrity, to fall in love with it.

I'm not talking here of the unquestioning love one feels for the familiar places of childhood, which I feel for Bangalore, but a clear-eyed, objective, ticks-all-the-important-boxes-and-therefore love which grows with time into a quite irrational passion. I miss loving my city with this second kind of love, the kind that natives like me can never fully enjoy without our own righteous selves pulling us up short with an accusatory 'Oh, come! You would feel quite differently about Bangalore if you hadn't grown up here.'

Would I? I'm not so sure. Because, you see, I did once believe there was something better out there. Once, long ago, I fled my then-small town, eager for the bright lights of seductive Xanadus – Delhi, London, Bombay, New York. All of them teased, flirted, grew me up in ways Bangalore could not, and finally exhausted – I was glad I had made memories with them, but they had no lasting power over me.

I returned to Bangalore 12 years later as the sort-of outsider, frankly terrified that I had made the wrong decision. Determined not to let my views be coloured by memory or nostalgia, I set out to discover the city in the same way I had 'discovered' every other city I had lived in – researching its history, walking its neighbourhoods, exploring its restaurants and cafés, meeting its people. Slowly, steadily, the incredible truth sank in: I had come home, in a way I hadn't done before, not with any city, not even this one.

This book is a collection of stories about my hometown that I learnt on this outside-in journey. I have more people and institutions to thank for the stories than would fit into these pages, but I shall be forever grateful for their incredible generosity in sharing what they knew; I have tried to do the same these past couple of decades. Fortunately, there are fewer people to thank for the book itself, and I shall proceed to do that without further ado.

Many, many thanks are due, then, to –

R. Sukumar, editor, *Hindustan Times*, who believed I was the right person to write a fortnightly column on the city for the new online Bangalore edition of HT in 2021 even though I had never written a column before;

Thomas Abraham, managing director, Hachette India, who has published most of the books I have written for children over the last 15 years, and who offered to publish this one, even though it isn't for children, with the same enthusiasm and conviction;

Vatsala Kaul Banerjee, my first editor, best mentor, and fast friend since I first started writing for children over three decades ago, who went out of her comfort zone to take on the editing of this book for adults, for no other reason than to support me, and did such a smashing job of it;

Priya Kuriyan, much-loved, much-fêted illustrator of more Indian children's books, including mine, than she herself can remember, besides a whole slew of books for adults, who not only designed the spectacular cover but also illustrated the book despite her ridiculous workload, in part perhaps because she is on her own journey of discovering her adoptive city, but in larger part, I like to think, because she loves Vatsala and me so much;

The lovely, lovely Bangalore celebrities – Rohan Bopanna, Raja Chandra Urs, Ramjee Chandran, Amoghavarsha and Hemamalini Maiya (in typical Bangalorean fashion, they behave like anything but celebrities), who agreed, with such alacrity, to read the manuscript of this book, and then proceeded to give it the warmest and most heartfelt testimonials;

And finally, to every Bangalorean – past, present, aspirational – who reacted and responded to the stories in the 'Beloved Bangalore' column, over the past four years, with so much wonder, enthusiasm, pride and affection, proving that to truly love something in the way it deserves to be loved – faults, imperfections, ugliness and all – one must first know it.